Miller Center Series on the American Presidency

WORKING IN THE WORLD

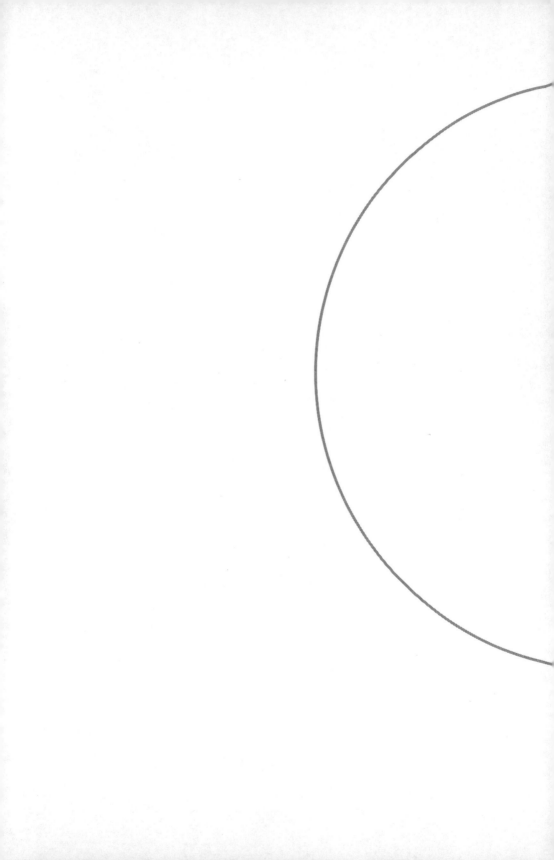

WORKING IN
THE WORLD

Jimmy Carter and the Making
of American Foreign Policy

ROBERT A. STRONG

Louisiana State University Press   *Baton Rouge*

Designer: Michele Myatt Quinn
Typeface: Granjon
Typesetter: Coghill Composition Co., Inc.
Printer and binder: Thomson-Shore, Inc.

Library of Congress Cataloging-in-Publication Data

Strong, Robert A., 1948–
    Working in the world : Jimmy Carter and the making of American
  foreign policy / Robert A. Strong ; with a foreword by James
  Sterling Young.
      p. cm. — (Miller Center series on the American presidency)
    Includes bibliographical references (p.) and index.
    ISBN 0-8071-2445-1 (cl. : alk. paper)
    1. Carter, Jimmy, 1924– . 2. United States—Foreign
  relations—1977–1981. I. Title. II. Series.
  E872.S79   1999
  973.926′092—dc21   99-16464
                                               CIP

Some material in chapter 6 is drawn from parts of *Decisions and Dilemmas* by Robert A. Strong,
copyright © 1993; reprinted by permission of Prentice-Hall, Inc., Upper Saddle River, NJ.
    Some of the chapters herein make use of material published previously, in different form, in *Miller Center Journal* and *Southeastern Political Review*.

The paper in this book meets the guidelines for permanence and durability of the Committee on
Production Guidelines for Book Longevity of the Council on Library Resources. ⊗

for Emily

Contents

Foreword

The Carter Presidency Project, undertaken in 1981–84 by the Miller Center at the University of Virginia, was the first systematic interview study of an outgoing presidency.[1] Unlike conventional oral history, the project was intended as a contribution to the biography of a presidency more than of an individual—an intimate biography, informed by extensive interviews with the former president and his principal White House associates, that would illuminate the sort of presidency the thirty-ninth was and why so. Emphasized were aspects of historical significance that did not make news during incumbency and that might escape the notice of researchers in the mass of official and personal records that come to light many years later.

The interviews revealed a picture of the Carter White House significantly different from the one that was widely circulated in the news media and that became the conventional wisdom. Drawing on the interviews, Charles O. Jones in *The Trusteeship Presidency* and Erwin C. Hargrove in *Jimmy Carter as President* contested the public perception of Carter and his aides as people who knew how to win an election against an incumbent president but not how to govern. These first two volumes in the Carter

---

1. A description of the project, the transcripts of which were donated to the Carter Presidential Library, may be found in the foreword to the companion volumes in this series (mentioned below).

presidency series showed that Carter had an unconventional but deliberate and methodical way of working his will on Congress and on policy; noted that it was consistent with his earlier legislative and gubernatorial experience and was suited to his personal strengths and skills as well as the nature of his own policy goals; showed how this governing style helps to explain the unusual successes as well as the unusual failures of his administration; and suggested new ways of evaluating presidential performance in Carter's time.

This first wave of revisionist scholarship on the Carter presidency had the considerable benefit of extended interviews with the principals uninhibited by the constraints of incumbency or the interviewers' intent to file news stories. But it did not have the benefit of access to documents in the presidential library, for these were not then available to researchers. In the decade following the publication of the volumes by Jones and Hargrove, many of the files, including the important President's Handwriting File, have been opened for research. Robert A. Strong has made extensive use of them in writing this third volume in the Carter series.

What he has discovered is a strong match between the picture of Carter's political methods, drive, and style that comes through in the documents and the picture that came through in the interviews. The nine detailed case studies presented in this book demolish the fiction that Carter was a president without a strategy of governance, not on top of foreign policy, indecisive, mired in details, unwilling or unable to practice the politics of persuasion and out of his depth in the high politics of state. That done, Strong asks how it could happen that the most transparent and open presidency in memory—no hidden hand, no stagecraft, no spinmeisters, never accused of deception—got so persistently and punitively fictionalized in public perception. Finding a good answer to this question would take another book. Strong points out promising places to look.

But *Working in the World* is more than a book about the real Jimmy Carter and the way he approached foreign policy in the world of his time. The case studies that follow also show the nature of presidential foreign policy work as it is almost all the time, from managing crises both real and false to politicking for Senate treaty votes and from peacemaking through personal diplomacy to battling for confirmation of appointees. *Working in the World: Jimmy Carter and the Making of Foreign Policy* gives scholars, journalists, and future presidents alike a needed reminder that the presidency is not just

Roosevelt I's "bully pulpit" or Roosevelt II's "preeminently a place of moral leadership" and that foreign affairs do not offer presidents escape from domestic drudgery and the constraints of Neustadt's "clerkship." Strong, like the president he has written about, is a realist in treating the presidency as a place of work.

James Sterling Young

Randolph P. Compton Scholar and
Director of the Presidential Oral History Project
Miller Center of Public Affairs

Acknowledgments

This book has taken a long time to complete and has been improved by the assistance of a great many people. All of my visits to the Carter Library in Atlanta were productive because that facility has an unusually competent and professional staff led by Donald Schewe. Many of the archivists at the library were helpful, but James Yancy in particular gave special time and attention to my research requests.

As a professor at Washington and Lee University and as a visiting scholar at the White Burkett Miller Center of Public Affairs at the University of Virginia, I have worked with a number of students who read drafts, checked footnotes, and helped with the collection of research materials. These research assistants included Elizabeth Detter, Millie Heatwole, Heather Olsen, Todd Peppers, Katherine Walther, and Marcia Widmer. Marshal Zeringue, who has been reading manuscript material for this project for longer than he may have wished, collaborated with me in the research and writing of an earlier version of the chapter on the neutron bomb controversy. That work was published, with joint authorship, in the *Southeastern Political Review*. A version of Chapter 4 was published in volume one of the *Miller Center Journal*. Chapters 8 and 9 first appeared as articles in the Washington and Lee University *Political Review*. A chapter in my last book, *Decisions and Dilemmas: Case Studies in Presidential Foreign Policy Making*, told the whole story of the Panama Canal treaty ratification process and, in a few places, overlaps with the account in this book of how the

White House dealt with Senator DeConcini and his controversial treaty amendment. All material for which others hold a copyright is here reprinted with permission.

A number of people who served in the Carter administration, including the president, agreed to be interviewed in the course of my research or corresponded with me about various issues. Their contributions are noted in the chapters that follow. Gary Sick, William Quandt, and Robert Pastor, who were among the foreign policy specialists on the National Security Council staff during the Carter years, read chapters, made comments, and in some cases provided documents in their areas of expertise. Zbigniew Brzezinski was exceedingly generous with his time in interviews and in the reading of draft chapters. Special thanks are also due to David Newsom, who served as under secretary of state in the Carter administration and later as a professor in the Department of Government and Foreign Affairs at the University of Virginia. Ambassador Newsom spoke with me on a number of occasions, read the entire manuscript at different stages in its development, and always offered detailed and thoughtful comments.

Other friends, colleagues, and professional reviewers who provided comments on chapter drafts include Peter Bourne, Douglas Brinkley, Dan Caldwell, David Clinton, Bill Connelly, Barry Machado, William Lee Miller, and Richard Neustadt. Portions of the manuscript were presented at conferences sponsored by the American Political Science Association, the Southern Political Science Association, the Southwestern Political Science Association, and Georgia State University.

From beginning to end this project was sponsored by the Miller Center at the University of Virginia, which, under the leadership of Kenneth W. Thompson, has become a major national resource for serious students of the American presidency. James S. Young, who served as the center's director of presidential research and organized a series of fascinating oral history interviews of Carter's senior White House staff, taught me how to do effective interviewing and to appreciate the complexity of presidential behavior. I have enjoyed a long association with the Miller Center throughout my academic career and hope that this book partially repays the substantial debt I owe to Professors Thompson and Young.

Finally, while these chapters were being researched and written, my wife, Elaine Chisek, and I welcomed our daughter Emily into the world and marveled at her seemingly endless energy and curiosity. Without her this book would have been finished much sooner and meant much less.

WORKING IN
THE WORLD

INTRODUCTION

This is a book about presidential work in the conduct of foreign affairs. To be more precise, it is a collection of case studies that examine the work that one president—Jimmy Carter—did in connection with a number of international issues that arose during his four years in the White House. It is not a book about the most important foreign policy problems of the late 1970s; nor is it about formal decision-making models as they have been developed by political scientists. The focus is both narrower than other books that have explored foreign affairs in the Carter era and broader than those that examine in detail a particular foreign policy issue with which President Carter was closely associated.[1]

1. For broad-scale reviews of Carter foreign policy, see David Skidmore, *Reversing Course: Carter's Foreign Policy, Domestic Politics, and the Failure of Reform* (Nashville, 1996); Jerel A. Rosati, *The Carter Administration's Quest for Global Community: Beliefs and Their Impact on Behavior* (Columbia, S.C., 1991); Timothy P. Maga, *The World of Jimmy Carter: U.S. Foreign Policy, 1977–1981* (West Haven, Conn., 1994); Alexander Moens, *Foreign Policy Under Carter: Testing Multiple Advocacy Decision Making* (Boulder, 1990); Gaddis Smith, *Morality, Reason and Power: American Diplomacy in the Carter Years* (New York, 1986). An excellent chapter on the Carter administration's foreign policy making process can be found in Erwin Hargrove, *Jimmy Carter as President: Leadership and the Politics of the Public Good* (Baton Rouge, 1988). For analysis of some specific issues, see Russell Leigh Moses, *Freeing the Hostages: Reexamining U.S.-Iranian Negotiations and Soviet Policy, 1979–1981* (Pittsburgh, 1996); William B. Quandt, *Camp David: Peacemaking and Politics* (Washington, D.C., 1986); George D. Moffett, *The Limits of Victory: The Ratification of the Panama Canal Treaties* (Ith-

The chapters that follow are organized around some deceptively simple questions. What is the work that presidents do when they make foreign policy, and how is that work done? Which portions of that work are literally presidential as opposed to the ministerial tasks performed by the staff and organizations that ostensibly serve the president? The literature on presidential foreign policy making is dominated by studies of process and crisis. Scholars of international relations and presidential foreign policy making have long been interested in how decision makers receive and interpret information; how psychological factors and group dynamics shape and distort the interpretation of problems and their possible solutions; and how institutional arrangements and bureaucratic politics can constrain the character and implementation of presidential decisions. Particular emphasis in these studies has been given to the behavior of leaders and institutions in crisis situations, when risks are high, time is short, and opportunities for dramatic policy changes are substantial. These are clearly important topics, but the emphasis on crisis management has led many scholars to neglect the day-to-day presidential business of foreign policy making, with its small steps and separated decisions arising from a wide array of circumstances and demands that are placed on presidential time and attention. Students of information processing do give consideration to routine foreign policy making, but are often more interested in bureaucratic politics and organizational behavior than in the thoughts and actions of the central decision maker. The students of both crisis management and information processing use case studies to illustrate their theoretical propositions.

The cases selected for this study were, however, not chosen to prove, or disprove, a particular hypothesis derived from an existing theory of presidential behavior or foreign policy decision making. They belong instead to a more exploratory stage of research in which the primary goal is to build a reliable and detailed record of political events that may have been neglected or misrepresented in previous accounts. Such a record may be useful to those who teach by the case study method. It may also contribute to the accumulation of accurate data about presidential performance in the conduct of foreign affairs and thereby provide the foundation for other scholars to explore new theoretical insights. Suggestions about some of the avenues for

aca, N.Y., 1985); Joshua Muravchik, *The Uncertain Crusade: Jimmy Carter and the Dilemmas of Human Rights Policy* (Lanham, Md., 1986).

theoretical development that emerge from the cases are noted in the conclusion.

In the nine case studies in this book we look at one president making foreign policy in a number of different settings, with regard to different issues, and in connection with very different kinds of presidential responsibilities or activities. The cases describe President Carter appointing an adviser, preparing official correspondence, meeting a head of state, drafting a speech, lobbying a member of Congress, dealing with advisers, talking to foreign leaders, traveling abroad, negotiating treaty language, leading an alliance, responding to the news media, and serving as commander in chief. These, and other kinds of work, are things that modern presidents regularly and routinely do. The presidential decisions and actions that constitute the work of foreign policy making are sometimes momentous and sometimes mundane, though the difference between the two can be difficult to ascertain at the time the work is being done. The topics and tasks that a president takes on are sometimes initiated by the chief executive himself or by senior members of his administration. More often, issues get to the president's desk because of actions by other consequential foreign or domestic actors. The work done by the president is typically, though not always, a collaborative effort that involves staff assistance, bureaucratic organizations, and consultation with such persons as the president may wish or be compelled to deal with regarding the matters at hand. The cases that follow are focused on what the president said and did in connection with a number of foreign policy making activities.

Some care was taken in the selection of cases to spread them chronologically across the life of the administration, to balance them with regard to perceived successes and failures, to include both routine and dramatic settings, and to avoid subjects—like the Camp David negotiations—that have been thoroughly treated by other scholars. The resulting mix of cases may strike some readers as odd. Nearly as many pages are devoted to a major military decision (the hostage-rescue mission) as are given to a minor piece of presidential correspondence (a one-page letter to Anastasio Somoza). This should not suggest that either the author or President Carter considered these matters to be of equal importance. Obviously, they were not. But presidential decisions to send troops on dangerous missions abroad are relatively rare when the nation is not at war and visits, conversations, and correspondence with other heads of state are common. The cases were consciously selected to include both ordinary and extraordinary presidential activities, since both play a role in the work of foreign policy making. In some instances the cases examine significant Carter administration accomplishments (like the Panama Canal treaties or the peace treaty between Israel and Egypt) by telling only a portion of those stories (how the president dealt with Senator Dennis DeConcini or what he did on his last-minute trip to Cairo and Jerusalem). In those instances, the narrower focus may help us to isolate Carter's personal contribution and involvement in some of the larger foreign policy enterprises of his administration. A number of the chapters deal with specific aspects of U.S.-Soviet relations and nuclear armaments (the Warnke nomination, the Annapolis speech, the neutron bomb, and the Soviet brigade in Cuba) without fully telling the story of what went wrong with arms control and détente in the late 1970s. Some effort is made in the conclusion to put these pieces together into a more coherent evaluation of Carter's foreign policy legacy, though the case study method places severe limitations on the general conclusions that can be drawn from very particular evidence.

As usually occurs in the case study method, there is an artificial coherence in narratives that isolate a single issue and examine its origins, development, and resolution over what may be a considerable period of time. Missing in such analysis is the fact that there are nearly always other matters, foreign and domestic, pressing for presidential action at the same time that the issue in the case study is being worked on. When those other demands and distractions are particularly relevant, I have tried to mention them, but a few references to the president's crowded schedule does not always do justice to the perennial presidential problem of finding enough time to develop a clear agenda and then to give adequate examination to the items on that agenda. The objective in selecting foreign policy activities from a variety of times, in a variety of settings, and with a wide variety of consequences is to capture, at least in part, the range of relevant presidential behavior in the conduct of foreign affairs.

All of the cases in this book come from one presidential administration. That fact simplifies the research project, since all of the stories told involve the same central character and many of the same secondary actors. It also matters that the one administration dealt with is Jimmy Carter's. Carter was an unusually hard-working and meticulous individual who did much of his work on paper, spending significant amounts of time reading and reviewing information and recommendations that crossed his desk. Many of those papers are now available in the Carter Library in the President's Handwriting File, which contains copies of the documents that the president reviewed in chronological order.[2] On almost all of those documents, President Carter recorded his initial in a conspicuous corner indicating that he had read what he had been given. On many pages he underlined the passages he thought to be important and wrote observations, comments, and instructions to his subordinates in the margins. More so than other modern presidents, Carter has left a paper trail that researchers can follow with some confidence that the underlining and notes in the president's handwriting are significant indicators of what he thought about a problem while he was working on it. Of course, the papers which the president read and marked can never tell the full story of White House deliberations. The frequent meetings, private conversations, and complicated personal relationships that exist in any modern White House obviously have an impact on how a president approaches and responds to an issue, and it would be impossible for all the factors that influence a decision to be clearly recorded in contemporary documents. Here memoirs and interviews can flesh out (or contradict) what the trail of paper teaches. The extensive diary that President Carter kept during his White House years, and has quoted from in his own books, is another important source of insights into the president's thoughts and reactions to important issues when he was confronting them.[3]

Perhaps no modern president, with the significant exception of Richard Nixon, has left as complete a record of his deliberations as has Jimmy Carter. Nixon's tapes may ultimately tell us more than we care to know about how he and his senior advisers did their work, but President Nixon spent considerable time and money after his resignation attempting to make sure

2. The President's Handwriting File, which is frequently cited in the chapters that follow, is not complete. Many of the memos that the president received which remain classified are not available to scholars, and some documents that the president reviewed are kept in other files.

3. Unfortunately, the president's diary is not available at the Carter Library, and the only portions of it used in this research project are those quoted by Carter and a few scholars with whom he has shared limited passages. The diary is reportedly six thousand pages of typed text transcribed by the president's secretary from tape-recorded comments he made on a daily basis. The original tapes were erased after transcription. Peter Bourne, *Jimmy Carter: A Comprehensive Biography from Plains to Post-presidency* (New York, 1997), 475.

that access to those tapes would be limited. Carter, whose records are less literal and voluminous than Nixon's, has made no such efforts. He has written books, granted interviews, encouraged researchers to use the materials in his presidential library, and participated in conferences that have evaluated the performance of his administration.[4] Despite this openness, Carter and many of his former White House assistants believe that his presidency is not well understood by the American people or by serious students of American politics.[5]

My own interest in the Carter administration began in the early 1980s, when I served as a research assistant for the Carter Presidency Project at the University of Virginia's White Burkett Miller Center. That project involved a group of presidential scholars, led by James S. Young, conducting extensive interviews with senior members of the Carter White House staff in the first year or two after they left office.[6] A clear theme in those interviews was the frustration that the Carter staff members felt regarding the misinterpretation and misrepresentation of their president and their administration in the media. Almost all modern presidents and White House staff assistants complain about press coverage, and sour grapes are likely to be on the menu for any group of people who lose a presidential campaign. Even so, the members of the Carter administration were adamant on this subject and thoroughly convinced that the public portrait of their president was badly distorted.[7]

4. See for instance the voluminous materials declassified and openly debated in the Carter-Brezhnev Project now available at the Carter Library.

5. There are some excellent books about the Carter administration, including Hargrove, *Jimmy Carter as President*, and Charles O. Jones, *The Trusteeship Presidency: Jimmy Carter and the United States Congress* (Baton Rouge, 1988), and more recently John Dumbrell, *The Carter Presidency: A Re-evaluation* (Manchester, Eng., 1993), but the public perception of Carter remains dominated by images of an inept and inexperienced chief executive who never fully had command of his administration. Those images are exaggerated or false and have led many commentators and citizens to miss or misjudge important aspects of the Carter presidency. For a review of how the Carter administration is treated in current textbooks on American government, see, J. M. Sanchez, "Awaiting Rehabilitation: The Carter Presidency in Political Science Textbooks," *Presidential Studies Quarterly* 27, no. 2 (spring 1997).

6. The interviews were transcribed and, with the permission of participants, made available to scholars conducting research at the Carter Library.

7. This is the theme in Jody Powell's White House memoir, which tries to explore why press accounts are often at odds with the truth and why White House press offices can have a difficult time correcting the prevailing account of events. Jody Powell, *The Other Side of the Story* (New York, 1984). Carter does not complain very much about media commentary

Of course, even if they were right that Carter had been misrepresented in the media coverage of his administration, there were good reasons to think that his presidency would be more susceptible to misinterpretation than others. After all, Jimmy Carter had come to the White House following a remarkably rapid rise to national prominence and was the only successful modern candidate for the presidency who began his campaign as a genuine dark horse. Moreover, Carter took up his duties in the national capital in the immediate aftermath of Watergate, when the media was confident, probably overconfident, about its ability to expose bad policy and uncover nefarious deeds. The president was little known, and Washington reporters were sure that they knew, or could easily learn, everything that was important about a White House occupant. Perhaps also, the alleged misjudgments of Jimmy Carter were related to important characteristics that made him different from other modern presidential politicians—his sincere religious convictions, his southern origins, his independence from the national party he came to lead. Whether, in the final analysis, Carter was responsible for whatever misunderstandings about himself and his administration that may have existed was less important to me than the possibility that an open and exhaustively examined modern presidency could be widely misjudged. For a young scholar participating in these interviews, evaluating the justice that might exist in the complaints regarding the misrepresentation of the Carter presidency became a kind of professional political science puzzle that seemed to raise important questions about how and where we find the right pieces to put together accurate portraits of recent White House occupants.

In many ways, the inspiration for writing this particular book about Carter's work as a foreign policy maker occurred when one of the familiar pieces in the Carter puzzle crumbled before my eyes. While searching at the Carter Library for documents dealing with the neutron bomb controversy, I asked the archivists for the files related to President Carter's speech on U.S.-Soviet relations that he delivered in Annapolis in the summer of 1978.[8] A frequently repeated anecdote about that speech had been reported by James Fallows in a long and very influential article that appeared in two

---

in his own memoirs, but probably took great pleasure in his successful law suit against the *Washington Post* for a false story it published during the Carter-Reagan transition.

8. Detailed accounts of the drafting of the Annapolis speech and the neutron bomb issue are found in Chapters 4 and 5.

issues of the *Atlantic Monthy* during the third year of Carter's presidency.[9] Fallows had been Carter's head speechwriter in the early years of the administration and reported that President Carter had casually put together his speech to the Annapolis cadets by stapling together two memos—one from his secretary of state, who wanted to preserve détente, and one from his national security adviser, who was growing increasingly wary of Soviet expansionism in the third world. The fact that the president would prepare an important foreign policy address in this careless manner was taken as evidence that he could neither recognize nor reconcile the significant differences between his principal foreign policy advisers. I had no particular interest in the speech itself, but wanted, out of idle and somewhat scholarly curiosity, to see the staple holes that Fallows had made famous. They were not there.

Instead, there was a large file of memorandums about proposed topics and language for the speech which the president had evidently read with care. The memos were heavily underlined. There was an outline written in the president's hand on multiple pages of legal pad and a draft of some thirty or forty pages that Carter had prepared, on his own, at Camp David on the weekend before the Annapolis commencement where he was scheduled to speak. There was no evidence to suggest that the speech had been slapped together, or even that Vance and Brzezinski were major contributors in the drafting process. Discovering that that often repeated and allegedly revealing anecdote about President Carter was, in fact, false encouraged me to look more closely at what he actually did in connection with a series of foreign policy actions and issues.[10] What documents did he read?

9. James Fallows, "The Passionless Presidency," *Atlantic Monthly,* May and June 1979.

10. The Fallows articles in the *Atlantic* tell another anecdote about the president spending his time scheduling the White House tennis courts that is even more famous than the one about the stapled speech. The president did make it a practice to let his secretary know when he would not be able to play on the courts so that others could use them, but the conclusion that some readers have drawn from Fallows's tennis court anecdote—that Carter gave inordinate time and attention to the trivia of White House management—is ludicrous. Even a casual reader of the President's Handwriting File or his appointment calendar in the Carter Library discovers that the president was spending almost all of his many working hours dealing with substantive aspects of the issues on his agenda. That agenda may have been too long or too ideologically diffuse to convey a clear picture to the American people about the principles and priorities of the administration (and Fallows makes those important

What did he think about the problems he was confronting? With whom did he consult? How did he do his foreign policy work?

This book then has a dual agenda. It uses Carter and his administration as examples to explore some general questions about the range and variety of things that presidents do in making foreign policy. At the same time it engages in some revisionism of what we know, or think we know, about what one particular president did while he was in the White House. Particular attention is paid to whether or not the contemporary public accounts of events in the Carter administration were accurate. These subjects require that we examine the selected case study materials in considerable, and some may think excessive, detail. But the devil, they say, is in the details; and that means that there are some devilishly complicated stories that need to be told about how President Jimmy Carter went about working in the world.

---

observations), but Carter was never wasting his time on White House recreational schedules while more pressing matters were overlooked.

1

LINING UP A TEAM
The Warnke Nomination

For every new president, but especially for one little known prior to the campaign, the appointment process can become an important vehicle by which the new chief executive introduces himself to Washington and the world. The people the president chooses, or passes over, for senior positions in the cabinet and the White House staff often indicates where policy in the new administration may be going and whether the administration will have the competence to get there.

The newly elected president in 1976 was required by law and custom to make approximately three thousand executive-branch appointments during the transition and early months of the new administration.[1] And, of course, many of those appointments required Senate confirmation and political consultation with individual senators and the committees on which they served. In order to put together a foreign policy team, Carter needed to select his secretaries of state and defense, a director of the CIA, a national security adviser, an assortment of deputy, under, and assistant secretaries, as well as ambassadors to the United Nations and to more than 150 nations and negotiating teams.

Jimmy Carter clearly realized the importance of the appointments he would have to make. He started thinking about the transition while the campaign was still under way and assigned a separate staff to do prelimi-

1. Stephen Hess, *Organizing the Presidency* (Washington, D.C., 1976), 19.

nary planning for his anticipated administration. Later he asked his long-time Georgia staff assistant and his most trusted campaign adviser, Hamilton Jordan, to take charge of the screening for major personnel decisions. Despite the early planning, Carter took his time in naming his cabinet officers and was slower to announce the full cabinet roster than any of his recent predecessors.[2]

The foreign policy team was a mixture of conventional and creative choices. For secretary of state, Carter selected a lawyer with broad experience in the Defense Department during the Kennedy and Johnson years and a record of involvement in sensitive negotiations. Cyrus Vance, Carter reports in his memoirs, was nearly everyone's first or second recommendation for secretary of state.[3] Harold Brown, who accepted the top position at the Pentagon, was another veteran of the McNamara-era Defense Department. He was a scientist by training, the president of a major university, and an expert on military technology. Like Vance, Brown was a popular choice for a senior foreign policy position. The selection of Zbigniew Brzezinski as national security adviser was more controversial.

Brzezinski, a professor of international relations at Columbia University and the author of numerous books on foreign affairs, had known Carter longer and supported him earlier than most of the people under consideration for senior appointments in the administration. But Brzezinski, unlike Vance or Brown, could be bold in his thinking and outspoken in his analysis of people and issues. The Polish-born academic was articulate, ambitious, and aggressive. According to one of his senior assistants in the Carter White House, Brzezinski put on heavy shoes when playing backyard soccer at the annual staff picnic. "When he charged the ball on the small playing field, others soon learned to get out of the way."[4] He could be just as combative in the game of making foreign policy.[5] But if there were concerns about Brzezinski's operating style, there were also good reasons for the president

2. Burton I. Kaufman, *The Presidency of James Earl Carter, Jr.* (Lawrence, Kans., 1993), 26. His successors were even slower.

3. Jimmy Carter, *Keeping Faith: Memoirs of a President* (New York, 1982), 50.

4. Gary Sick, *All Fall Down: America's Tragic Encounter with Iran* (New York, 1986), 358.

5. Clark Clifford reports that he advised President Carter not to appoint Brzezinski to the NSC post. When Carter asked Clifford what job he should give to Brzezinski, Clifford jokingly replied, "Make him the first American Ambassador to the Bermuda Triangle." Clark Clifford, *Counsel to the President* (New York, 1991), 621.

to appoint him as national security adviser. The same staff assistant who noted the aggressive play at the picnic believed that Brzezinski possessed an "irreverent inventiveness" that made him extremely valuable to Jimmy Carter.[6] He could give the president new ideas, perspective on world events, and the intellectual stimulation of a first-class teacher of international politics. Moreover, Brzezinski, unlike many of the senior White House staff members, was Carter's peer in age and was both willing and able to confront him with bad news and criticisms. The president was happy to have a national security adviser who would speak his mind, and he understood that Brzezinski might have some difficulty deferring to a secretary of state.[7]

Carter was satisfied with his two senior appointments in foreign affairs even though they may have embarrassed Hamilton Jordan. The president's senior political adviser had foolishly said during the campaign that "if, after the inauguration, you find a Cy Vance as Secretary of State and Zbigniew Brzezinski as head of National Security, then I would say we failed. And I'd quit."[8] The point Jordan was trying to make with his ill-chosen examples was that Carter would not be a conventional establishment president and that coming to Washington as an outsider would inject some creativity into the foreign policy appointment process. Jordan's point may not have been apropos in the naming of the secretary of state or the NSC adviser, but he was right about some of the other national security nominations Carter made. Two of the president's nominees—Andrew Young as UN ambassador and Theodore Sorensen as CIA director—were particularly creative.

Young, a protégé of Martin Luther King, Jr., a civil rights activist, and a Georgia politician, had no experience in foreign affairs. But the appointment of an African American to this important ambassadorship, which also carried cabinet rank in the Carter administration, suggested a new direction in U.S. policy regarding Africa and made Young the most prominent black in the new administration. Later, some of his less than diplomatic remarks and meetings he held with Palestinians would cause problems for the president, but Young fully fulfilled the expectations that he would be an unconventional UN ambassador with special credibility and effectiveness in dealing with the third world. Other Carter nominees with experience in the

6. Sick, *All Fall Down*, 358.
7. Carter, *Keeping Faith*, 52–54.
8. Hamilton Jordan, quoted in David S. McLellan, *Cyrus Vance* (Totowa, N.J., 1985), 24.

civil rights movement, particularly Patricia Derian, became active proponents of the president's human rights agenda and brought a genuinely new, if not always well received, perspective to the foreign policy bureaucracies.

Sorensen, a speechwriter and special assistant to President Kennedy, was another unconventional choice. He had no experience in intelligence work other than his years as a White House consumer of CIA briefings, which made his appointment a break with the tradition of selecting directors who had some background in the intelligence community. That tradition had already been violated by President Ford's appointment of George Bush, but Bush at least had wartime military credentials, which Sorensen lacked. Moreover, questions were raised immediately after he was selected about Sorensen's having been a conscientious objector during the Korean War. Though there were other questions raised, including questions about his legal career, his use of classified materials in the writing of his book about the Kennedy administration, and affidavits filed on behalf of Daniel Ellsberg in the Pentagon Papers trial, it was probably his personal decision to seek exemption from the draft in the late 1940s that put his nomination at risk in the Senate.[9] After Sorensen appeared before the Senate Select Committee on Intelligence to defend his reputation, he withdrew his name from further consideration for the post. The president later nominated Admiral Stansfield Turner, an Annapolis classmate with a distinguished military record, to be director of the CIA.

Though Carter abandoned Sorensen as soon as controversy arose about his nomination, he stuck with another controversial national security nominee to the end and secured a favorable confirmation vote for Paul Warnke as director of the Arms Control and Disarmament Agency and chief negotiator for the Strategic Arms Limitation Talks (SALT).[10] Along the way the president encountered many of the problems that accompany the appointment and confirmation processes. His nominee's public positions on various defense and arms control issues were treated as harbingers of the decisions that the president would make about weapon systems and arms limitation treaty provisions. The assumption made by Warnke's critics on Capitol Hill

9. "Controversial Nominations in 1977," in *Presidency 1977*, by Congressional Quarterly, Inc. (Washington, D.C., 1978), 40.

10. Warnke would also be in charge of the other arms control negotiating teams dealing with the Soviet Union on a comprehensive test ban, restrictions on anti-satellite weapons, and other issues, but the SALT delegation was his most important negotiating assignment.

was that the personnel and policy decisions of the new administration would be intertwined. In fact, in the area of arms control, they were disjointed; and the Senate debate over the Warnke nomination went on at precisely the same time that the president was developing a dramatic arms control proposal that was intended to satisfy both Warnke and Warnke's staunchest critics.

The Two Pauls

During the 1976 presidential campaign, when Carter was asked to name the people he consulted on matters of national security and arms control, he often mentioned Paul Nitze and Paul Warnke.[11] They were among the names most likely to be mentioned by any Democratic candidate for the presidency in the mid-1970s. Like Cyrus Vance, both Nitze and Warnke were former Defense Department officials in the Johnson administration. They came to Washington from successful careers in the legal and financial communities that had long supplied the leading members of the foreign policy establishment. When not in office, they were frequent authors, lecturers, and congressional committee witnesses on current issues in national security and foreign affairs. Nitze's public service dated back to the Roosevelt administration and included the directorship of the State Department's Policy Planning Staff under President Truman. Though Nitze had also served as an arms control negotiator during the Nixon years and initially supported Senator Henry "Scoop" Jackson in the 1976 Democratic presidential primaries, he and Warnke were both courted by the Carter campaign. In July of 1976 they were, along with Brown, Vance, and others, part of a group of foreign and defense policy experts who met with Carter in Plains and were invited to contribute ideas to the campaign staff.[12] After the November election, the two Pauls were high on the list for prominent positions in the new administration. In the normal course of events, they could easily have become colleagues serving the president who succeeded in bringing their party back to power. But 1977 was not a normal year within

11. For evidence of influence by Nitze and Warnke in the 1976 campaign, see Jules Witcover, *Marathon: The Pursuit of the Presidency, 1972–1976* (New York, 1977), 319; and Strobe Talbott, *The Master of the Game: Paul Nitze and the Nuclear Peace* (New York, 1989), 150.

12. For an account of this meeting see Talbott, *The Master of the Game*, 147–150; and Paul Nitze, *From Hiroshima to Glasnost: At the Center of Decision, a Memoir* (New York, 1989), 347–350.

the community of experts on arms control and national security. It was, in some ways, the year that that community came apart.

The international control of nuclear weapons and the systems used to deliver them to enemy territory had been on the U.S. foreign policy agenda since the Truman administration, but the first decade of the cold war provided little opportunity for progress in any arms reductions. Serious negotiations with the Soviet Union began only after the Cuban missile crisis, when both superpowers realized the dangers of confrontation in the nuclear age. Even then, the early agreements often dealt with limited aspects of the ongoing arms race and were presented as small steps in a long journey that would later lead to reductions in the superpower nuclear arsenals. A hot line was established for reliable emergency communications; nuclear testing in the atmosphere (but not underground) was prohibited; a non-proliferation treaty was signed; and agreements were negotiated to prohibit placement of nuclear weapons in outer space, on the seabeds, or in Antarctica (locations neither side particularly wanted to use anyway). Though several of these agreements had important international consequences, particularly those dealing with testing and proliferation, none of the early arms control achievements placed effective limits on the size or capabilities of the growing nuclear arsenals acquired by the United States and the Soviet Union. That subject would not receive serious discussion until the late 1960s and early 1970s.

The detailed planning for strategic arms limitation and what came to be called the SALT process began in the McNamara Pentagon. Paul Nitze and Paul Warnke were both present at the creation of SALT. They took part in the earliest government deliberations about what might be accomplished in superpower negotiations on the size and makeup of strategic arsenals. Warnke remembers their conversations, often over lunch at the Pentagon, about the exciting prospects of talking with the Soviets about the offensive and defensive strategic weapon systems that were at the heart of the nuclear balance.[13] The secretary of defense they worked for wanted to limit both offensive weapons and anti-ballistic missile systems to ensure a stable strategic relationship between the two cold war rivals. McNamara raised some of these subjects at the brief Glassboro, New Jersey, meeting between Johnson and Kosygin, but without much success.

13. Paul Warnke, interview by author, Washington, D.C., February 16, 1995.

When the initiation of formal U.S.-Soviet strategic arms limitation talks was postponed following the Soviet invasion of Czechoslovakia in 1968, the task of securing limits on superpower strategic systems fell to the Nixon administration. Arms control for Nixon and his national security adviser, Henry Kissinger, became part of a larger effort to transform U.S.-Soviet relations. The SALT process was the centerpiece of détente and the best evidence for President Nixon's claim that the era of confrontation between the United States and the Soviet Union had ended and the era of negotiation begun. The first SALT agreements, completed near the end of Nixon's first term, involved a permanent treaty limiting anti-ballistic missile (ABM) systems and an interim agreement freezing, for a five-year period, the number of strategic missile launchers on land and at sea that each superpower could possess. The expectation was that, during the five years that the interim limitations would be in effect, a permanent treaty on offensive strategic weapon reductions would be negotiated. Though these agreements and the 1972 Moscow summit at which they were signed were popular with the American public, détente failed to develop in Nixon's second term. Distracted and eventually destroyed by Watergate, Nixon could not bring his foreign policy efforts during his second administration to fruition. But even without the president's domestic political problems, improving relations with the Soviet Union would have been problematic.

In the mid-1970s the foundations of détente were cracking. A major confrontation between the superpowers occurred in the Middle East during the Yom Kippur War, and Soviet-backed forces gained ground in Africa and Southeast Asia. The negotiations for a follow-on agreement to SALT I were also in trouble. The discussions between U.S. and Soviet negotiators were long, complicated, and inconclusive. During the ratification of the SALT I accords, Senator Jackson secured passage of a resolution requiring that future strategic arms agreements include equal numbers of weapons for each side. Because of differences in geography, technology, and alliance structures between the United States and the USSR, and because of different choices the superpowers had made in the procurement of strategic systems, this would be a difficult criterion to meet. Jackson worked to undermine détente in other ways as well. The passage of the Jackson-Vanik amendment, requiring Soviet officials to loosen policies on Jewish emigration (something they refused to do) before receiving normal trade arrangements with the United States, effectively slowed the expansion of détente from arms control into other spheres of cooperation. President Ford, originally enthusiastic about the prospects for arms control during his brief 1974 meeting with Brezhnev in Vladivostok, was later challenged for his party's nomination by Ronald Reagan, and postponed the completion of a SALT II treaty until after the election. On the larger issue of détente, Ford backed away from the grandiose claims about a new generation of peace that had been made by Nixon in 1972 and even called on his campaign staff and administration to refrain from using the word *détente* to describe U.S.-Soviet relations.

The political decline of détente in general was accompanied by a decline in public support for arms control. Dissatisfaction with arms control found expression on both the left and right in American politics and within the Democratic Party. Paul Nitze and Paul Warnke became leading spokesmen for the two distinct sets of criticisms that were commonly made about superpower arms control negotiations. For Nitze, there was a growing suspicion that the Soviet Union was using arms control and détente to cover an effort to win the arms race by acquiring effective nuclear superiority. Americans in the 1950s and 1960s had not been terribly excited about the question of whether nuclear superiority mattered, as long as they had it. But when the Soviet nuclear arsenal grew rapidly in the 1970s, despite the SALT I agreements and the SALT II negotiations, conservative observers began to fear that the Soviet Union did not accept the American goal of parity or equivalence in strategic forces. Some suspected that the Soviet Union genuinely sought a usable nuclear superiority. In January of 1976, an influential article by Nitze published in *Foreign Affairs* warned that Soviet numerical superiority and advantages in missile throw-weight (the technical measure of how many payload pounds a missile could carry), combined with the improvements in missile accuracy that both sides would eventually achieve, would make American land-based missiles vulnerable to preemptive attack. Such an attack, or the knowledge that it was feasible, would give the Soviet Union a greater chance of prevailing in a nuclear war or, more importantly, the ability to put effective pressure on the United States in a crisis short of war.[14]

In 1976, at roughly the same time that he was being courted by the Car-

14. Paul Nitze, "Assuring Strategic Stability in an Era of Détente," *Foreign Affairs* 54, no. 2 (January 1976).

ter campaign, Nitze was asked by then CIA director George Bush to join a team of outside experts who would review the current CIA estimates of Soviet military strength. The so-called Team B that Nitze joined produced a report which concluded that Soviet military spending was far higher than previously assumed and that the Soviet strategic threat was greater than had previously been acknowledged. The obvious policy to follow, if these things were true, was for the United States to increase its defense budget and either suspend arms control negotiations with the Soviet Union or radically revise our existing negotiating positions and demand deep cuts in the Soviet arsenal. Nitze favored both new arms and new arms control policies. He hoped that a Democratic administration would avoid the dangers of détente and pursue these objectives. Naturally, his candidate in 1976 was Senator Jackson, who had been politically aggressive in raising questions about the SALT negotiations and the whole direction of détente. When Jackson's campaign faltered early in the primary season, Nitze was left without a candidate he could enthusiastically support. He did not know Carter, but at the urging of his children sent him a campaign contribution and copies of some of the things he had written about national security.[15] After their July meeting in Plains, he submitted a long memo on strategic issues that, much to his surprise, Carter read with care.[16]

On the left, the disillusionment with détente and arms control had a different set of arguments and a different set of advocates. According to critics of the SALT II negotiations like Paul Warnke, arms control was failing to do enough to stem the quickening pace of an arms race driven largely by technological progress rather than Soviet desires to achieve a war-winning nuclear capability. Though the ABM treaty had for all practical purposes eliminated an entire class of weaponry (missile defense systems), the interim SALT agreement did little to reduce offensive strategic arms. It capped each side at the number of missile launchers held or under construction in 1972,

15. Talbott, *Master of the Game*, 147–48.

16. Nitze, *From Hiroshima to Glasnost*, 349–50. The July meeting in Plains was the first time during the election year that Carter and Nitze had an opportunity to have a substantive conversation. Peter Bourne, a longtime Carter associate, tried to arrange a Washington lunch for Carter and Nitze in the spring of 1976, but Carter's campaign staff canceled that commitment to give their candidate more time to shake hands with crowds in the Maryland suburbs. When Bourne called Nitze to inform him that the lunch had been canceled, he sensed that Nitze was offended. Peter Bourne, interview by author, Atlanta, Ga., February 21, 1997.

even though many analysts considered those numbers to be unnecessarily high, and it allowed older missiles to be replaced with newer and more effective ones. Furthermore, SALT I said nothing about missiles with multiple warheads, or multiple independently targetable reentry vehicles (MIRVs) as they were officially called in the Pentagon, which were dramatically increasing the lethal capabilities of existing strategic systems. When the Vladivostok accords were signed, liberal arms control observers were even more distressed. The documents approved by Ford and Brezhnev provided for equal, but extremely high, numbers for each side. They included some limitation on multiple warheads but not enough to prevent the land-based missile vulnerability problem that so concerned Paul Nitze and other right-wing critics of the SALT process. For arms control advocates like Paul Warnke, SALT had become a way for the two superpowers to plan and manage the continuing growth of their nuclear arsenals. Radical new steps were needed to produce genuine arms reduction. In 1975, Warnke proposed that the United States attempt to break out of the slow-paced and low-yield SALT II negotiations and announce a temporary unilateral act of restraint in the development or deployment of a new strategic system. If the Soviet Union responded in kind within a reasonable period, then further restraints could be announced.[17] Warnke's candidate in 1976 was Morris "Mo" Udall, but his candidacy (which lasted longer than Jackson's) also fell to the little-known former Georgia governor who surprised everyone in the Democratic primaries.

In the summer of 1976, Jimmy Carter found himself at the head of a party containing both liberal and conservative critics of Ford administration policies toward arms control and the Soviet Union. In the campaign he played a balancing act in which his criticisms of Nixon, Ford, and Kissinger were designed to be appealing to both wings of his political party. This was, no doubt, partly a matter of campaign strategy, but it may also have been a reflection of Carter's genuine independence from any doctrinaire national security positions, liberal or conservative. Carter was a candidate, and later a president, who defied simple ideological labeling. He believed that he could take the best elements from the wide variety of ideas within the Dem-

17. Warnke's 1975 ideas about new techniques in arms control negotiations were reprinted during the confirmation battle two years later. Paul C. Warnke, "Arms Control, Before Time Runs Out," *New York Times*, February 9, 1977.

ocratic Party and use them in shaping his own policies and decisions. After the election, he continued to consult with both the liberal and conservative critics of arms control without making it clear which side of the debate about the SALT process and détente he would eventually take. Early in the administration, he gave indications that might have been interpreted as steps to the right or left. In fact, he was simultaneously moving in both directions.

In his inaugural address Carter surprised many observers by calling for a truly radical arms control objective: the elimination of nuclear weapons from the planet. In the same speech, he also called for greater attention to human rights. Early in the Carter administration, criticisms of Soviet human rights violations were made in public and taken as signs that the president would take a hard line on détente. The president's public pronouncements and gestures of support for dissidents within the Soviet Union were, however, accompanied by frequent comments about the importance of arms control and the reduction of the danger of nuclear war. When Carter reviewed candidates for high-level positions in the administration, he considered both Nitze and Warnke.[18] When he wanted advice on SALT, he consulted with all the opinion leaders within the Democratic Party.

Two weeks after his inauguration, Carter had a long private meeting with Senator Jackson. He asked the senator for his suggestions about arms control and SALT; Jackson responded by having his foreign policy assistant, Richard Perle, produce a twenty-three-page, single-spaced memorandum of recommendations for SALT II, which was delivered to the White House on February 15.[19] Paul Warnke, by then the president's announced nominee as Arms Control and Disarmament Agency (ACDA) director and chief SALT negotiator, read the Perle memo and gave Carter his reactions in a brief handwritten note.[20] The president also had Secretary of Defense

18. Zbigniew Brzezinski, *Power and Principle: Memoirs of the National Security Advisor 1977–1981* (New York, 1983), 11.

19. Henry M. Jackson to Jimmy Carter, "Memorandum for the President on SALT," February 15, 1977, Henry M. Jackson Papers, accession no. 3560–5, box 315, folder 35, University of Washington Libraries. A copy of the memo can also be found in the conference papers on file at the Carter Library for the conference titled "SALT II and Growth of Mistrust."

20. Paul Warnke to the President, February 19 [1977], Office of the Staff Secretary, President's Handwriting File, Box 9, Folder 2/23/77, Carter Library, Atlanta. Talbott reports that

Brown and Secretary of State Vance circulate the memo widely within their departments and gave instructions that it was to be given a respectful response. To Senator Jackson, the president sent a personal note in which he wrote, "Your SALT memorandum is excellent, and of great help to me."[21] Carter was attempting to show some sympathy for the arms control critics of both the left and the right. That was more than they were able to show for each other.

The Nomination

Paul Warnke came highly recommended for the two positions for which he was named on February 2, 1977. Both Brzezinski and Vance suggested him for positions in the administration.[22] He was a distinguished attorney educated at Yale and Columbia and a former partner in the influential Washington law firm of Covington and Burling. During the Johnson administration he had served in the Defense Department under Robert McNamara and Clark Clifford. He was general counsel to the Department of Defense and then assistant secretary for international security affairs—the same job Paul Nitze had held earlier in the Kennedy-Johnson years. Those two positions gave Warnke exposure to a wide range of defense and national security issues. He was one of the Defense Department officials who opposed the continuation of the Vietnam War and supported Secretary Clifford in his efforts to persuade Lyndon Johnson that America's only hope was some sort of negotiated settlement. When Johnson left office, Warnke joined a new law firm headed by his former boss, Clark Clifford, and combined an active legal practice with frequent public statements and Capitol Hill testimony on issues related to national security and defense. Along with several other members of the new administration, including the president, Warnke had

---

Warnke called the Perle memo a "first-class polemic." Strobe Talbott, *Endgame: The Inside Story of SALT II* (New York, 1979), 53. Warnke does not recall describing the document in that terminology. Warnke, interview.

21. Jimmy Carter to Senator Jackson, handwritten note, February 17, 1977, Zbigniew Brzezinski Collection, Box 40, Folder "SALT [Jackson, Senator Henry M. 3/77–6/77]," Carter Library. (Information in brackets in citations of Carter Library manuscript material, here and in subsequent notes, refers to a folder within a folder, in accordance with the style recommended by the staff of the Carter Library.)

22. Cyrus Vance, *Hard Choices: Four Critical Years in Managing America's Foreign Policy* (New York, 1983), 43.

been a member of the Trilateral Commission established by David Rockefeller and administered by Brzezinski that explored new avenues of international cooperation among the United States, the major European powers, and Japan.[23]

Carter reports that Warnke, despite his obvious qualifications, twice declined the ACDA and arms control negotiator nominations before finally accepting.[24] His hesitancy may have come from the substantial financial sacrifices involved in leaving private legal practice for government service at a time when he had three children in college, or the separation from home and family that would clearly be involved in serving as the nation's chief arms control negotiator.[25] Carter eventually persuaded Warnke to join the administration at a Saturday morning meeting in the White House. The combined appointment as ACDA director and chief SALT negotiator would make Warnke a key arms control adviser to a president who placed that issue high on his foreign policy agenda. Carter made his decision to name Warnke on January 29,[26] but delays in the White House clearance process held up a public announcement for several days. In the meantime, speculation about the forthcoming nomination appeared in the press along with early indications that the nominee would be controversial on Capitol Hill.[27]

The controversy centered on some of the statements Warnke had made or written in his years as an active critic of both the slow-moving SALT process and the conservative claim that the Soviet Union was winning the

23. The other former trilateralists in Carter's cabinet were Secretary of Defense Harold Brown, Secretary of State Cyrus Vance, Secretary of the Treasury Michael Blumenthal, and National Security Adviser Brzezinski. At the time of Warnke's nomination, there were fourteen former members of the commission in the administration.

24. "Press Conference February 8, 1977," in *Public Papers of the Presidents of the United States, Jimmy Carter 1977* (Washington, D.C., 1977), 94.

25. There was also speculation in the press that Warnke was disappointed in not being named secretary of defense. Lee Lescaze, "Warnke to Head Arms Control Agency," *Washington Post*, February 1, 1977. Warnke reports that he never expected the top Pentagon post, but did have an interest in serving as deputy secretary of state. He fully supported Warren Christopher's nomination to that position and hesitated to accept the arms control appointments for the reasons listed above. Warnke, interview.

26. The President to Jody Powell, handwritten note, January 29, 1977, White House Central File, Subject File, Executive, Box FG-209, Carter Library.

27. "Warnke to Head Arms Control Agency," *Washington Post*, February 1, 1977.

arms race. A vivid writer, Warnke once described the decisions of the United States and the Soviet Union in the procurement of new strategic arms as comparable to the behavior of "apes on a treadmill." Much effort and not much intelligence was being expended by both sides in a process that was going nowhere.[28] This was provocative language.

One of the people provoked by Warnke's views on arms control was his former associate in the Johnson administration, Paul Nitze. Early in 1977, Nitze was in the process of shifting his energies from being an expert on the inside of national security affairs to becoming a critic on the outside. He had resigned from his last full-time position in government, as a member of the SALT negotiating team in 1974, and was on record as being skeptical about the value of the Vladivostok accords and the general direction that Kissinger and Ford were taking on détente and arms control.[29] Though he supported Carter in the 1976 presidential election, he wanted more spending on strategic arms than either candidate called for in the campaign. His advice was solicited and considered, but according to Strobe Talbott, Nitze's confident, perhaps even arrogant, style of presenting his views at the July 1976 meeting in Plains did not impress Carter and kept the president from extending any invitation for Nitze to join the new administration.[30] Late in the fall of 1976 Nitze, along with Carter energy adviser James Schlesinger, became a founding member of the Committee on the Present Danger, an organization established to lobby for more hard-line policies in defense spending and U.S.-Soviet relations. This organization would later prove to be an effective opponent of SALT II and a number of other arms control initiatives, but Nitze's first important public criticism of the Carter administration was his opposition to the Warnke nomination.

On the weekend after Warnke's name was officially announced for the ACDA and SALT negotiator posts, Nitze made several phone calls to prominent members of Congress and composed a blunt letter to the chairman of the Senate Foreign Relations Committee calling into question Warnke's fitness to hold two important arms control positions in the new administration. "I am concerned," Nitze wrote, "that Mr. Warnke, who has

28. Paul Warnke, "Apes on a Treadmill," *Foreign Policy*, no. 18 (spring 1975).

29. Paul Nitze, "The Vladivostok Accord and SALT II," *The Review of Politics* 37, no. 2 (April 1975).

30. Talbott, *Master of the Game*, 147–50.

spoken with such certainty on matters of military requirements, weapons capabilities, and strategy, may nevertheless not be a qualified student or competent judge of any of these matters. . . . I cannot bring myself to believe that the Senate would be well advised to give its consent to Mr. Warnke's appointment."[31] Nitze reports in his memoirs that when he contacted Senator Jackson about his Warnke reservations, the senator had no plans to actively oppose the nomination.[32] Though questions had been raised about Warnke as soon as his name appeared in the press (including the circulation of an anonymous memo on Capitol Hill listing and attacking some of Warnke's controversial statements),[33] Jackson did not immediately speak out against the president's nominee. He evidently changed his mind when Nitze's letter and public testimony guaranteed an open battle within the national security community. In that battle, Paul Nitze was the self-appointed general in charge of the assault on his former Pentagon colleague, his longtime acquaintance, his occasional dinner guest, and his fellow member of the foreign policy establishment, Paul Warnke.

The Hearings

The controversy surrounding the Warnke nomination dealt primarily with the nominee's record as a commentator on issues of national security after leaving the Department of Defense in 1969. There were several less important issues raised in the course of the hearings before the Senate Foreign Relations and Armed Services Committees—whether Warnke had been involved in the unauthorized release of the Pentagon Papers, whether his legal representation of the government of Algeria had been proper and advisable, and whether it was wise to have a single individual serve as both

31. The full text of the letter is reprinted in U.S. Senate, Committee on Armed Services, *Consideration of Mr. Paul Warnke to be Director of the U.S. Arms Control and Disarmament Agency and Ambassador*, 95th Congress, 1st sess., February 22, 23, 28, 1977, 165–66. (Hereinafter cited as *Consideration of Mr. Paul Warnke.*) Nitze sent President Carter a short note and a copy of the letter on the same day he sent it to Senator Sparkman. Paul Nitze to the President, February 7, 1977, White House Central File, Name File, Warnke, Paul C. ACDA Director Nomination Against 2/1/77–2/18/77, Carter Library.

32. Nitze, *From Hiroshima to Glasnost*, 354.

33. "Warnke Draws Senate Fire on Nuclear Arms Remarks" *Washington Post,* February 2, 1977. Warnke recalls that the anonymous memo that quickly made the rounds on Capitol Hill had been prepared by a staff member in Senator Daniel Patrick Moynihan's office without the senator's knowledge or approval. Warnke, interview.

ACDA director and head of the SALT negotiating team. These secondary matters were adequately answered by the nominee or by other witnesses and were always less important than the questions raised about Warnke's public positions on weapon systems and arms control negotiations. In the 1970s, Warnke had spoken out against a number of strategic weapon systems, including the B-1 bomber and the Trident submarine. He advocated cuts in defense spending and called the arms competition between the United States and USSR senseless, proposing controversial techniques to break the momentum of the arms race. The long list of Warnke public statements about excessive defense spending and inadequate arms control measures led one of his critics to say that choosing Warnke for an important national security position was "like choosing a boll weevil to head the Department of Agriculture."[34]

At the hearings, Warnke turned out to be an articulate and forceful witness. He defended his public positions by arguing that while he opposed certain weapon systems, he certainly did not wish the United States to be defenseless. In the case of both the B-1 bomber and the Trident submarine, he had recommended the acquisition of new bombers and submarines that were less expensive than the systems selected by the Nixon and Ford administrations.[35] Though he did not favor B-1 or Trident when there were alternative systems under consideration, he testified that he could support them in 1977 when they were actively under development and the only available options for improving the airborne and sea-based components of America's strategic arsenal.[36] In general, he defended the provocative character of his public statements in the early 1970s by pointing out that individuals not in office tend to take more extreme positions than they do when they are working in government in order to draw attention to their ideas and stimulate public debate.

In the Senate Foreign Relations Committee, the nomination hearings—despite Nitze's highly critical testimony—went well and resulted in a favor-

34. Mark Lockman of the Liberty Lobby, quoted in "Debate on Warnke Sharpens," *Washington Post*, February 10, 1977.

35. Warnke supported the Trident missile, but not the large submarine from which it was to be launched. Warnke, interview.

36. The future of the B-1 bomber was a special case, since the Carter administration had not yet made a final decision about its procurement, and Warnke testified that he would support the president's decision when it was made.

able recommendation of the nominee by a vote of 14 to 2 as chief arms control negotiator and 15 to 1 as ACDA director. Only two senators, Republicans John Danforth and Robert P. Griffin, opposed Warnke's appointment as chief arms control negotiator. Several Republican members of the committee, especially Jacob Javits, actively supported the nominee. The real controversy came before the Armed Services Committee, which did not have jurisdiction over the nomination but elected to hold hearings in order to explore Warnke's views on defense and arms control issues. Armed Services chairman John Stennis, who would eventually vote against the Warnke nomination, agreed to help the administration by making sure that there was no vote on the nominee or recommendation sent to the floor from his committee.[37] Nevertheless, the second round of committee hearings did provide a forum for critics of the Warnke appointment. They also delayed the Senate vote and enhanced the controversy surrounding the nominee. In the two sets of hearings, Paul Nitze was the star witness opposed to the nomination, and Senator Jackson was Warnke's most hostile questioner. In an extensive series of aggressive questions about Warnke's views on various weapon systems, Jackson listed thirteen new strategic weapons that the United States had elected to procure against Warnke's advice. The senator from the state of Washington wondered how an individual who was on record as being against nearly every new strategic weapon entering the U.S. arsenal could effectively negotiate the future of those systems with the Soviets. Warnke provided detailed answers to Jackson's questions, which were followed up by several Republican and Democratic members of the committee.[38] In addition, he prepared written responses to specific questions Jackson raised about Warnke's past positions.

Warnke argued that he had two main reasons for opposing some new strategic weapon systems. Sometimes, as was the case with the B-1 bomber, he felt that the unit cost of each new plane would be too high and that as a result the air force would be unable to build an adequate number of them. Warnke preferred a cheaper model that could be produced in larger numbers and, by those larger numbers, frustrate Soviet defensive or preemptive plans. Much the same argument was made by Warnke about the new gener-

37. Lee Lescaze, "Senate Armed Services Forces Decide Against Warnke Vote," *Washington Post*, March 1, 1977.

38. *Consideration of Mr. Paul C. Warnke*, 16–20.

ation of missile-carrying submarine. Warnke wanted the United States to abandon plans for the Trident submarine and build a much larger fleet of smaller and quieter subs. The other reason Warnke gave for his opposition to new strategic arms was his belief that arms control could successfully foreclose the need for new and potentially destabilizing technologies. He lamented the fact that the United States had not been more aggressive in negotiations to prevent the placement of multiple warheads on strategic missiles. Though the United States benefited from that development in the short run, once the Soviet Union began to make the same improvement to their much larger and more plentiful land-based missiles, the United States faced new problems in vulnerability. Warnke opposed other new technologies, like the development of highly accurate warheads, on similar grounds. It would be better to negotiate an agreement to forgo new weapon systems or technological improvements in existing systems than it would be to enjoy a brief strategic advantage.[39]

The other line of questioning that proved to be contentious involved Warnke's published proposal that arms control negotiating deadlocks might be overcome by unilateral initiatives—for instance an announcement by the United States that it would postpone production of the B-1 bomber in the expectation that the Soviet Union would curtail a comparable strategic program in response. Warnke's position was stigmatized as "unilateral disarmament," arms reductions without reciprocal and matching reductions by the other side. Unilateral disarmament had traditionally been the pet project of radical peace groups on the fringes of the public policy debate about arms control. One of the conservative committees quickly organized to oppose the Warnke nomination called itself the "Emergency Coalition Against Unilateral Disarmament."[40] Warnke defended himself by pointing out that he had never favored unilateral disarmament. Instead, he advocated limited unilateral restraints that would be publicly announced and subsequently withdrawn if they failed to produce favorable reciprocal actions from the other side. In defending this tactic he cited several historical precedents in which unilateral initiatives led to successful permanent agreements—the

39. Response to Senator Byrd, in *Consideration of Mr. Paul C. Warnke*, 35.

40. The organization, headed by General Daniel Graham, former director of the U.S. Defense Intelligence Agency, and John M. Fisher, president of the American Security Council, ran a full-page ad opposing the Warnke nomination in the *Washington Post* on February 23, 1977.

moratoriums on atmospheric testing that preceded the limited test ban agreement, and the reduction of permitted ABM sites from two to one that was first incorporated in congressional legislation before it became an agreed-on addendum to the ABM treaty.[41]

When President Carter was asked at a press conference whether he supported unilateral initiatives, he reminded Warnke's critics that the president, not the ACDA director or the chief arms control negotiator, would make the important decisions about administration policy and that Warnke's views expressed in the past would not be decisive. Without criticizing Warnke's call for U.S. unilateral arms control restraints, Carter effectively defused the issue by turning it around and suggesting that the Soviets would be well advised to show some restraint in the deployment of their new medium-range and long-range mobile missiles.[42]

The high, or low, point of the hearings came when Senator Thomas McIntyre, a Democrat from New Hampshire and a Warnke supporter on the Armed Services Committee, tested the intensity of Nitze's opposition to the nominee. The senator asked the witness whether or not he considered himself to be a better American than Paul Warnke. Nitze's answer was, "I really do."[43] It was an inappropriate answer to an inappropriate question. Both Warnke and Nitze were intelligent and distinguished public servants who had worked in a variety of government appointments. Both were hard-working and honest individuals who held legitimate positions about the nature of nuclear deterrence and the role of arms control in American foreign policy. But if it was wrong to ask Nitze to reduce his differences with Warnke to a claim to superior patriotism, it was also revealing. In a way, it got to the heart of the matter. Paul Nitze did not think that he had a mere difference of opinion with Paul Warnke. He and the other conservative critics of strategic arms control policy and détente thought that the safety of the republic was at risk and that the growing Soviet military capabilities would be translated into cold war confrontations in which the United States would be forced to back down much as the Soviets had done over Cuba in 1962.

41. *Consideration of Mr. Paul C. Warnke*, 23–24.

42. *Public Papers of the Presidents of the United States, Jimmy Carter 1977*, 96.

43. After the hearing, Nitze requested permission to revise his answer and submitted the following elaboration: "I really do take exception to what I believe to be inconsistent and misleading testimony by Mr. Warnke." See *Consideration of Mr. Paul C. Warnke*, 183. For Nitze's views on this episode, see Nitze, *From Hiroshima to Glasnost*, 354–55.

This was not a minor matter, and in the long run responding to real and imagined Soviet military and political challenges would be one of the most important foreign policy issues facing the Carter administration.

At the outset of the administration, the White House political strategy for dealing with the Warnke confirmation controversy was basically to weather the storm.[44] Though some members of the Armed Services Committee, particularly Senator Gary Hart, wanted even longer hearings and a parade of witnesses enthusiastic about the Warnke nomination, the White House preferred a shorter list of witnesses and an earlier vote. With Democrats in control of the Senate by a 62 to 38 majority, the president was prepared to put his nomination to the test.

The Vote

In general, the four days of Senate floor debate over the Warnke nomination focused on the same issues that had been raised in the heated exchanges before the Armed Services Committee. Again the central question was whether or not Warnke's public positions on strategic issues in the years between his Pentagon service in the Johnson administration and his appointment by Carter were within the mainstream of national security discourse. In addition, accusations were made that the statements Warnke had recently made before the Foreign Relations and Armed Services Committees were inconsistent with his earlier positions. Critics of Warnke questioned the wisdom of his views or the honesty of his confirmation testimony. Some questioned both.

For a day or two, headline stories in major newspapers during the Senate debate discussed a controversial punctuation mark in one of the documents Warnke submitted to Senator Jackson. In detailed answers that Warnke prepared for Jackson, he included a number of long quotations from his speeches, articles, and statements on various strategic issues. One of the quotations came from the transcript of oral testimony before a Senate committee in 1972. In the transcript, Warnke had said that with regard to the superpower arms competition, there was "no purpose in either side's achieving a numerical superiority, which is not translatable into" military

---

44. This conclusion is based on the administration's behavior and not on documents. Many of the files dealing with personnel decisions remain closed at the Carter Library.

or political advantage.[45] In the quotation, the comma before "which" was omitted, then subsequently added. Senator Jackson claimed the changes in punctuation were a deliberate attempt to alter the meaning of the nominee's sworn statement. With the comma, the sentence suggested that nuclear superiority could not be translated into a military or political advantage; without the comma, the sentence left open the possibility that numerical superiority could, on at least some occasions, create an advantage for the side that had it. Did Warnke believe that nuclear superiority was useful in superpower confrontations or did he not? The answer, Jackson claimed, depended on the proper punctuation of the nominee's 1972 testimony, and the misplaced comma was evidence of an intentional attempt to doctor the historical record on this important issue.[46]

In fact, somewhere behind the complicated comma confusion, there was a difference of opinion between Jackson and Warnke on a real issue. Senator Jackson, and Paul Nitze for that matter, firmly believed that nuclear superiority could and should be achieved for the purpose of winning cold war showdowns. It was critical, they would argue, that the United States had strategic nuclear superiority at the time of the Cuban missile crisis and important that it not face some future crisis with the Soviets in possession of superior strategic power. Paul Warnke was more skeptical about the value of numerical superiorities in the huge nuclear arsenals that had been accumulated by the United States and the Soviet Union.

So was Henry Kissinger when he responded in frustration to hostile questions about the SALT I agreements (which temporarily allowed more missile launchers for the Soviet Union than for the United States). At a late night Moscow press conference after the signing of SALT I, Kissinger answered charges that the agreement left the Soviets in a better strategic position by asking, "What, in the name of God, is strategic superiority? What is the significance of it, politically, militarily, operationally, at these levels of

45. Warren Weaver, Jr., "Comma Now a Focus of Fight on Warnke," *New York Times*, March 9, 1977.

46. Thomas W. Scoville, as assistant to Mr. Warnke during the confirmation process, reports that Warnke's answers to Jackson's written questions were carefully drafted and proofread, but the quotations from his previous writings and statements were not. When they were later checked, the quotations contained numerous typographical errors. The missing comma was one of them. Thomas W. Scoville, telephone interview by author, March 20, 1995.

numbers? What do you do with it?"[47] Kissinger came to regret those questions, and the implication that he belonged in the camp that thought nuclear superiority of little value. Warnke took the Kissinger questions seriously. He was also not convinced in 1972 that either side had meaningful nuclear superiority over the other. Moreover, the SALT I agreements counted missile launchers at a time when the United States was well ahead of the Soviet Union in the development and deployment of multiple warheads. If you counted warheads in 1972 instead of launchers, and added in bombers, which were not included in the interim SALT I limits, the United States arguably possessed nuclear superiority—whatever that might mean—over the Soviet Union.

In his confirmation testimony before the Armed Services Committee, Warnke expressed the opinion that the nuclear balance in 1977 was best described as "rough equivalence." In a serious exchange with Senator Sam Nunn, he conceded that the Soviet Union might derive political advantage from the ability to destroy "a very substantial part of our land-based missiles."[48] Selected quotations from Warnke's past commentary on arms control and the strategic balance could make his exchange with Nunn appear to be a fundamental shift in his position. However, a full and fair review of the record showed that Warnke had always been dubious of both our ability to precisely measure strategic superiority and the capacity of either side to convert whatever superiority might exist into military or diplomatic leverage. He recognized the need for "cosmetic comparability" between the two sides for psychological and political reasons, but rejected the Jackson and Nitze claims that in either 1972 or 1977 the United States was in danger of losing the arms race to the Soviet Union.[49]

The fact that this important and complicated question regarding the meaning of strategic superiority became reduced to a discussion of the proper punctuation in a single sentence of testimony delivered five years be-

47. The quotation is from a Moscow press conference immediately after the completion of negotiations for SALT I. Henry Kissinger, quoted in William G. Hyland, *Mortal Rivals: Superpower Relations from Nixon to Reagan* (New York, 1987), 72.

48. *Consideration of Mr. Paul C. Warnke*, 10. For a summary of the hearing highlights, see "Warnke Said to Alter Views on Arms Policy," *Congressional Quarterly Weekly Report*, February 26, 1977, 348–49.

49. The term "cosmetic comparability" was used by Warnke to describe his position years after the nomination battle. Warnke, interview.

fore Warnke's nomination exemplifies the trivialization of policy debates that often occurs in Washington. Hubert Humphrey, defending the president's nominee in the floor debate, saw little merit in Jackson's claims that the allegedly altered punctuation was a worthy subject for Senate deliberation. He pointed out to his colleagues that there were numerous typographical errors in the voluminous material gathered by the committees that reviewed the Warnke nomination. This was certainly not surprising, "given the way our schools are teaching today."[50] Years later, Warnke observed that in his controversial sentence from the transcript of his 1972 testimony, he should have used the word "that" instead of "which."[51] That change would have removed any controversy from Warnke's statement in 1972. Warnke would then have been saying that no nation seeks nuclear superiority unless that nation thinks that such superiority is worthwhile. This is obviously true and misses the point. No matter how Warnke's sentence from 1972 was punctuated or worded, there was a real issue in his confirmation about the nature of nuclear superiority and the ability of either superpower to achieve it or use it. That real issue was hard to find and follow in the floor debate about the comma.

In public statements and in private consultations, Carter fought to win Senate confirmation for Warnke to both of the positions for which he had been named. At news conferences on February 8 (the day that Nitze began his public testimony against Warnke) and March 9 (the day of the Senate vote) Carter praised his nominee, expressed his confidence in Warnke's qualifications, and reminded the public that the president, not the ACDA director or the chief SALT negotiator, would make the important decisions about arms control policy.[52] At the March 9 press conference, the president attacked Warnke's opponents by saying that many of them "just don't want to see substantial reductions in nuclear weapons," a statement which was challenged by several senators who planned to vote against the nominee.[53]

Behind the scenes, Carter actively lobbied a long list of senators for

50. Weaver, "Comma Now a Focus of Fight on Warnke."
51. Warnke, interview.
52. *Public Papers of the Presidents of the United States, Jimmy Carter 1977*, 93–96, 345.
53. "Warnke Confirmed to Both Arms Posts Despite Harsh Debate," *Washington Post*, March 10, 1977. Moynihan sent Brzezinski a personal note complaining about the president's statement. White House Central File, Subject File, Executive, Box FG-209, Folder FG264/A, Carter Library.

Warnke's confirmation. On February 16, he wrote to Senator Richard Schweiker of Pennsylvania answering public statements Schweiker had made that Warnke would become the administration's "disarmament czar." Carter assured the senator that Warnke would not be the chairman of a Verification Panel, the organization that controlled arms control policy in the Nixon and Ford years. That panel had been eliminated in the early re-organization of the National Security Council which Carter had approved. Brzezinski, as head of the newly established Special Coordinating Commit-tee (SCC), would have responsibility for coordinating arms control policy. The next day, the president called Senators Russell Long, Jennings Ran-dolph, Robert C. Byrd, Henry Bellmon, Howard Cannon, John McClellan, and Richard Stone urging them to vote for Warnke. Carter paid particular attention to Robert Byrd, the Senate majority leader, who waited some time before eventually announcing that he would vote for Warnke. On the 17th, the vice president sent Carter a brief memo describing his breakfast conver-sation with Byrd, who was then still undecided, but promised not to use his leadership position to oppose the president's nominee.[54]

The following day, Carter wrote a note to Senator Orrin Hatch, again offering assurance that the president alone would be making the important decisions about the SALT negotiations. Prior to the Senate vote, additional phone calls were made to Senators Bellmon, Robert Byrd, Cannon, James Eastland, John Glenn, J. Bennett Johnston, Long, McClellan, Daniel Pat-rick Moynihan, Randolph, and Milton Young. Each received follow-up let-ters from the president, several with Carter's handwritten personal notes. On March 4, Carter spoke with Senator Lawton Chiles in the Oval Office and asked for his support on the Warnke vote. Both Florida senators, Chiles and Stone, who would eventually vote against the nomination, were being heavily lobbied with negative constituent mail and full-page ads opposing Warnke in major Florida newspapers.[55]

The president's congressional liaison staff gave Carter regular updates on the head count for the upcoming confirmation vote. Even after the Armed Services Hearings and Stennis's announcement that he would vote against

54. Walter Mondale to the President, memorandum, February 17, 1977, Office of the Staff Secretary, President's Handwriting File, Box 9, Folder 2/18/77 [1], Carter Library.

55. Documents relating to the president's activities in support of the nomination are found in the White House Central File, Subject File, Executive, Box FG-209, Folder FG 264/A 1/20/77 to 3/18/77, Carter Library.

the nominee, there was no doubt that the president had the votes to win on the Senate floor.[56] However, Warnke opponents kept interest in the vote alive by arguing that the confirmation process should be seen as a test for how well the new administration would be able to pursue its future arms control policies. If opposition to Warnke could be found among one-third of the Senate members plus one, they contended, the capacity of the administration to win ratification of a controversial SALT II treaty would be demonstrably limited.

In the end, there were 58 votes for Warnke as head of the SALT negotiating team, including 48 Democrats and 10 liberal Republicans (among them Edward Brooke, John Chafee, Mark Hatfield, Javits, Charles Mathias, and Charles Percy). Twelve members of the Democratic majority voted against the president's nominee—Jackson, both Georgia senators Nunn and Herman Talmadge, Armed Services Committee chairman Stennis, and Senators James Allen, Harry F. Byrd, Cannon, Chiles, Walter Huddleston, Moynihan, Stone, and Edward Zorinsky. In a separate vote, Warnke won appointment as ACDA director by the much larger margin of 70 to 29. Newspaper commentators noted, as opponents of the nomination hoped they would, that the first vote for confirmation fell short of what would be needed for ratification of a SALT II treaty.[57] The vote was, therefore, interpreted as only a partial victory for the administration.

On the first day after the vote, Warnke attended a meeting of the Special Coordinating Committee working on SALT negotiating positions and was greeted by comments about his "landslide" confirmation.[58] In his remarks at Warnke's swearing-in ceremony, Carter noted that his new arms control negotiator had been "trained for tough negotiations by some of the distinguished Senators behind me and their fellow Senators."[59] He went on to say that Warnke would be joining Secretary of State Vance on a trip to Moscow with a scheduled departure in just a few days. "This week the National Security Council, which has been working on the question of SALT negotia-

56. Frank Moore to the President, memorandum, March 5, 1977, Jordan Files, Box 59, Folder Feb 1977 [CF,O/A 67] [5], Carter Library.
57. "Warnke Confirmed to Both Arms Posts Despite Harsh Debate," *Washington Post*, March 10, 1977.
58. Talbott, *Endgame*, 57.
59. "Remarks at the Swearing in of Paul C. Warnke as Director, March 14, 1977," *Public Papers of the Presidents of the United States, Jimmy Carter 1977*, 379.

tions for a number of weeks with me, will evolve a fairly final position that Secretary Vance and Director Warnke will take with them."[60] That new SALT position had been developing within the administration throughout the Senate hearings and floor debate on the Warnke nomination, with very limited participation from the embattled nominee. It would give the new ACDA director and SALT negotiator his first important task and the clearest indication that Carter really wanted to bridge the gap between the positions that Warnke and Nitze represented during the confirmation confrontation.

The Deep Cut Proposal

When the Carter administration entered office, strategic arms limitation talks with the Soviet Union had been going on for eight years. There was a complicated record of negotiating positions taken by both sides and a stalemate on a number of issues. The agreements reached at Vladivostok placed equal and high ceilings on the number of missile launchers each side could have (2,400) and a subceiling on the number of MIRVed launchers (1,320) that would be permissible. These numbers did not represent any real reductions for the United States and tended to ratify the substantial Soviet strategic buildup of the 1970s rather than reverse it. Moreover, new weapon systems—cruise missiles in the United States and the Backfire bomber in the Soviet Union—raised difficult problems about how to define a strategic system and how to limit technological developments not previously on the SALT agenda.

When Carter asked for proposals from the bureaucracies on where to go in the SALT negotiations, as he did in Presidential Review Memorandum No. 2,[61] he received a variety of complicated policy options that were essentially revised versions of Vladivostok. One proposed option was a quick conversion of the Ford and Brezhnev numbers into a treaty with a deferral of the unresolved issues raised by cruise missiles and the Backfire bomber. This was something Carter had endorsed during the campaign and in statements to the press during the early days of his administration. It was also included as a suggestion to Brezhnev in a secret letter that Carter sent to

60. Ibid., 380.
61. Presidential Review Memorandum No. 1 dealt with the renegotiation of the Panama Canal treaties. Both documents are described in Talbott, *Endgame*, 43–44.

the Soviet leader during his first week in office. Other options contained modest ideas for adding to Vladivostok by counting or not counting Backfire and trading off some Soviet concession on the new bomber for limitations on the still-undeployed cruise missiles.[62]

If Carter was thinking about ratification of the Vladivostok limits early in his presidency, he did not consider that to be a substantial accomplishment. Finishing up the treaty outlined by Ford and Brezhnev would only be meaningful if it were a quick step toward more serious limitations to follow. When the president met with the staff members working on SALT proposals, he reportedly showed real intensity. In these early arms control deliberations he said that he was serious about ridding nuclear weapons from the earth as he had said in his inaugural address and called progress in arms control his "most cherished hope" for the new administration.[63] As president-elect he met with the Joint Chiefs of Staff and reportedly asked why the United States needed a nuclear arsenal with thousands and thousands of warheads. Wouldn't two hundred be sufficient to deter the Soviet Union?[64] That question, frequently quoted as evidence of Carter's national security naïveté, also demonstrated his ambitions for a bold arms control agenda. Trained in the nuclear navy, Carter was the first modern president to come to the White House with personal, working-level knowledge of nuclear weapons and nuclear deterrence.[65] In his White House diary, he noted how "sobering" it was as commander in chief to review the complete inventory of U.S. nuclear warheads.[66]

In February and March of 1977, three members of the president's senior foreign policy team also wanted more from arms control than would be provided by a mere conversion of the Vladivostok accords into a SALT II treaty. Brown, Brzezinski, and Brzezinski's assistant David Aaron all pushed for a new set of negotiating guidelines that would go well beyond

62. For a full account of Carter administration SALT negotiations in addition to Talbott's, see Raymond Garthoff, *Détente and Confrontation: American-Soviet Relations from Nixon to Reagan* (Washington, D.C., 1985), 801–27.

63. Talbott, *Endgame*, 43.

64. Ibid.

65. Eisenhower, of course, was in charge of nuclear forces deployed in Europe when he served as SACEUR, but the rest of Carter's modern White House predecessors had their military careers in the pre-nuclear forces of World War II.

66. Carter, *Keeping Faith*, 212.

the Vladivostok agreements and immediately address issues that others thought would be part of a SALT III negotiation. In a series of meetings of the SCC, chaired by Brzezinski and closely followed by the president, the new administration came up with a package of proposals calling for real reductions in strategic arms, especially on the Soviet side. The old Vladivostok totals of 2,400 strategic systems would come down to something between 1,800 and 2,000, with MIRVed systems being held to 1,100 or 1,200, instead of 1,320. Moreover, the Soviets would be asked to dismantle half of their 300 very large ICBMs, which, because of their size and ability to carry many warheads each, posed the greatest threat to America's land-based forces. Both sides would forgo the development and deployment of any new ICBMs and limit the testing of existing land- and sea-based missiles. The new cruise missiles, under development in the United States, would be limited in range to 2,500 kilometers.[67] If they were deployed on aircraft, they would count in the overall limitations imposed on MIRVed strategic systems. Cruise missiles deployed on land or at sea would not be counted. Nor would the Backfire bomber (in one of the few concessions to the Soviets) so long as the Russians guaranteed that its potential as a long-range weapon would not be enhanced. Vance was also given permission to offer additional concessions to the Soviets in the form of American cancellation of the B-1 bomber and the Trident submarine, if they expressed interest in the deep-cut initiative.[68]

This was an ambitious package. In 1977, it was probably attractive to Harold Brown because it solved, or at least postponed, the missile vulnerability problem that animated Paul Nitze and some of the strategic analysts in the Pentagon. If the Soviets would be willing to reduce their missile forces, particularly their large modern missile systems, fears that they were seeking a usable strategic advantage over the United States would considerably diminish. Brown never took those fears as seriously as Nitze did, but as the chief Pentagon planner he had to be sensitive to the worst-case analysis of Soviet capabilities. Acceptance of the deep-cut proposals by Soviet leaders would have made the most dire interpretations of the Soviet strate-

67. According to Talbott, the range limit was higher than many arms control experts or Pentagon officials thought wise or necessary. Talbott, *Endgame*, 61–62.

68. Hyland, *Mortal Rivals*, 212. These additional concessions were a closely held secret in Vance's instructions for the Moscow trip. They had been approved by the president, but were not known widely in Washington.

gic buildup far less plausible. For Brzezinski and Aaron, the radical SALT proposals being considered by the Carter team early in 1977 would have produced major political accomplishments. If the proposals had been taken seriously by the Soviets, the administration would have answered the arms control critics of both the right and left. They would be taking a strong response to the Soviet threat while making a commitment for both superpowers to accept meaningful reductions in their strategic forces. Moreover, if the porposals had led to a SALT II agreement, it would have given the Carter administration an early and major accomplishment that went well beyond anything produced, or even contemplated, under President Ford.

Vance, arms control and Soviet expert William Hyland, and even Warnke when his appointment was finally confirmed were all more cautious about the developing proposals. Their concerns involved the likelihood that the Soviet Union would reject a bold new arms control plan and the consequences of that rejection. Warnke warned that if the new Carter arms control proposals were turned down by the Soviets, the real reductions they contained would establish a benchmark against which other, more modest SALT II arrangements could be measured and criticized.[69] Vance, who eventually supported the deep-cut proposals, insisted that there be additional backup negotiating positions, including something like a quick ratification of Vladivostok, that could be offered if the more ambitious and deeper cuts were not well received. All the reservations expressed by senior Carter advisers were set aside after a Saturday White House meeting in which Carter heard a review of the arguments for and against the deep-cut proposals and made his decision to go ahead with them.[70] That secret meeting, attended by principals only on March 12, set in motion the final preparations for the Vance and Warnke trip to Moscow at the end of the month.

In Moscow, the deep-cut proposals were summarily dismissed, and the world quickly learned of the gap between Carter and the Kremlin leadership in Moscow press conferences held by Vance and Gromyko. Each side blamed the other for the impasse. The administration's first high-level discussions with the Soviet Union ended in failure. Commentators at the time

---

69. Talbott, *Endgame*, 57.

70. To Warnke it was perfectly clear from the president's remarks and demeanor at the Saturday meeting that he wanted the deep-cut proposal to be taken to Moscow, and no one thought there was much point in opposing a strongly held presidential conviction. Warnke, interview.

were inclined to believe that the administration's highly publicized human rights campaign and its decision to publicly reveal the essential elements of the deep-cut proposal before Vance had a chance to present them in Moscow were responsible for the arms control setback, but there is some evidence from former Soviet sources to suggest that this analysis may not be correct.[71] Instead, the key to the Soviet rejection was their commitment to Vladivostok, their surprise that the new president was asking for much more than the quick ratification of Vladivostok that he had previously endorsed, and their suspicion that there were ulterior motives behind the new proposals that Vance and Warnke brought to Moscow.

Conclusions

Both the leaders of the Soviet Union and the members of the United States Senate were very busy early in 1977 trying to figure out what the new president and his foreign policy team were all about. As it turned out, the battle over the Warnke nomination, which possessed an intensity never anticipated by the president or his senior advisers, was hardly a watershed event in the early days of the new administration. While the president's nominee was publicly defending his record of arms control policy statements against the attacks of Paul Nitze and Senator Jackson, Carter and the rest of his foreign policy advisers were busy in private developing an ambitious SALT negotiating position that contained some of the provisions that Nitze and Jackson would have been likely to recommend had they been part of the president's inner circle.

After the Soviets rejected the deep-cut proposals, the administration put the SALT negotiations back on track with the more conventional objective of seeking improvements and refinements to the Vladivostok accords. The SALT II treaty took two more years to negotiate. Though it contained some very significant provisions, particularly in the area of verification, and lower limits than those agreed to at Vladivostok, it was a long way from the ambitious objectives contained in the package Vance and Warnke had taken to Moscow in March of 1977. In the deteriorating atmosphere of U.S.-Soviet

71. Vladislav M. Zubok, "An Offered Hand Rejected? The Carter Administration and the Vance Mission to Moscow in March 1977," in Herbert D. Rosenbaum and Alexej Ugrinsky, eds., *Jimmy Carter: Foreign Policy and Post-Presidential Years* (Westport, Conn., 1994), 357–67.

relations two years later, the SALT II achievements were increasingly difficult to explain and defend to a Senate and American public less enthusiastic about strategic arms control. In fact, the new SALT treaty was opposed by both liberals and conservatives for many of the same reasons that both groups had earlier attacked the Vladivostok accords.

When the ratification debate over SALT II began in the Senate, Paul Warnke was no longer a member of the Carter administration. He resigned in October 1978 to resume the private practice of law. In accepting his appointment in 1977, Warnke had made it clear to the president that he could not serve for the full four-year term, and by the end of 1978 the broad framework for SALT II was completed and the other arms control negotiations with the Soviet Union were bogged down and not likely to see much progress in the near future.

Warnke was replaced by two individuals, at ACDA by General George Seignious and as chief SALT negotiator by Ralph Earle II. At the time of his appointment, Seignious was president of the Citadel in South Carolina and a close friend of Senator Fritz Hollings, one of the conservative Democratic senators whose vote would be needed if the SALT II treaty was to pass. Earle was an experienced arms control negotiator, who had served from the beginning of the Carter administration and led the U.S. SALT II delegation whenever Warnke was not in Geneva. Earlier in his career, he had been a protégé of Paul Nitze. Though both Warnke and Carter note that Warnke's resignation in 1978 was for personal reasons,[72] his replacements were individuals more likely to win easy confirmation and help the administration in the forthcoming SALT II ratification debate.

What did the confirmation battle over Warnke's nomination in 1977 really mean? For Nitze and some senators, it was largely a vehicle for announcing their opposition to the direction they presumed policy under Carter would take. Their presumptions were wrong, but perhaps understandable in the uncertainties that accompanied a party change in the White House and the arrival in Washington of a president little known on Capitol Hill. Carter's biggest frustration in the debate over the Warnke confirmation was probably the difficulty he had in persuading senators and the public that he would, in fact, be in charge of his own administration. Whatever

72. Dan Caldwell, *The Dynamics of Domestic Politics and Arms Control: The SALT II Treaty Ratification Debate* (Columbia, S.C., 1991), 60.

Warnke may have said in the past, or whatever may have been said by Vance, Brown, or Brzezinski for that matter, would not automatically become administration policy. The president would make the important decisions, and Carter fully intended to be an activist president who made lots of important decisions. That was the central theme in Carter's public statements about the Warnke nomination and throughout his private consultations with senators.

The president's problem was to convey the message that he was in charge of arms control and foreign affairs, an obvious message as far as Jimmy Carter was concerned. Warnke's problem was similar if somewhat more serious. He had to convince his critics that he was, as he always thought he had been, a respectable member of the community of experts on arms control and national security. Warnke was surprised by the opposition that his nomination brought out, and disappointed that it was led by an individual who was a former colleague, a fellow Democrat, and a social acquaintance.[73] The controversial comma in his confirmation documents and the insult to his patriotism in Nitze's testimony were the headline stories in the Senate battle, but the important question throughout the confirmation process was whether or not Paul Warnke was a mainstream appointee. His educational pedigree, legal credentials, and Washington experience were thoroughly mainstream—probably making him the kind of nominee Hamilton Jordan hoped his outsider president would ignore. But Carter did not ignore those qualifications, and during the whole confirmation controversy the president's most mainstream foreign policy adviser, Secretary of State Vance, was also Warnke's most loyal supporter. The real issue about the Warnke nomination had to do with the acceptability of the nominee's public positions on arms control and national defense. They too were mainstream, if somewhat left of center, and certainly legitimate for the administration official expected to serve as an advocate for arms control solutions to national security problems.

But the Warnke nomination came before the Senate when the American mainstream on arms control and national security was experiencing considerable political turbulence, as two new paths were being dug on either side

73. Years later, Warnke could not explain Nitze's decision in 1977, and praised his performance as an arms control adviser in the Reagan administration, observing that "Paul was always better in office than he was out of office." Warnke, interview.

of a barrier built up around some of the most fundamental assumptions in the cold war and the nuclear age. On one side of the emerging barrier were those who saw the Soviet Union as a devious and implacable foe in the midst of a dangerous strategic nuclear buildup, a foe that could only be kept in check by substantial U.S. defense spending and hard-line responses. This was the path that fed the foreign policy decisions and rhetoric of the first Reagan administration. On the other side of the rising barrier were those who feared that the military might being acquired by both sides in the cold war was the root of our greatest national security problem. They believed that miscalculations by suspicious superpower leaders could produce the nightmare of nuclear war. This was the path that fed the nuclear freeze campaign in the early 1980s. As the Washington experts in national security affairs, already divided by the Vietnam War, were navigating around the new barriers in mainstream thinking about U.S.-Soviet relations and arms control policy, the Warnke nomination got caught in the swirl.

It was a swirl that had not been foreseen by Carter, Jordan, or any of the other members of the administration who reviewed and approved Warnke's selection for the ACDA and SALT negotiator positions.[74] The nominee may have been even more surprised by the controversy his appointment generated and by the personal price that he had to pay in publicly defending his competence and integrity when he thought neither would be challenged. In the 1980s and 1990s, a number of presidential appointees, particularly those selected for the Supreme Court, would find themselves in the midst of confirmation battles with organized political activists on both sides and painful personal allegations being made against them. Warnke did not face the degree of organized opposition that Robert Bork would later encounter, nor did he confront the kinds of personal charges that filled the John Tower and Clarence Thomas confirmation hearings. Nonetheless, his experiences before the Senate could not have been pleasant or productive. His longer than expected confirmation kept him away from most of the deliberations that led up to the earliest and boldest arms control initiative of the administration he would serve.

74. Again, many documents in the Carter Library dealing with personnel matters are not now available to scholars, but it is logical to conclude that the controversy surrounding Warnke was not foreseen. Carter made special efforts to get a reluctant Warnke to accept an invitation to join the administration. He probably would not have done so if he had known the difficulties the nomination would produce.

Though surprises are a regular, if relatively rare, feature of the nomination and confirmation processes, presidents, particularly in their first few weeks in office, hardly ever make an explicit decision to invite battle with the Senate. For this reason everyone is usually caught off guard when they arise. Carter may be even more justified in his surprise that the Warnke battle took place, since the most intense opposition to his nominee came from within his own political party. Richard Neustadt and Ernest May have criticized Carter for his attempts to placate Jackson in both the early and later SALT II negotiations. They argue that a better understanding of Jackson's personality and the sometimes deceptive demeanor of a powerful senator might have led to an earlier and healthier appreciation of the likelihood that Jackson would be hostile to anything that Carter might negotiate with the Soviet Union.[75] Carter did not use the Warnke nomination battle as an excuse to cut communications with Jackson. Nor did he give ground to Jackson and withdraw his nominee.

There is no evidence that the president ever considered abandoning his controversial arms control adviser.[76] He fully supported Warnke in public statements and in private communications with senators, though he never called or sent a note to his embattled nominee while he was being attacked in Capitol Hill hearing rooms or on the Senate floor.[77] President Carter did not really know Paul Warnke until they began to work together after his confirmation. All presidents must appoint people to positions of trust who are outside their circle of friends and associates, but Carter came to Washington with fewer friends and associates in the nation's capital and among the policy-making elites than most of our modern presidents. As a result, he could be caught off guard by the revelations about Sorensen's draft status or by the level of controversy that Warnke's public record would produce, and he could not back down in response to every revelation about his nominees. Having already abandoned the fight over Sorensen, it would have been politically harder for Carter to do the same in the Warnke confrontation. Moreover, the reception Warnke received in the Senate was fundamentally unfair. He was being examined as if he would be the principal

75. Richard E. Neustadt and Ernest R. May, *Thinking in Time: The Uses of History for Decision Makers* (New York, 1986), 199–204.

76. Zbigniew Brzezinski, interview by author, Washington, D.C., February 17, 1995.

77. Warnke, interview.

decision maker in matters of arms control when the president had understandably reserved that position for himself. And Warnke was being criticized for being one-sided in his thinking about national security and arms control when the president was actively consulting with all sides in the preparation of his first major arms control decision.[78]

Throughout the Warnke nomination fight and the later fight over SALT II, Jimmy Carter characteristically refused to treat the growing divisions in the arms control and national security communities as an occasion for making a fundamental choice to join one side or the other. Instead, he tried to forge substantive arms control and national security policies that would bring both sides together. That was a noble objective. The Warnke nomination should have given the president an early indication of just how hard it would be to achieve.

78. A week after the Senate vote on Warnke, the president received a detailed letter from Paul Nitze offering advice on the new arms control policy that would become the deep-cut proposal. Paul Nitze to the President, March 16, 1977, White House Central File, Executive, Box FG-209, Folder FG 264/A, Carter Library.

2

FACE TO FACE

Meeting the Shah of Iran

Arms control and relations between the United States and the Soviet Union may well have been the most important foreign policy issues confronting the Carter administration. The ratification of new canal treaties with Panama and the negotiation of permanent peace agreements between Israel and Egypt were the president's greatest foreign policy achievements. But in foreign affairs, the fate of the Carter presidency was not decided in Moscow, Central America, Camp David, Israel, or Egypt. The fortunes, and many of the misfortunes, of the thirty-ninth presidency rested on the shifting sands of Iran. There the opposition to the shah and his fall from power surprised the administration and the world, exacerbating an international energy crisis; there U.S. diplomats were taken hostage and held for more than a year; there the military mission to rescue the captured Americans was aborted; and there, when the hostages were finally released immediately after Ronald Reagan's inauguration, the transition from one administration to the next had its most dramatic moment.

So much in the Carter presidency revolved around events in Tehran that it may be surprising to note that President Carter sat face-to-face with the shah of Iran on only two occasions—once when the Iranian leader came to Washington in November of 1977 and again about six weeks later, when Carter briefly stopped in Tehran during a nine-day overseas trip to Europe, Africa, and Asia. Both visits between heads of state received the kind of careful preparation, protocol-filled ceremony, and media attention that one might expect; both meetings involved public speeches and private conversations; and both failed to produce a solid personal relationship between two leaders whose fates were more intertwined than either could have known in the first year of the Carter presidency.

The United States and the Shah

When Jimmy Carter took the oath of office as president of the United States, the shah was in his thirty-sixth year as the ruler of Iran. Mohammad Reza Shah Pahlavi was the son of a soldier who led a coup against the Qajar dynasty and in 1925 installed himself as shah. The elder Pahlavi wanted to unify his nation and end foreign influence over its internal affairs, but his alleged ties to Nazi Germany and the strategic location of Iran led to an Anglo-Soviet takeover in 1941. His eldest son, educated in Switzerland and at the Iranian military academy was, at the age of twenty-one, placed on the Peacock Throne as a constitutional monarch. The younger Pahlavi did not fully dominate Iranian politics until a CIA-supported coup overthrew the government of Prime Minister Mohammad Mossadegh in 1953. After the coup the shah ruled Iran with something softer than an iron fist. He did have his secret police, SAVAK, which kept tabs on his political enemies, and frequently those enemies were arrested, tortured, and deported. The shah's eventual nemesis, the Ayatollah Khomeini, was arrested twice in 1963 and forced to leave the country in 1964 for preaching anti-government messages and inciting riots. Though the shah was capable of cracking down on his opposition, Iran was not a totalitarian regime, and Pahlavi, like his father before him, saw himself as a reformer and modernizer of his nation. In what he called the White Revolution, to distinguish it from the red variety, the shah used Iran's considerable oil revenues to finance improvements in education, housing, medical facilities, and roads and to develop a modern economy for his citizens. He liberalized the treatment of women, despite the criticism of Khomeini and other religious leaders. He carried out a program of land reform, encouraged students to study abroad, and invited Western businesses to Iran. The shah also built a large, well-paid, and elaborately equipped military force that would defend Iran against its regional rival, Iraq, and the ever-present danger of Soviet expansionism.

Northern Iran had been occupied by Russian troops during the Second World War. When the war was over, one of the earliest cold war confrontations between the United States and the Soviet Union involved the slowness of Soviet forces to carry out their promised withdrawal from Iranian territory. In that confrontation, the United States took the side of Iranian independence and began to replace Great Britain as the most influential Western power in the Persian Gulf. Liberal Iranians were initially enthusiastic about the new role that might be played by the United States. For the first time, a major power appeared to be taking the side of Iranian sovereignty and self-rule. The coup against the Mossadegh government ended any hopes that America would be different from the other powerful nations that had long dominated Iranian domestic politics. Though the actual U.S. participation in the Mossadegh coup was relatively limited and had no lasting place in American public consciousness, it was a crucial event for Iranians and set the stage for a level of anti-U.S. feelings that would surprise many Americans in the 1979 revolution.

After the coup, the shah requested massive military assistance, which the Eisenhower administration partially provided. Throughout the 1950s and 1960s, the shah's demands for armaments usually exceeded America's willingness to supply them. Early in the Kennedy years, there was a general effort to improve U.S. standing with the third world by moving away from indiscriminate American support for friendly dictators. However, Iran's location atop major oil reserves and between the southern border of the Soviet Union and the waters of the Persian Gulf made it of great strategical importance to the United States and thus prevented any president from doing much that would offend the shah. The mixed signals that occasionally came from Washington were an irritant to Pahlavi and may have encouraged some of the shah's critics to demand more political liberalization. But they did not change the fundamentals of U.S.-Iranian relations.[1]

Those fundamentals, rooted in shared interests in oil and anti-communism, were glorified in the Nixon years. Nixon had known the shah since his first trip to Tehran as Eisenhower's vice president, and he both liked and respected what others saw as the shah's exaggerated fear of the Soviet threat. Moreover, the oil embargo that accompanied the 1973 war in the Middle East demonstrated how important it was to have an American friend in Tehran. Iran happily raised prices with the rest of the oil-

1. For a general review of U.S.-Iranian relations see, Barry Rubin, *Paved with Good Intentions: The American Experience in Iran* (New York, 1981), and Gary Sick, *All Fall Down: America's Tragic Encounter with Iran* (New York, 1986), 3–24.

exporting nations but did not participate in the embargo and even sold petroleum products to Israel. With Iran's growing importance in the politics of oil and its stalwart stand against Soviet expansion, the shah was a natural ally for Richard Nixon. The declaration of the Nixon Doctrine, in the wake of Vietnam, increased American dependence on powerful regional allies. The Nixon administration considered support for Iran to be one of the "pillars" of U.S. foreign policy in the Middle East. The United States gave the shah the green light he had always wanted to purchase whatever American weapons he might wish with his rapidly growing oil wealth. Iran became the largest buyer of U.S. arms in the world.

In the 1976 presidential campaign, without saying much about Iran in particular, Jimmy Carter challenged the U.S.-Iranian relationship by raising the general issue of human rights and by questioning the wisdom of supplying developing countries with extensive, elaborate, and expensive armaments.[2] Even before those issues became the stuff of Democratic campaign speeches, members of the Ford administration were expressing some of the same concerns. Ford's secretary of defense, James Schlesinger, was worried that the level of arms shipments to Iran exceeded the capacity of that country to absorb them and called for a reexamination of the arms trade between Washington and Tehran. In the United Nations, Ambassador Patrick Moynihan called for greater attention to democratic values and fundamental freedoms. And on Capitol Hill, new legislative requirements were enacted to establish an office of human rights in the Department of State, mandate the production of an annual report on the status of those rights in the nations of the world, and make performance in this area a factor in policy decisions regarding U.S. assistance and trade.

The shah had been able to read these new signals from Washington and responded with a series of modest steps toward liberalization. Both before and after Carter's election he approved changes in Iranian law, policy, and personnel that were designed to appease his domestic and foreign critics. He reshuffled his cabinet, released a number of political prisoners, promised to end the torture of inmates, allowed greater freedoms for the press and polit-

2. Carter's chief campaign speechwriter reports that the candidate deleted a specific reference to Iran from his major human rights speech in 1976 because he did not want such a reference to "tie my hands" in future dealings with the shah. Patrick Anderson, *Electing Jimmy Carter: The Campaign of 1976* (Baton Rouge, 1994), 102.

ical opposition groups, and changed the law regulating military prosecutions to give those accused more access to due process.[3] After the election of Jimmy Carter, he watched as the president moved to implement his campaign commitment to give greater attention to global issues like arms sales, human rights, and nuclear non-proliferation. In developing those new policies, the Carter administration was realistic about the need to balance strategic and regional interests with progress on the new global agenda. That willingness to compromise broadly stated policy objectives with the realities of individual cases was sensible, and necessary in the case of an important nation like Iran, but it led to persistent accusations of hypocrisy and indecision with every step the administration took. To liberals who wanted dramatic changes in American foreign policy, the administration was never able to do enough; to conservatives committed either to automatic anticommunism or the realpolitik of the Kissinger era, the administration was always doing too much.

When Secretary of State Vance went to Tehran in May of 1977 in the first high-level contact between the new administration and the shah, he talked about the importance of human rights, but he also delivered a formal invitation for the shah to visit Washington in November. This was one of the shah's highest priorities and clearly pleased him.[4] The shah's other major concern was arms, and on that subject, Vance brought more good news. The secretary of state promised that the United States would go ahead with the sale of 160 F-16 fighter aircraft that had been under discussion at the end of the Ford administration; the shah promptly asked to purchase 140 more. Vance also promised support for the Iranian request to purchase sophisticated radar-equipped aircraft called AWACS, which would provide Iran with early warning of incoming planes and the ability to monitor traffic and control combat in Iranian airspace.

Carter later scaled back the shah's request from ten to seven AWACS

3. R. K. Ramazani, *The United States and Iran: The Patterns of Influence* (New York, 1982), 93–94. See also "Statement by Charles W. Naas, Director of the Office of Iranian Affairs, Made Before the Subcommittee on International Organizations of the House International Relations Committee," October 26, 1977, reprinted in Yonah Alexander and Allan Nanes, eds., *The United States and Iran: A Documentary History* (Frederick, Md., 1980), 451–53.

4. Cyrus Vance, *Hard Choices: Four Critical Years in Managing America's Foreign Policy* (New York, 1983), 318–19.

planes. However, he personally approved the sale under new procedures outlined in Presidential Decision Memorandum 13 (PD-13), which established specific goals for the reduction of U.S. arms sales and required all large-scale transactions to receive White House approval. PD-13 exempted certain nations (NATO members, Australia, New Zealand, Japan, and Israel) from the new executive review procedures, and the Iranian ambassador to the United States complained that Iran was not included among the exempted countries.[5] In practice, however, the absence of Iran from the exemption list made very little difference in the flow of arms from America to Iran. The pipeline of deliveries from orders placed under Nixon and Ford was already full. In addition to the new fighters and the AWACS aircraft, President Carter approved a package of over a billion dollars in spare parts and support equipment needed by Iran to keep its previously purchased military hardware in good working order. Iran's problems in continuing to secure arms from the United States did not come from the Carter White House. They came from Capitol Hill.

Legislative reforms passed before Carter came to office gave Congress an active part to play in the arms sale process and the right to veto any sale that was opposed by resolutions passed in both houses. Sales involving countries in the Middle East that might pose a threat to Israel garnered the most opposition. The public announcement of the AWACS deal with Iran triggered a wave of congressional criticism that was more acrimonious than the administration had expected. When the House Foreign Affairs Committee voted to reject the sale, in part, because of fears that Iran could not safeguard sensitive AWACS technology, the administration had to renegotiate the details of its agreements with Iran and lobby extensively for a reversal of the House committee vote. The first direct communication between the president and the shah was an angry letter from Pahlavi complaining about the delayed congressional action on the AWACS sale.[6] The final result was favorable, but the extended Capitol Hill battle produced embarrassing public statements about the shah, standard accusations of administration hypocrisy, and fuel for the shah's suspicions that the new administration in Washington could not be trusted.

Establishing greater trust between the leaders of Iran and the United

5. Ibid., 319.
6. Jimmy Carter, *Keeping Faith: Memoirs of a President* (New York, 1982), 434.

States would require some personal contact and careful diplomacy. That process would take place in the exchange of high-level visits between Washington and Tehran that occurred at the end of 1977.

The Shah Comes to Washington

When he came to see Jimmy Carter, the shah of Iran was already a veteran White House visitor. Before his trip to Washington in November 1977, he had come to the United States as an official head of state eleven times.[7] He met with every American president who held office after he assumed the throne and hosted three of those presidents—Roosevelt, Eisenhower, and Nixon—during their visits to Iran. But if the shah was accustomed to talking to American presidents and walking the halls of the White House, nothing from his previous visits prepared him for the welcome he received in 1977.

In many ways the most important event in the shah's first visit with Jimmy Carter was a mishap on the White House lawn that marred his arrival. As the formal greeting ceremonies began in mid-morning, noise from anti- and pro-shah demonstrators just outside the White House grounds could clearly be heard. When fighting broke out between the two groups, the tear gas used by police to bring the crowds under control drifted across the lawn, where members of the press and the dignitaries on the platform were unable to disguise their discomfort or hold back their tears. Both Carter and the shah completed their prepared welcoming remarks, but they were visibly affected by the fumes, and the newspaper photos and television coverage of the welcoming ceremonies made their tears the lasting visual image of the visit.

Following the tear-filled welcome, the president and the shah entered the White House for another ceremonial gathering. The shah presented the United States with a tapestry portrait of George Washington that was Iran's bicentennial gift to the American people. The two leaders went next to the Cabinet Room for the first of two high-level discussions. The president was joined by Vice President Mondale, Vance, Brzezinski, Assistant Secretary of State for Near Eastern and South Asian Affairs Alfred Atherton, U.S. Ambassador to Iran William Sullivan, and Gary Sick, the NSC staff mem-

7. Ramazani, *The United States and Iran*, 96.

ber with responsibility for the Persian Gulf.[8] The shah was accompanied by his foreign minister and the Iranian ambassador to the United States. The meeting lasted ninety minutes and is described in at least seven different memoirs or books written by those in attendance.[9] The published accounts of what was said vary considerably.

The meeting began with the shah talking at some length about the serious Soviet threat in the world and in his region, a threat that justified substantial Iranian military preparations. From the shah's point of view, the Soviets were attempting a "pincer movement to encircle the Arabian peninsula and the Persian Gulf" with one side of the pincer in the Horn of Africa and the other in Afghanistan.[10] Hamilton Jordan reports that the shah spoke for nearly an hour without notes in a *tour d'horizon* of the strategic threats facing the West and the importance of U.S.-Iranian relations. "It was more than a presentation," Jordan notes, "it was a performance."[11] Cyrus Vance was less impressed. The shah, he observes, was a member of the "grand design" school, whose members found more systematic Soviet involvement and planning in international events than Vance thought warranted.[12] Brzezinski recalls that the shah had a great deal to say about the importance of Afghan neutrality for both the United States and Iran, a feature in the shah's presentation that was not noted by any of the other participants.[13]

The exchange of views on security issues was serious and probably useful to both sides. It also produced one minor misunderstanding. According to Ambassador Sullivan, the shah's command of the English language was excellent but did involve an occasional mispronounced word. When combined with the president's accent, there was some potential for confusion. During their White House conversations, the president told the shah that Soviet ac-

8. Hamilton Jordan writes about this meeting as if he were there, but his name is not included in the official record of those present. Hamilton Jordan, *Crisis: The Last Year of the Carter Presidency* (New York, 1982), 89.

9. The public accounts of the meeting are found in books cited here by Carter, Brzezinski, Vance, Sullivan, Jordan, Sick, and the shah.

10. William Sullivan, *Mission to Iran* (New York, 1981), 128.

11. Jordan, *Crisis*, 89.

12. Vance, *Hard Choices*, 322.

13. Zbigniew Brzezinski, *Power and Principle: Memoirs of the National Security Advisor 1977–1981* (New York, 1983), 356.

tivities in the Horn of Africa should first be addressed by the Organization of African Unity (OAU). The shah replied that he considered the OAU to be "impotent." President Carter, evidently believing that the Iranian leader had just called the OAU an *important* organization, promptly expressed his agreement, demonstrating that in diplomacy a single syllable can make a considerable difference.[14]

On the larger issues that the president wished to raise, the talks went well. Carter, according to Vance, had two topics he wanted to pursue. One was a detailed explanation of the AWACS controversy on Capitol Hill, which had ended a month before the shah's visit but not without leaving behind some political fences that needed mending. On this subject, the shah appeared to understand the president's problems with the Congress and agreed to provide some long-range planning about his anticipated military needs to help avert future congressional surprises. Later in the day, the shah would have a meeting on Capitol Hill with leaders from both political parties at which further efforts would be made to explain the legislative process and minimize the diplomatic harm that might have been done by the open and vigorous debate that took place on the AWACS issue. The other presidential topic was the price of oil and the prospects for a price freeze at the upcoming December OPEC meeting. Here the shah pledged that he would support a freeze, but argued that this was not likely to solve the long-term energy problems in the West.[15] At a press conference following his visit to Capitol Hill the shah publicly endorsed the goal of securing an OPEC price freeze. This announcement gave the administration some favorable news coverage—a gift that was of much more immediate political value than the Washington tapestry.[16]

The official White House statement released after the first Washington talks reports that the two leaders also exchanged views on the plans for a Middle East peace conference in Geneva, the general situation in the region (where Sadat had just announced his intention to visit Jerusalem), developments in Africa and South Asia, and the current negotiations between the United States and the Soviet Union on SALT and military forces in the In-

---

14. Sullivan, *Mission to Iran*, 129.

15. Vance, *Hard Choices*, 321–23.

16. "Shah, Shifting Stand, Pledges to Oppose Increase in Oil Price," *New York Times*, November 17, 1977.

dian Ocean. The two leaders also discussed nuclear non-proliferation and the shah's hope that Carter would visit Iran in the near future.[17] There were no real surprises in the first round of Washington talks. Most of the subjects under discussion between Carter and the shah had already been rehearsed in meetings the shah had in Tehran with Ambassador Sullivan.[18]

Vance and Sullivan, in their memoirs, provide the most detailed description of the substantive discussions in the Cabinet Room; Carter offers mostly personal observations. To the president, the shah appeared to be more "calm" and "self-assured" than might have been expected after the disruptions of the teargassed reception. But the shah was also "modest in demeanor" and expressed himself with an "air of reticence" that Carter found surprising given the fact that he had dealt with every American chief executive from Franklin Roosevelt on.[19] The combination of calm and reticence was something of a puzzle that Carter does not explain and may not have fully understood. Asked years later whether or not the president and the shah had been successful in getting to know each other during their first face-to-face visit, presidential adviser Gary Sick replied that "very few people ever got to know the Shah."[20]

A second session of high-level discussions took place the following morning, with the same list of participants again gathered in the Cabinet Room of the White House. This time the topics included a general review by Carter of "his approach to human rights throughout the world"; some detailed examination of issues related to the peaceful use of nuclear energy and non-proliferation, issues important to the shah because of his hopes to purchase nuclear reactors from the United States; and further discussion of "military supply issues" and "Iran's security needs."[21]

After the second general session, the president invited the shah into a private room near the Oval Office for a discussion without any advisers present. This is a customary part of meetings between heads of state, designed to facilitate sensitive conversation. Even if such conversations do not take

17. *Public Papers of the Presidents of the United States, Jimmy Carter 1977* (Washington, D.C., 1978), 2028–29.

18. Sullivan, *Mission to Iran*, 124.

19. Carter, *Keeping Faith*, 434.

20. Gary Sick, interview by author, Charlottesville, Va., January 27, 1992.

21. *Public Papers of the Presidents of the United States, Jimmy Carter 1977* 2033. Jordan did attend this meeting.

place, the inclusion of a fully private meeting on a visitor's agenda can be read as evidence at home and abroad of the importance of the guest and the level of intimacy between leaders. In the case of Carter and the shah serious conversation did take place.

Carter reports in his memoirs that he had carefully rehearsed what he would say when he spoke to the shah alone. The subject would again be human rights, but this time the president would raise specific human rights concerns affecting Iran. Carter spoke politely, but bluntly, about the fact that "a growing number" of Iranian citizens are "claiming that these [human] rights are not always honored in Iran." The president said that he understood that "most of the disturbances have arisen among the mullahs and other religious leaders, the new middle class searching for more political influence, and students in Iran and overseas," but he pointed out that "Iran's reputation in the world is being damaged by their complaints." He asked directly whether or not there was "anything that can be done to alleviate this problem by closer consultation with the dissident groups and by easing off on some of the strict police policies." The shah paused and said, "No, there is nothing I can do. I must enforce the Iranian laws, which are designed to combat communism."[22] Before the shah's visit, the Iranian ambassador to the United States, Ardeshir Zahedi, had confidentially expressed his concern about the growing isolation of the Iranian leader. Carter had that warning in mind when the shah insisted that his opposition was very small and made up entirely of Communists. That portion of their private conversation gave the president some indication that perhaps the shah was out of touch with the political realities in his own country.[23]

Hamilton Jordan records in his book, *Crisis*, that Carter told him later that "the Shah had been very 'forthcoming' in his response, promising a renewed effort on human rights and democratization."[24] That account of the private conversation between heads of state is rather different from Carter's version in *Keeping Faith*. Even if the shah did not give the assurances that Jordan reports, the president may well have been pleased with the fact that the subject of human rights in Iran had been dealt with in a serious fashion,

22. Carter, *Keeping Faith*, 436. Carter provides another brief account of his first meeting with the shah in his book *The Blood of Abraham: Insights into the Middle East* (New York, 1985), 12–13.

23. Jimmy Carter, interview by author, Atlanta, Ga., April 11, 1995.

24. Jordan, *Crisis*, 89.

without public embarrassment or personal rancor. In fact, the public ceremonies, after the first disastrous encounter on the White House lawn, went
exceedingly well.

On the night of November 15, between the two sessions of high-level
talks, a formal state dinner was held in the White House. The detailed
planning for official White House entertaining of foreign dignitaries was
done by the First Lady and her staff in consultation with the Department
of State, members of the NSC staff, and the Washington embassy representing the visiting guest. Rosalynn Carter recalls that White House decora-
tions, menus, and entertainment were at all times selected on the basis of
known preferences for the expected visitors. Helmut Schmidt's wife, an
avid botanist, found the White House decorated with a flower she had ad-
mired on a previous trip to the United States. Anwar Sadat, a devoted
reader of American Wild West novels, was entertained by a country and
western singing group. The president of Venezuela enjoyed his preferred
ballet. The daughter of the Japanese prime minister warned the First Lady
that anything classical would put her father to sleep and that his tastes ran
to popular American music. At his visit the entertainment was provided by
Bobby Short.[25]

The protocol file on the shah of Iran and his wife, Empress Farah, was
probably one of the most complete Rosalynn Carter encountered. The preferences of the Iranian couple would have been well known to Washington
officials long before November 1977. In fact, the empress had already made
one official visit to the Carter White House, in July of 1977, when she was
traveling in the United States. That visit had elicited its own "Death to the
Shah" chants from Iranian students demonstrating at the White House welcoming ceremony. The empress said she had come to expect such demonstrations in all of her foreign travels; the First Lady had the same reaction.
"We had been in Washington for only a few months," Rosalynn Carter
writes in her memoirs, "and had already become accustomed to some kind
of demonstration in front of the White House almost every day."[26]

In his toast at the state dinner honoring the shah and his wife, President
Carter began with some humorous observations about the events earlier in

25. For a general description of preparations and protocol at state dinners, see Rosalynn
Carter, *First Lady from Plains* (New York, 1984), 204–22.
26. Ibid., 289.

the day. "There is one thing I can say about the Shah," Carter said, "he knows how to draw a crowd." The president went on to praise the shah's courage and strength in getting through the arrival ceremonies and observed that his own speech on the White House lawn had been one of the briefest he had ever given and that he "was glad to turn the microphone over to the Shah."[27] Carter then went on to deliver, extemporaneously, a warm statement about the accomplishments of the White Revolution in Iran and the significant improvements in education and economic prosperity for Iranian citizens that had occurred under the shah's reign.[28] He said nothing about human rights and a great deal about the importance of Iran to the United States and to the other states in the region. The president praised the charitable and cultural endeavors of the shah's wife and complimented her beauty in another humorous remark. He speculated that a movie company executive attending the state dinner was probably interested in making the empress the star of his next picture. If that were so, the president promised to buy the first ticket.[29] President Carter's remarks at the state dinner were so generous and gracious that they reportedly brought tears to the shah's eyes for the second time that day and, on this occasion, without the aid of crowd-control gases. On Thursday, at the formal luncheon that concluded the state visit, the shah referred to the previous day as "tears in the morning and tears at night."[30]

The state dinner was followed by entertainment in honor of the shah and the empress, who were known to be fans of American jazz. The official program included performances by Sarah Vaughan and Dizzy Gillespie, and was followed by an unscheduled jam session between Gillespie and jazz great Earl Hines, who was a guest at the state dinner. Gary Sick describes what happened next. When the president and Mrs. Carter went up on stage to congratulate both the scheduled and unscheduled performers, they were

27. *Public Papers of the Presidents of the United States, Jimmy Carter 1977,* 2030.

28. Carter did receive a memo from head speechwriter James Fallows with talking points for his toast to the shah. He underlined some of the material in this memo and wrote some additional notes in his own hand on that document. This would appear to be the basis for his remarks at the state dinner. Jim Fallows and Jerry Doolittle to the President, memorandum: "Talking Points for Toast to Shah, Nov. 15," November 10, 1977, Office of the Staff Secretary, President's Handwriting File, Box 59, Folder 11/15/77 [1], Carter Library.

29. *Public Papers of the Presidents of the United States, Jimmy Carter 1977,* 2031.

30. Sick, *All Fall Down,* 33.

joined by the shah and his wife only after the empress "virtually propelled" the shah "toward the stage, where he shook hands all around, in evident discomfort." For Sick, this was an incident that provided some insight into the shah's character. The shah, he concluded, was "basically a shy man. No politician in the Western sense, he lacked the common touch. Although impressive in the orchestrated ritual of statecraft, when confronted with the unexpected and the need for improvisation, he froze."[31]

The emotional tears shed by the shah at the state dinner and his subsequent discomfort in thanking the entertainers were, like the calm and reticence that Carter had seen earlier in the day, hints at the complexity, and perhaps contradictions, in the shah's character. But they were hardly evidence that he was close to the end of his days as the ruler of Iran. When Carter reciprocated the shah's visit with his own trip to Tehran, he made even stronger public statements than he had in Washington about the strength of the Iranian leader and his importance to the United States. In both meetings, the president and all in his entourage missed whatever signs there may have been of the shah's underlying weakness and political vulnerability.

The President Goes to Tehran

The stop in Iran was not originally on the president's itinerary for an overseas trip that was supposed to include a large number of nations in Europe, Africa, Asia, and Latin America, but when a decision was made to shorten the list of destinations, an opening occurred on the calendar for New Year's Eve. The presidential party needed a resting place between the planned stop in Poland and the visit to New Delhi. A last-minute decision was made to include a very brief visit (roughly twenty-four hours) in Tehran. The shah was disappointed about the brevity of the visit, but thrilled that it would take place so soon after his own trip to Washington. The timing, he believed, would demonstrate that the new administration was serious about the kind words of support spoken in Washington. The president's advance team wanted the Tehran stop to be informal, with plenty of time to allow the presidential party to rest before the next leg of the journey. The shah, however, wanted a formal meal at a royal palace that would match the state dinner he had attended in Washington, and he hoped to spend as much

31. Ibid.

time as possible in meetings and social events with the president. Compromises were negotiated. The president would spend no more than one day in Iran, but more of the hours in that day would be devoted to ceremonies and discussions than the travel planners originally preferred.[32]

In Tehran the two leaders greeted each other at the airport in the afternoon on New Year's Eve and proceeded to a meeting in one of the shah's several palaces in the capital city. Because of the recent Washington discussions, there was relatively little new business for the two nations to conduct at the highest level. Carter was able to inform the shah that his request to purchase American-made nuclear reactors would be approved and there was some discussion of armaments and the shah's recently updated wish list for future purchases. These were not new subjects, and the combination of giving the shah something he wanted while expressing reservations about future purchases was the expected pattern of exchange after the Washington talks.

The agenda in Tehran was broadened when late in the day and early the next morning King Hussein of Jordan joined the president and shah in their meetings. Hussein, a close friend of the shah, had met with Carter in Washington the previous spring and was an important figure in the Middle East peace process that was gaining momentum. Carter appreciated the opportunity to speak with Hussein and lobby for Jordan to join the negotiations that would eventually lead Egypt and Israel to Camp David. The Jordanian king made no promises in this regard, but gave Carter an opportunity to explore what was rapidly becoming one of the highest priorities on the president's foreign policy agenda.

In Iranian protocol, the Jordanian monarch outranked the American president and, therefore, did not attend the New Year's Eve dinner in Carter's honor. That event, which the president had wanted to be an informal meal, turned out to be a lavish affair. The presidential party, together with the shah's large family, sat for a sumptuous dinner including "Dom Pérignon, caviar, kebabs, a pilaf of diced partridge, fruit salad, fabulous wines, and, the pièce de résistance, flaming ice cream in honor of which the lights were lowered."[33] Entertainment was provided by traditional Iranian folk

32. Sullivan, *Mission to Iran*, 130–32.
33. William Shawcross, *The Shah's Last Ride: The True Story of the Emperor's Dreams and Illusions, Exile, and Death at the Hands of His Foes and Friends* (New York, 1988), 129.

dancers and singers in a separate room, where King Hussein joined the party.[34] Later in the evening, as midnight approached, there was also some informal entertainment provided by the shah's teenage son, who acted as the disc jockey for some impromptu holiday dancing. The prince, along with his younger sister, demonstrated the latest disco steps for the king of Jordan and the presidential party.[35]

Though the private discussions about arms, the sale of nuclear power plants, and the prospects for a Middle East peace may have been the most important diplomatic exchanges of the visit, most of the attention subsequently given to this presidential visit has involved the formal toasts delivered at the dinner hosted by the shah. As in Washington, Carter's toast was a mixture of personal greetings, self-deprecating humor, and unreserved support for the shah and for continued close ties between the United States and Iran. He did not use the toast that had been prepared by the embassy staff in Tehran and instead spoke from a few notes he had written on an official program prepared by the Iranian government for his visit.[36] The notes were partly based on two pages of suggested remarks prepared by one of the speechwriters, Garrett Smith, assigned to this overseas trip.[37]

The president began by apologizing for an error he had made in his arrival remarks at the airport when he mentioned the shah's twenty-seven years in power. The correct number was thirty-seven, and the president thanked the empress for bringing the mistake to his attention, though he observed that the "Shah said he felt 10 years younger when I did that."[38] He went on to comment about the glories of the ancient civilizations that had existed in Persia and the striking difference in age between one nation that had recently celebrated its 2,500th anniversary and another that had

34. Sullivan, *Mission to Iran*, 134.

35. Shawcross, *The Shah's Last Ride*, 131.

36. Programme of the Official Visit of the Honourable Jimmy Carter The President of the United States of America and Madame Carter to Iran December 1977, Office of the Staff Secretary, President's Handwriting File, Box 66, Trip to Mideast & Europe 12/29/77–1/6/78, [4], Carter Library. Sullivan, *Mission to Iran*, 134.

37. Smith's notes include a reference to Iran as "an island of stability in a turbulent corner of the world." The Saadi quote discussed below was inserted into Smith's proposed "Tehran Dinner Remarks," but it is not clear who discovered or suggested this quotation. Staff Office Files Speechwriters, Chronological File, Box 13, Folder "12/31/77—Iran Remarks GS," Carter Library.

38. *Public Papers of the Presidents of the United States, Jimmy Carter 1977*, 2220.

just passed its bicentennial. Carter's comments about the age and beauty of Persian culture also allowed him to make a subtle and effective reference to the issue of human rights. Quoting a popular Iranian poet, Saadi, Carter read the following passage: "Human beings are like parts of a body, created from the same essence. When one part is hurt and in pain, others cannot remain in peace and quiet. If the misery of others leaves you indifferent and with no feeling of sorrow, then you cannot be called a human being."[39] The message in the quotation was clear, but because it came from a respected indigenous author and showed the president's respect for Iranian culture, it was delivered with minimal discomfort to the shah.

The president's toast also contained a line about the stability of Iran, which Cyrus Vance described as "the usual effusiveness typical of such occasions."[40] It would be the most remembered sentence in the president's visit to Tehran largely because it would turn out to be spectacularly wrong in the year that lay ahead. "Iran," the president said, "because of the great leadership of the Shah, is an island of stability in one of the most troubled areas of the world." In the closing of his toast, Carter was even more effusive:

> Our talks have been priceless, our friendship is irreplaceable, and my own gratitude is to the Shah, who in his wisdom and with his experience has been so helpful to me, a new leader.
>
> We have no other nation on earth who is closer to us in planning our mutual military security. We have no other nation with whom we have closer consultation on regional problems that concern us both. And there is no leader with whom I have a deeper sense of personal gratitude and personal friendship.[41]

The British ambassador to Iran found the president's toast to be "mawkish," but the shah was very pleased with what Carter had to say in Tehran.[42] In his memoirs, written in exile after his fall from power, he reported that he had "never heard a foreign statesman speak of me in quite such flattering terms." To the shah, "Carter appeared to be a smart man" who left Tehran

39. Ibid., 2222.
40. Vance, *Hard Choices*, 323.
41. *Public Papers of the Presidents of the United States, Jimmy Carter 1977*, 2222.
42. Anthony Parsons, *The Pride and the Fall: Iran, 1974–1979* (London, 1984), 59.

having improved the favorable impression he had already made in Washington.[43]

If that was the purpose of the president's visit to the Iranian capital, it was amply accomplished. But making a good impression with a leader who would, within a year, fall from power was an accomplishment of limited value. Moreover, as in Washington, what was said may have been less important than what was seen. The first meeting of the two heads of state had generally gone well, but the television cameras in the American capital broadcast the dramatic images of world leaders awkwardly exchanging tear-filled greetings while demonstrators clamored in the distance. The substantive discussions and words of support during their second meeting in Tehran may also have constituted a diplomatic success, but the citizens of Iran, if they saw all of the ceremonies connected with the president's visit, would have seen images that may have been just as unsettling as the tear gas in Washington. The president of the United States and the shah of Iran were lifting crystal glasses filled with French champagne as they toasted the New Year. To American eyes that would have been, and was, a scene of friendship; but to an Iranian audience it would have been odd, perhaps even offensive, to see the shah commemorate a Western holiday that Iranians do not observe with the consumption of an alcoholic beverage forbidden to the faithful under Islamic law.[44]

One week after Carter's visit to Tehran Iranian police opened fire on an anti-shah demonstration, killing a number of protesters in the holy city of Qom. The demonstration had been organized by religious opponents of the regime upset by the publication of a scurrilous newspaper attack on their hero, the Ayatollah Khomeini. Though it was not recognized at the time, those shots are now seen as the first in the Iranian revolution that ended the shah's reign on the Peacock Throne.[45]

43. Mohammad Reza Pahlavi, The Shah of Iran, *Answer to History* (New York, 1980), 152.

44. The observations about how the ceremonies would have appeared to Iranian eyes come from Minou Reeves, *Behind the Peacock Throne* (London, Eng., 1986), 167. In the Reeves account, it is implied that the New Year's Eve events were televised in Iran. Gary Sick does not believe that there were any cameras present for that portion of the ceremonies or that Iranian officials would have allowed the broadcast of the champagne toasts in the shah's private library at midnight. Gary Sick, letter to author, March 15, 1995.

45. Sick, *All Fall Down,* 40.

Conclusions

The president would later criticize the intelligence community for its failure to provide timely warning of the pending revolution in Iran.[46] It was a valid if slightly unfair criticism. It is true that the CIA was unable to foresee the fall of the shah until it was apparent to nearly everyone, but the CIA was not alone in this failure. The intelligence agencies of other countries missed the signs of early revolutionary activity in Iran. So did most scholars of Iranian politics in the West.[47] So did the president and his senior advisers in their two high-level meetings with the shah. There were two important elements in this collective failure of vision. One involved the shah, the other the politics of developing countries.

The mistake made about the shah was the assumption that he would divide, repress, or buy off his opposition in the late 1970s as he had done in the past. In Iran, the shah had long been opposed by a variety of political groups—the democratic reformers of the Mossadegh era, who felt betrayed by the 1953 coup; the Communists, who called for a Marxist revolution; the Kurds and other ethnic minorities mistreated at various times by the central government; and the mullahs and religious leaders unhappy with the modernization of Iran. In the past, the shah had always been able to introduce enough new political reforms, or arrest enough members of the Communist party, or produce enough promises for the Kurds or bribes for the mullahs that his collective opposition would remain divided and weak. He did some of the same things in the late 1970s, but more half-heartedly and less successfully than in the past.

Why did the shah fail to deal effectively with his opposition in 1977 and 1978? Part of the answer is that in the late 1970s, the Shah was a different man. He was dying of cancer. Diagnosed in 1974 with chronic lymphocytic leukemia, the shah had secretly received examinations and treatments in

46. Stansfield Turner, *Secrecy and Democracy: The CIA in Transition* (New York, 1985), 113–18. See also, Brzezinski, *Power and Principle*, 367. David Newsom recalls that "after the September 1978 riots, the State Department sent three young officers, one of whom, at least, was a Farsi speaker, to tour Iran. They came back with a report that the situation was deteriorating. Dr. Brzezinski would not permit them to give their report; he felt the State Department, and particularly, Henry Precht, the country director, was trying to undermine the shah. He put more stock in what the Iranian Ambassador Zahedi, was saying. Not everyone in the government was caught by suprise." David Newsom, letter to author, April 5, 1998.

47. Rubin, *Paved with Good Intentions*, 203.

France, Switzerland, and Tehran. He occasionally experienced pain connected with a temporary enlargement of the spleen and regularly took a drug called chlorambucil. There is no evidence that he was experiencing any immediate health problems when he met with Carter late in 1977 and early in 1978.[48] But according to one report, his French doctors told him shortly after the second visit with the new American president that his cancer had become much more life threatening.[49] Carter had no information in November or December of 1977 (or for that matter for all of 1978 and most of 1979) that there was any serious question about the shah's health.[50] The fact that the shah was entering a new year not knowing if it would be his last and concerned about how he would transfer power to his teenage son was an important key to much of what would follow. His condition would affect his personality and behavior and make him more likely to hesitate about using levels of force against his enemies that would cloud his reputation or make the succession of his son harder to carry off.

The failure of American officials to learn about the declining state of the shah's health was understandable. The shah was reportedly not told by his own physicians that he had cancer until 1976 and remained extremely secretive about his condition. He disguised his trips to receive Western medical attention with other purposes, preferred French doctors because of their presumed discretion, and prevented his twin sister from learning that he had cancer until early in 1979.[51] But even before disease began to change the shah's personality, there were hints about his inability to handle the growing opposition to his regime. Carter was impressed with the shah's calm response to the indignities of welcoming ceremonies held under a cloud of tear gas but was surprised by his modesty and reticence in their subsequent conversations. Ambassador Sullivan found the shah he first met in Tehran after delivering his diplomatic credentials to be quite different from the shah he had read about in the government's psychological profile of the Iranian leader. The profile had led him to expect an arrogant and authoritarian personality, but the shah was, in fact, informal, soft-spoken, and "almost

48. Shawcross, *The Shah's Last Ride*, 230–34.
49. Rubin, *Paved with Good Intentions*, 204.
50. Sick, *All Fall Down,* 212–15.
51. Shawcross, *The Shah's Last Ride*, 234–38.

tentative in the manner in which he presented conclusions."[52] Gary Sick saw something of the same thing in the shah's hesitancy and inability to improvise a response to the evening's entertainment at the White House state dinner in November 1977.

For several of the policy makers watching the shah carefully early in the Carter administration, the Iranian leader was a bit like the Wizard of Oz. Behind the curtain of his imperial public presence he was surprisingly meek, mild, and indecisive. But if the president and several members of his administration were able to occasionally peek behind the curtain, they were never able to fully pull it aside or reach the conclusion that the weaknesses glimpsed on the far side were the relevant personality traits for an accurate assessment of the shah's political future. In fact, it was such an unthinkable proposition that the shah's days on the Peacock Throne might be numbered that very few Iranian experts inside or outside the government were thinking about that prospect in 1977.

That was the second source of the failed vision about Iranian revolutionary prospects. Hardly anyone who had studied Iran suspected that a broad-based coalition could be assembled against the shah or that its charismatic leader would be an aging Islamic cleric. The importance of religion was supposed to decline as a society entered the modern age, and a revolution that would call for the creation of an Islamic constitution, the restoration of the veil and the rest of traditional female dress, the closing of movie theaters and bars, and an end to contact with foreign businessmen was not supposed to happen in a country whose citizens were becoming richer, more urbanized, better educated, and more likely to come in contact with Western culture. But it did. While American officials debated the importance of human rights in Iran, they gave little attention to the subject of Islamic rights and the degree to which Iranian modernization was undermining traditional values and practices. Westerners were inclined to criticize the shah for not moving fast enough in his modernization program or for attempting to modernize the educational system and economy without creating compara-

---

52. Sullivan, *Mission to Iran*, 55. According to an interview William Colby (CIA director under Ford) gave to two researchers in 1986, the intelligence community personality profile on the shah did portray him as a weak man. Gregory F. Treverton and James Klocke, "The Fall of the Shah of Iran," Pew Case Studies in International Affairs, Case 311 (Washington, D.C., 1994), 4.

bly modern political institutions. It did not occur to most outside observers that the shah's real problem may have been that he was reforming his country too quickly and gradually losing the support of a population easily swayed by fundamentalist religious teachings. The Iranian revolution surprised the Carter administration in part because it surprised a world used to the dominance of Western values over those of other cultures and predisposed to discount the importance of religion in world affairs. It is perhaps ironic that Jimmy Carter, arguably the most devoutly religious occupant of the White House in modern times, would be confronted by a religious revolution that neither he nor any of his advisers adequately anticipated or understood.

The two meetings between Carter and the shah helped neither leader to see or understand the events that were forthcoming in Iran. Nor did either meeting establish a close personal rapport that would be useful in the crisis to come. In fact, despite the glowing description of the shah as one of his closest personal friends when Carter spoke in Washington and Tehran, the two leaders rarely communicated with each other after their official visits. They spoke on the phone only twice after the meeting in Tehran, and the shah denied that one of those conversations ever took place.[53]

Words of friendship between heads of state are, of course, not always to be taken literally. The things Carter said in Washington and Tehran were intended to publicly reassure an important American ally that his nation would continue to receive the support of the United States. Though Carter wanted to reduce overall international arms sales and make genuine progress in the improvement of human rights for all the citizens of the world, he was realistic enough to understand that America's strategic and regional partners needed to be handled with care. Carter gave the shah special attention. He agreed to sell Iran most of the weapons the shah wanted, including the highly controversial AWACS aircraft, but did not give him a blank check or an unrealistic assessment of the political problems that would be likely to accompany the approval of major arms transactions on Capitol Hill. Carter wanted to convey to the shah that his concerns about human rights were real and substantive, but without embarrassing an important world leader or failing to recognize the progress he was making. In these balancing acts Carter appears to have done a good job.

53. Sick, *All Fall Down,* 60–62. Mohammad Reza Pahlavi, *Answer to History,* 161.

In private, he raised some specific complaints about human rights in Iran; in public, he praised the shah. That praise may have been effusive, and perhaps even hyperbolic, but it was not all that different from the language used by Lyndon Johnson in 1967, or by Richard Nixon in 1969 and 1973, or by Gerald Ford in 1975.[54] Visits between the shah of Iran and presidents of the United States tended to be occasions when the ample supplies of political superlatives in the files of presidential speechwriters were freely dispensed. Carter's official toasts to the shah may, in fact, have been better than most because they were extemporaneous, humorous, personal, and free from the formality that is often evident in the work of State Department protocol officers or White House speechwriters. Carter's problems in meeting the shah were not in the words of praise he used to describe an ally who truly had been "an island of stability in one of the most troubled areas of the world," but in the unfortunate fact that they were spoken months before the instability of the shah's regime began to appear.

Moreover, the pictures shown of the first meeting between Carter and the shah conveyed the image of two leaders under siege. The president was forced to rub his eyes, the shah needed a handkerchief to wipe away his tears; both leaders and their wives were clearly affected by the tear gas wafting across the south lawn. This was not the image that either leader would have wished to present at the outset of high-level talks between the new administration and an important American ally. Gary Sick later learned that news of the tear gas incident may have emboldened some members of the shah's opposition in Iran because they assumed that the Carter administration must have intentionally staged the incident in order to humiliate the shah.[55] Nothing could have been further from the truth, but truth was hard to see from either side of the gulf that separated American policy makers and Iranian revolutionaries. From the president's perspective it would have

54. See for example, *Public Papers of the Presidents of the United States, Lyndon B. Johnson 1967* (Washington, D.C., 1968), 803–804; and *Public Papers of the Presidents of the United States, Richard Nixon 1973* (Washington, D.C., 1975), 662–63. In some ways the toasts Carter gave in 1978 to Romanian president Nicolae Ceaușescu and Yugoslav president Tito are better examples of his effusive style in such ceremonies and of the danger of giving too much public praise to leaders whose policies and practices in gaining and keeping power were repugnant to a serious advocate of human rights. See *Public Papers of the Presidents of the United States, Jimmy Carter 1978* (Washington, D.C., 1979), 475–76, 738–40.

55. Sick, *All Fall Down*, 36.

been infinitely better if the tear gas problem had never occurred, but the violence outside the White House gates on November 15 was, like so much else in the story of U.S.-Iranian relations, hard to anticipate. Protests against the shah by students studying in the United States were fairly common in the mid-1970s; they took place in connection with the earlier visit of the Empress and were expected for the shah's visit in 1977.[56] But the size of the crowds (estimated at 4,000 anti-shah and 1,500 pro-shah demonstrators) were larger than the Washington, D.C., police were prepared for, and the exchange of blows between the two groups, which necessitated the use of tear gas, was completely unanticipated.[57]

It is impossible to say whether better White House planning could have avoided this unfortunate aspect of the welcoming ceremony,[58] but it is true that the senior officials on Carter's White House staff were less attentive than their counterparts in the Reagan administration to the power of visual images and the need to plan presidential appearances with care. There was no Michael Deaver in the Carter White House and no comparable communications strategist with a high-level White House appointment and a close personal relationship with the president. One could speculate that such a staff member might have taken extra precautions for the shah's visit, but the evidence for that speculation is thin. There were in November 1977 no compelling reasons for anyone in the Carter White House to treat the shah's pending visit to Washington any differently from his earlier visits in 1975 or 1973 or his two visits in 1969. A visit from the shah of Iran was routine business for the White House.

In his first year in office, according to a study done by Hamilton Jordan, President Carter met with over forty heads of state—more than Kennedy, Johnson, or Nixon in comparable periods in their administrations.[59] By another count, in Brzezinski's files, the president's first meeting with the shah in November was his sixty-sixth personal contact with either a head of state

56. Sullivan, *Mission to Iran*, 125.

57. Crowd numbers from Rubin, *Paved with Good Intentions*, 200.

58. Sullivan reports that as the helicopter carrying the shah to the White House reception flew over the demonstrators, he was surprised to see how narrow and poorly policed the area between the two groups was. Demonstrators the previous day in Williamsburg, Virginia, were successfully kept apart. Sullivan, *Mission to Iran*, 127.

59. Jordan, *Crisis*, 88.

or a head of government in 1977.[60] The First Lady reports that in her first twenty months in Washington, there were a hundred presidents, prime ministers, and kings or queens who made official visits to the White House.[61] These meetings and the accompanying social events absorbed a great deal of presidential time and energy with rather mixed results. The president formed an early friendship with Anwar Sadat that was very important in the development of Middle East diplomacy and the Camp David achievements. He liked and respected President Pérez of Venezuela and developed an unusual working relationship with General Torrijos of Panama. But he also got off to a bad start with Helmut Schmidt, after which things never got much better, and his only summit with a Soviet leader came late in the administration and at a time when Brezhnev's declining health made it difficult for the two leaders to do much beyond the ceremonial signing of a belated SALT II treaty. In Hamilton Jordan's view, however the private and public meetings between heads of state may have turned out, the president was spending too much time on foreign affairs and not enough on domestic policy issues.[62]

As a president new to issues of foreign policy with almost no acquaintances among world leaders, Jimmy Carter may have felt that he needed to devote more time to meetings with heads of state than other presidents would have required. In 1977, the least imperial of modern American presidents urgently needed to meet and assess the highly imperial shah of Iran. The shah was an important player for many of the issues that were prominent on Carter's agenda—international energy supplies, Middle East peace negotiations, conventional arms transactions, and human rights. The coming unrest in Iran would have profound effects on the policies and politics of the new administration. Though the two leaders met twice in the last months of Carter's first year in office, it was not enough. Neither head of state came away from those meetings with an accurate assessment of the other or the kind of personal relationship that might have helped them

60. "President Carter's Contact with Heads of State & Government in 1977," Zbigniew Brzezinski Collection, Box 34, Folder "National Security Council 1/77–10/80," Carter Library.

61. Rosalynn Carter, *First Lady from Plains*, 209.

62. Carter rejects this conclusion and estimates that he spent three-quarters of his time on domestic issues. He does admit that he found foreign policy more interesting and freer from restraints and restrictions than domestic affairs. Carter, interview.

weather the storms that lay ahead. But it may not have been possible for any president in 1977, whether new to the international scene or well established on it, to fully fathom the secretive and sensitive man who had been the undisputed ruler of his nation for decades and was himself oblivious to the grave political dangers he was about to face.

3

A TALE OF TWO LETTERS
Human Rights, Sakharov, and Somoza

On February 17, 1977, Andrei Sakharov—the nuclear physicist who helped develop the Soviet Union's hydrogen bomb and then became an internationally renowned critic of his nation's political system—stood in front of the U.S. embassy in Moscow posing for photographers with a piece of paper in front of his chest. The Nobel Peace Prize–winning dissident had just received a letter about human rights from the president of the United States. On July 21, 1978, the American ambassador in Managua delivered another letter dealing with the same subject, from the same president, to the Nicaraguan dictator Anastasio Somoza. The letter praised one of the regular offenders of human rights in the Western Hemisphere for a few positive steps he had recently promised to take. In a manner of speaking, the Somoza letter would be held up to public view much as the Sakharov letter was, but for rather different purposes and with rather different results.

The two letters have a number of things in common. Both were small pieces of presidential work in the administration's sustained commitment to the cause of human rights. Both letters were drafted for Carter's signature and occupied very little presidential time. To the extent that there were questions about the wisdom of sending these communications, the debates that accompanied their preparation were not always deemed sufficiently important to merit the president's personal attention. In each case, Carter decided to send a letter, then read and reworked the drafts he was given.

He signed them and sent them on their way for delivery through diplomatic channels. In some ways, this was routine business for a president who probably put his name on hundreds, if not thousands, of communications touching on matters of human rights.

But these instances of presidential communication are, nevertheless, worthy of our consideration. Both produced significant, though admittedly hard to measure, consequences. One played a role in the development of U.S.-Soviet relations in the early months of the new administration; the other reverberated in the revolutionary forces gathering momentum in Central America. Both involved private communications which became public. Both were used by administration critics as examples of the president's naïveté in foreign policy making. And both serve as reminders that the White House often acts as a monumental magnifier, giving a few presidential words or actions large, and not easy to anticipate, international repercussions.

Jimmy Carter and Human Rights

Carter's emphasis on human rights in the 1976 presidential campaign is often described as a political strategy for unifying a Democratic Party torn apart by Vietnam and as a way of finding an effective foreign policy issue for a candidate and party generally supportive of the major international accomplishments of the Nixon and Ford administrations. There is some truth to this claim.

In 1976, human rights was a unifying theme in the Democratic Party and a rallying cry in the nation at large. Liberals wanted to limit U.S. support for right-wing dictators around the world, like Marcos in the Philippines, Somoza in Nicaragua, and the shah of Iran. They complained that too much of American foreign policy in the cold war, including our involvement in Southeast Asia, involved attempts to defend democracy where it had never existed and to ally the United States with dictators whose only virtue was the fact that they did not abuse their citizens in the name of Karl Marx. Conservatives liked human rights as well. They wanted to abandon détente and step up attacks on the Soviet Union for its flagrant violations of economic and political liberties and its suppression of independence in the captive nations of Eastern Europe. In the American bicentennial year, and in the wake of disillusionment over Vietnam and Watergate, there was a natural appeal to the notion that the fundamental political principles in the

Declaration of Independence should be given new prominence in the conduct of foreign affairs. Human rights was a platform plank on which George McGovern and Henry Jackson could stand side by side without much distance or discomfort between them.

Human rights was also an issue where Democrats could claim some distinctiveness from their Republican opponents without challenging the popular and constructive accomplishments of the Kissinger era. In many respects, Carter administration foreign policy would be a continuation and advancement of ideas and efforts initiated by Carter's Republican predecessors. The SALT process, after the false start with the deep-cut proposal, picked up where Ford left off in Vladivostok. The Panama Canal treaties were based on the negotiating framework announced by Henry Kissinger and Panamanian foreign minister Juan Tack in 1974. The dramatic transformation in U.S. relations with China set in motion by President Nixon's trip to that country in 1972 reached its conclusion in the official recognition and exchange of ambassadors that took place under Carter. In the Middle East, after failing to organize a general peace conference in Geneva, the Carter administration returned to Kissinger's step-by-step approach, including some very productive presidential shuttle diplomacy between the Camp David cabins occupied by Anwar Sadat and Menachem Begin.

The basic continuity between Carter and his Republican predecessors in foreign affairs may have been good for the nation, but it was not very useful in presidential politics. Campaigns thrive on differences and distinctions, not commonalities and continuities. In 1976, human rights became one of the important lines of demarcation between President Ford and his challenger Jimmy Carter.[1] Of course, both candidates were in favor of promoting freedom and democracy around the world, but Carter could effectively attack the realpolitik rhetoric of Henry Kissinger, the U.S. role in overthrowing Allende in Chile, the American tilt toward Pakistan in its 1973 war with India, and Ford's refusal to meet with the exiled Soviet author Alexander Solzhenitzyn. But human rights for Jimmy Carter was much more than a convenient campaign issue in 1976. It had deep roots in his personal experiences and his early political career. It had a central place in his world view.

1. The other major foreign policy issue in the campaign was style. Carter repeatedly and effectively criticized Henry Kissinger's dominance of foreign affairs under Nixon and Ford and promised that there would be no "Lone Ranger" in his administration.

Respect for human rights and for the power that could come from political ideas and democratic reforms came naturally to a southerner who had lived through the civil rights movement of the 1960s. The revolution in race relations that took place in the nation, but particularly in the South, was the defining political event in Jimmy Carter's adult life. His mother had long been a vocal critic of race relations in her community and was, in her personal behavior, a kind of dissident to the social norms of the segregated South. When the Supreme Court decided to end the separate but never very equal public schools in the nation, the Carter family did not join in the resistance to integration that was a common reaction in their community. Jimmy Carter, serving as a member of the local school board when there was growing national pressure to implement the Brown decision, refused to join the White Citizens' Council that actively opposed integration. As a result, the family business was subjected to a boycott. The Carters were outcasts again when they opposed a decision by their church congregation to close its doors to any black worshipers who might wish to attend their services.[2] When another Supreme Court decision mandated the democratic principle of "one man, one vote" in state elections, the reapportionment of the Georgia state legislature created an opportunity for Carter to enter state politics that had not previously been available.[3]

Throughout his careers in farming, business, and Georgia politics, Jimmy Carter was both a witness to and a participant in the major social and political transformations that accompanied the civil rights movement. Those transformations occurred more rapidly and more peacefully than most observers expected. The lessons he learned from that period in his life were important to his thinking about international human rights. Carter understood the benefits that might come from the simple act of drawing attention to injustices long ignored. If the American South could end legal segregation in a matter of years, through processes that were largely non-violent, perhaps it would be possible for other parts of the world to enjoy similar social and political changes.[4]

2. Jimmy Carter, *Why Not the Best* (New York, 1976), 72–78.

3. Jimmy Carter, *Turning Point: A Candidate, a State, a Nation Come of Age* (New York, 1992).

4. The chapter on human rights in Carter's presidential memoirs begins with a discussion of civil rights in the South. Jimmy Carter, *Keeping Faith: Memoirs of a President* (New York, 1982), 141–44.

Jimmy Carter never thought that talking about human rights was merely good politics. In many cases, particularly after he was in the White House, it was politically controversial. But he kept talking about fundamental freedoms and democracy throughout his years in office and beyond. He talked about human rights in his inaugural address, in his first speech to the United Nations, and in the major foreign policy address delivered during his first year in office. At the Notre Dame commencement in May of 1977, he listed the five major objectives for foreign policy in his administration. The promotion of human rights was the first and most important of those objectives. In the Notre Dame speech, one of the few to which he devoted considerable time and attention at every stage of drafting, Carter admitted that there were limits to what could be accomplished by moral suasion, but he also reminded his audience that it was "a mistake to undervalue the power of words and of the ideas that words embody. . . . In the life of the human spirit, words *are* action, much more so than many of us may realize who live in countries where freedom of expression is taken for granted. The leaders of totalitarian nations understand this very well. The proof is that words are precisely the action for which dissidents in those countries are persecuted."[5]

Carter would be careful about the words he would use in his efforts to promote human rights. And he would back up his words with other kinds of action. He staffed the Human Rights Bureau in the Department of State with dedicated activists and set up mechanisms to ensure that performance in the areas of human rights was considered in connection with decisions concerning foreign aid, arms sales, and diplomatic contacts. In virtually all of his own meetings with ambassadors and heads of state representing countries with human rights problems, those problems were the subject of high-level conversation and negotiation.

And from time to time, President Carter wrote letters to those who suffered, and to those who perpetrated, violations of human rights around the world.

Sakharov

For the community of Soviet dissidents in Moscow, the winter of 1976–77 was a time of both hope and dread. The hope came from a growing interna-

5. *Public Papers of the Presidents of the United States, Jimmy Carter 1977* (Washington, D.C., 1977), 958.

tional attention to human rights. Language guaranteeing fundamental freedoms had been included in the 1975 Helsinki accords signed by the Soviet Union, the United States, and European nations on both sides of the Iron Curtain. Nobel Prizes in literature and peace had been awarded to Alexander Solzhenitzyn and Andrei Sakharov, drawing worldwide attention to the dissident movement within the Soviet Union. Moreover, new legislation passed by the American Congress and a new president elected in 1976 were making human rights increasingly prominent in American foreign policy.

The dread came from signs that despite the new international interest in human rights, or perhaps because of it, a new crackdown against the most active critics of the Soviet regime was about to begin. Early in January the home of Yuri Orlov was searched by internal-security officers. Orlov was a leader in the Moscow-based Helsinki Group, a self-appointed organization monitoring Soviet compliance (or the lack of compliance) with the human rights commitments that were part of the 1975 agreements signed in Finland. Others in the organization also had their homes searched and papers and property confiscated. In the immediate aftermath of the searches, Sakharov appealed to all the heads of state who had signed the Helsinki documents, including Gerald Ford. On January 8, a bomb exploded in a Moscow subway resulting in deaths and injuries for innocent passengers. A few days later, Sakharov learned that reports being circulated by Soviet officials blamed dissidents for the explosion. In his mind, the combination of the recent searches and the allegations of sabotage were indicators that an "all out attack on the dissident community" was forthcoming.[6]

In mid-January, Sakharov issued a statement to foreign correspondents calling for an international investigation of the bombing incident and warning that the explosion might be used as an excuse for a crackdown on nonviolent and peaceful human rights advocates. This statement attracted some attention in the West. Not surprisingly, it was also noticed by officials in the Soviet government. Near the end of January, Sakharov was called in to see a deputy prosecutor, who warned him that criminal proceedings might be initiated as a result of his international pronouncements concerning the subway incident.[7]

6. Andrei Sakharov, *Memoirs* (New York, 1990), 463.

7. Sakharov, *Memoirs*, 465. Sakharov uses the term "procurator" rather than prosecutor, but it is clear from the context that he was being threatened with criminal prosecution by an official comparable to a prosecutor in Western legal terminology.

Between the issuing of his statement to foreign correspondents after the January 8 bombing and his visit to the prosecutor's office, Sakharov wrote a letter to Jimmy Carter. It was actually his third communication with the new American president. During the campaign he had sent a message to Ford and Carter calling on both candidates to work to advance the cause of human rights and the Helsinki principles. After Carter won the election, Sakharov sent a brief telegram congratulating the victorious candidate and commending his "unambiguous statements in defense of human rights throughout the world."[8] Neither of these messages was answered by Carter. Because of its timing and method of delivery, Sakharov's third message to the new president got more attention and a personal response.

On January 21, Sakharov and his wife, Elena Bonner, were visited in their Moscow apartment by an American attorney, Martin Garbus, who had come to the Soviet Union to represent a "refusnik" (the name given to those who sought permission to emigrate from the Soviet Union and were routinely refused). It was the day after President Carter's inauguration. The new American chief executive had said in his inaugural address that "our commitment to human rights must be absolute" and that "the passion for freedom is on the rise. Tapping this new spirit, there can be no nobler nor more ambitious task for America to undertake on this day of a new beginning than to help shape a just and peaceful world that is truly humane."[9]

When Garbus offered to carry a letter to President Carter and suggested that his host name the ten political prisoners whose cases should receive special attention from the new administration, Sakharov immediately agreed. Though he usually prepared his correspondence and public statements with some care, on this occasion he was rushed. Garbus was at the end of his trip to the Soviet Union, and his flight out of Moscow was only hours away when he arrived at the Sakharov apartment. In the limited time available, Sakharov wrote praising Carter's stand on human rights and asking for his help on behalf of sixteen (he could not limit himself to ten) individuals in the Soviet Union and Eastern Europe who were currently in prison or under arrest. He reiterated his warning that a new round of arrests and "attempts to discredit dissidents" was beginning, including "the persecution of

8. Both communications are described and reprinted in Edward D. Lozansky, ed., *Andrei Sakharov and Peace* (New York, 1985), 203–205.
9. *Public Papers of the Presidents of the United States, Jimmy Carter 1977*, 1–4.

the members of the Helsinki Watch Groups in Moscow and the Ukraine." He reminded the president about the repression of religion in the Soviet Union, and mentioned his own problems in communicating with the West. "The question of communications is basic to my public activity and the entire human-rights movement in this country. I ask you to take steps at the international level in this connection."[10] His plea for help in communicating with the West was Sakharov's only appeal in his own behalf. The rest of the letter gave the names of those already imprisoned (some of whom urgently needed medical care) and a shorter list of some dissidents who were threatened in the latest round of government harassment.

As Sakharov wrote, his wife and perhaps one of their other guests translated the letter from Russian into English.[11] In the rush to get it done, there was evidently some misunderstanding about how the letter was to be delivered. Sakharov was under the impression that he was sending a private message to the new president, but Garbus thought he was at liberty to deliver the letter in whatever way would maximize its impact.[12] After his return to the United States, Garbus asked for an appointment in the White House to deliver the letter and Sakharov's message directly to the president. His request was refused. When he met, instead, with Under Secretary of State Philip Habib, he was not convinced that the letter would be given the priority it deserved. Fearful that it would get buried in the State Department bureaucracy, Garbus left his meeting with Habib determined to ensure that Sakharov's words were heard. He gave a copy of the letter to the *New York Times*.[13] It was published in the January 29, 1977, issue of the newspaper, together with related stories about the letter's significance, the current status of human rights in the Soviet Union, and an appeal sent to world leaders on Sakharov's behalf in connection with the threatened pros-

10. These quotations are from Lozansky, ed., *Andrei Sakharov and Peace*, 206–208.

11. In Sakharov's memoirs the translation is done by Bonner. Sahkarov, *Memoirs*, 464. In another version of this meeting at least two people do the translation and produce two versions of the letter with paragraphs in different orders and slight variations in the names mentioned for Carter's consideration. Lozansky, *Andrei Sakharov and Peace*, 205. Garbus recalls that he drafted some of the general language in the letter while Sakharov prepared the list of dissidents whose cases deserved presidential attention. Martin Garbus, telephone interview, April 8, 1996. A full account of these events from Garbus's perspective can be found in Martin Garbus, *Traitors and Heroes: A Lawyer's Memoir* (New York, 1987).

12. Sakharov, *Memoirs*, 464.

13. Garbus, telephone interview.

ecution for the public statements he had made about the Moscow subway bombing.[14] This was front-page headline news. The most prominent dissident active within the Soviet Union, and a recent recipient of the Noble Peace Prize, was writing directly to the president of the United States about the foreign policy issue the new president had adopted as his own. There was immediate speculation about how Carter would answer.

His first answer was accidental and disappointing to Sakharov. It involved the kind of minor mishap that commonly occurs in the first few days of any new presidential administration. After Sakharov had been called into the prosecutor's office on January 24, but before his letter to Carter appeared in the press on January 29, the State Department issued a brief statement on January 27. It said, "Any attempt by the Soviet authorities to intimidate Mr. Sakharov will not silence legitimate criticism in the Soviet Union and will conflict with accepted standards of human rights." The new secretary of state, Cyrus Vance, heard about his department's public support for Sakharov when the Soviet ambassador to Washington, Anatoly Dobrynin, called to complain about U.S. interference in the internal affairs of his nation.[15] Vance, who fully supported the president's commitment to human rights and the statement about Sakharov, was momentarily more concerned about internal affairs within his own department. He made it known that, in the future, the secretary of state expected to be informed about statements regarding Soviet dissidents by someone in the State Department and not by Ambassador Dobrynin.

The next day Carter was asked about the minor State Department flap and made an understandable remark supporting his senior cabinet officer. To a reporter interviewing him on a helicopter ride to Pennsylvania, where the president would visit some hard-hit locations in the bitter winter of 1976–77, Carter said that it would have been better if an important statement about a Soviet dissident had been made by himself or his secretary of

14. The text of the letter is reprinted in several places in addition to the January 29 *New York Times*. The *Los Angeles Times* also printed the letter on January 29. A more complete copy appears in Sakharov, *Memoirs*, 686–87, and Lozansky, ed., *Andrei Sakharov and Peace*, 206–208. The copy in the Carter Library, which was delivered to the Department of State and then sent to the White House, is the incomplete handwritten Bonner translation; see White House Central File, Name File, "Sakharov," Carter Library.

15. "Moscow Rebuts U.S. on Sakharov Praise," *New York Times,* January 30, 1977.

state.[16] When that comment was reported in the international press and made its way to Moscow, it appeared to Sakharov that the new president was not fully endorsing the State Department's message of support.[17] In fact, Carter also said during his informal helicopter interview that the statement on Sakharov, made without prior approval from the senior members of the administration, reflected his own attitude in this instance and that it was important for the Soviet Union to understand "our deep commitment to human rights."[18]

The full account of what the president said on January 30 evidently did not reach Sakharov, and the Soviet dissident was bitterly disappointed. Years later he would write,

> Carter may have had nothing more in mind than the need to coordinate policy, but it was a mistake to air such differences in public. It's mind-boggling to hear Western statesmen picking each other to pieces, washing their dirty linen for all to see; or, even worse, tailoring their positions on international issues to win points in domestic or party politics. Their adversaries note any sign of discord, inconsistency, naïveté, or cynicism, and capitalize on it. With the world situation as precarious as it is, the West and its politicians cannot afford to behave as though they exist in isolation. Perhaps I am making too much of a chance remark, but this seems as good a place as any to air my very strong feelings on this subject.[19]

Sakharov does make too much of a chance remark, particularly when he heard, or remembered, only part of what the president said and, as a result, fundamentally misunderstood Carter's position. Had their communications

16. "Carter Says Warning on a Soviet Dissident Reflected His Views," *New York Times*, January 31, 1977.

17. Sakharov, *Memoirs*, 465.

18. "Carter Says Warning on a Soviet Dissident Reflected His Views." This story also reports that the president talked about air sickness, a problem that was evidently of urgent importance to several of the passengers taking a rough ride on the presidential helicopter.

19. Sakharov, *Memoirs*, 465. Sakharov's misunderstanding of what Carter said during his helicopter interview evidently stems from an article that appeared in the *Times* of London on February 1, 1977. The article, by Bernard Levin and titled "Mr. Carter Offers Peanuts to Dr. Sakharov," includes a very incomplete and distorted version of what Carter had said about the Soviet dissident. The *Times* did much better in its news story printed the day before under the headline "Mr. Carter Not Told of Sakharov Statement."

ended here, there would have been a very unfortunate misunderstanding between the new president and the Soviet dissident, but Sakharov would soon receive a very different and much less ambiguous message from President Carter.

According to Brzezinski, there was no serious question about responding to the Sakharov letter that was published on January 29. Having complained in the campaign about Ford's failure to meet with Solzhenitzyn, it would have been awkward, to say the least, for Carter to allow a letter from another world-famous Soviet dissent to go unanswered. After the president rejected a State Department recommendation that a low-level American official meet with Sakharov in Moscow, a presidential letter to the Soviet dissident was jointly drafted by Vance and Brzezinski.[20] It thanked Sakharov for his January 21 letter; quoted one of the key sentences in the president's inaugural address ("Because we are free, we can never be indifferent to the fate of freedom elsewhere"); and in very general language promised both to continue "to seek the release of prisoners of conscience" everywhere and promote a world in which "nations of differing cultures and histories can live side by side in peace and justice."[21]

Carter's letter, dated February 5, 1977, and delivered in person to Sakharov when he was invited to the U.S. embassy on February 17, did not mention any of the names that Sakharov had included in his letter or any of the recent events in the Soviet Union that were the current focus of his concern. Instead, it discussed the president's commitment to human rights in general and global terms without specific reference to problems in Moscow or the Eastern bloc. Nevertheless, the fact that the president had replied at all was taken by Sakharov, and the world, as a statement of support for his stand on human rights. In this case, as in many others, the fact that a presidential letter had been sent was more important than the words it contained.

Like the earlier statement supporting Sakharov issued by the Department of State, Carter's letter was not well received by the Soviet leadership. Dobrynin met with State Department officials to register his nation's objections to interference in their internal affairs as soon as the letter to Sakharov

20. Zbigniew Brzezinski, *Power and Principle: Memoirs of the National Security Advisor 1977–1981* (New York, 1982), 156; Robert Kaiser, "Right Improvisation Strains Détente," *Washington Post*, February 27, 1977.

21. The letter appears in Sakharov, *Memoirs*, 687; and Lozansky, ed., *Andrei Sakharov and Peace*, 210.

became public. Brezhnev, who had his own correspondence with Carter early in the administration, sent a letter on February 25 with a much more negative tone than he had used in his first letter to the new American president. The Soviet leader took particular offense at Carter's direct communication with Sakharov, calling the Soviet dissident "a renegade who proclaimed himself an enemy of the Soviet state."[22] The harsh tone of Brezhnev's letter disappointed Carter, but did not change his behavior.

The human rights theme in the 1976 presidential campaign continued to be translated into presidential words and actions. At the end of February, the administration announced cuts in military aid to Argentina, Ethiopia, and Uruguay because of abuses in human rights. On the first of March, the president and vice president met with the exiled Soviet dissident Vladimir Bukovsky in the White House. Though no photographers were present and the visit did not appear on the president's official schedule, it quickly became known to the press. In the middle of March, Carter spoke to the United Nations General Assembly, making human rights one of the principal themes in that speech. He continued throughout his administration to speak out on this subject in speeches, press conference statements, and in both public and private diplomatic communications to leaders throughout the world.

Sometimes his personal attention and words of censure or praise led to improvements in human rights; sometimes they did not. Sometimes they produced complicated consequences in Washington and elsewhere in the world that were hard to foresee. In the case of Anastasio Somoza, a brief presidential letter to the Central American dictator created a minor battle in the administration's foreign policy bureaucracies, an embarrassing press leak in Washington, and considerable confusion in Latin America.

Somoza

Like the shah of Iran, Anastasio Somoza Debayle was a second-generation dictator who had been in power for years when Jimmy Carter was elected president in 1976. The founder of the family dynasty, Anastasio Somoza Garcia, was an early leader of the Nicaraguan National Guard, which the United States had helped to create in 1932. It had been hoped that the guard would provide the country with enough military stability to allow for the

22. Quoted in Brzezinski, *Power and Principle,* 155.

development of democratic political institutions and end the need for interventions by American marines. The National Guard did provide Nicaragua with a kind of stability, but not the sort that most Americans or Nicaraguans would have wanted. The guard became the most powerful institution in Nicaraguan politics and the principal subverter of whatever prospects for democratic reform that country may have had.

As head of the National Guard, and sometime president of the nation, the senior Somoza amassed a multimillion-dollar family fortune that involved huge landholdings, monopolies, and substantial interests in many sectors of the Nicaraguan economy.[23] Political opponents of the regime were harassed, bribed, and sometimes killed by Somoza and his agents in the national guard. Honest officeholders who tried to reign in the power of the Somoza family were forced to resign, and guerrilla fighters like Augusto Sandino were assassinated.

The senior Somoza, who lived by the bullet, also died by it. He was shot on September 21, 1956, and survived for only a few days thereafter. He was succeeded as president by his eldest son, Luis, who, like all the children in the Somoza family, had been educated in the United States. In 1966, the younger son, Anastasio, a West Point graduate, was elected president in the rigged polling process that passed for democracy in Nicaragua. Whether from inside or outside the presidential residence in Managua, Anastasio Somoza ruled Nicaragua for the next thirty-nine years. He and his brother continued to build the family fortune by using their political power for private profit. When the capital city was rocked by a devastating earthquake in 1972, Somoza took control of the international relief pouring into the country and used much of it to promote his own personal wealth and power. When a new generation of guerrilla opponents, who called themselves Sandinistas (in honor of the slain hero from an earlier era), began fighting in the hills, he increased defense spending to oppose them. When a popular opposition leader and outspoken newspaper editor, Petro Joaquin Chamorro, was killed early in 1978, it was presumed that Somoza was responsible.

23. According to one estimate, in 1961, a few years after the death of the elder Somoza, the family earned 10 percent of the entire Nicaraguan gross national product and controlled 40 percent of its sugar and alcohol output, 10 percent of the coffee crop, 100 percent of the national airline, and 50 percent of the cement business. Bernard Diederich, *Somoza: and the Legacy of U.S. Involvement in Central America* (New York, 1981), 73.

Throughout the two generations of dictatorship in Nicaragua, there were complicated relationships between the hemisphere's only superpower and one of its smallest and weakest nations. In the 1930s the policy of the United States was to be a "Good Neighbor" in Latin America, which meant that it would refrain from carrying out the kind of military interventions that had been commonplace earlier in the century. The United States did this even if some of its Latin American neighbors, like Nicaragua, were governed by military dictators. As American attention was increasingly drawn toward the much more dangerous dictatorships in Europe and the Far East, the good neighbor was often an indifferent neighbor preoccupied with problems elsewhere in the world. After the Second World War, relations with Latin America were again secondary to the global challenge of communism and the cold war contest with the Soviet Union. The highest priority in the hemisphere was to prevent the spread of communism; the most important nation was Castro's Cuba. When nations like Nicaragua were helpful to the CIA in overthrowing a leftist regime in Guatemala or providing training facilities for Cuban refugees before the Bay of Pigs, the United States was grateful. In a much repeated, but probably apocryphal, statement Franklin Roosevelt is reported to have observed that the elder Somoza may have been a son of a bitch, but he was, at least, "our son of bitch."[24]

At the height of the cold war, the United States had friendships with a rather long list of international sons of bitches, and Carter was elected, in part, for his promise to distance the United States from some of its more unsavory and less essential allies. But Carter had no intention of returning to the days of regular Marine Corps invasions of the nations of Central America. He wanted to promote human rights but was not going to use force for that purpose. When he spoke to the Organization of American States about human rights in April 1977, he promised to "respect the individuality and sovereignty of each Latin American and Caribbean nation."[25] Other nations in the region, particularly Panama and Venezuela, did provide aid to the Sandinistas, but the United States did not. The president

24. Roosevelt scholars make a convincing case that FDR never said those words, but they are still repeated as illustrative of the relationship between the United States and Nicaragua. Both Pastor and Lake repeat the quote with notation that FDR may never have said it.

25. *Public Papers of the Presidents of the United States, Jimmy Carter 1977*, 612.

criticized human rights abuses in Nicaragua, approved a proposal to cut off military assistance to the regime (a proposal that was actively opposed on Capitol Hill by some powerful friends that Somoza had in Congress), and monitored progress and prospects for fundamental freedoms in a variety of ways.

Carter reviewed the annual State Department report to Congress on human rights in all the countries of the world, read reports from nongovernmental organizations like Amnesty International, and followed day-to-day events with some care. In addition to certain daily newspapers, Carter read each morning a White House press office–prepared collection of clippings and summaries from papers across the country, the wire services, and network news broadcasts. There was also a daily package of intelligence briefing materials that summarized important developments in the world's capitals during the previous twenty-four hours. Prepared by the staff in the White House situation room, where world events were monitored round the clock, and delivered to the president each morning by the NSC adviser, the intelligence summary frequently contained information not included in the newspapers or clippings the president read.

That was the case on June 21, 1978, when Carter saw a brief intelligence report on some recent public statements made by Anastasio Somoza in Nicaragua. Earlier in the week, the Nicaraguan dictator had indicated a new willingness to cooperate with the Inter-American Human Rights Commission and to consider ratification of the Inter-American Convention on Human Rights. In addition, Somoza had said that the leaders of an opposition group that operated in exile and called itself "The Twelve" were free to return to Nicaragua. All of these promises, if carried out, would constitute progress in Nicaragua's otherwise dismal human rights performance. Carter, independent of any advice from his staff, decided to send a letter to Somoza commending these announcements and instructed Brzezinski to have such a letter drafted.

Brzezinski referred the president's request to the National Security Council's Latin American specialist, Robert Pastor, who immediately objected. Somoza had a habit of boasting about his close connections with members of Congress and presidents. He had been a dinner guest in the Nixon White House and regularly used real or alleged American support to his advantage in domestic politics and in regional foreign policy. If the administration wanted to distance itself from Somoza's regime, it was better, Pastor thought, not to have the president communicate directly with the Nicaraguan dictator. Somoza might interpret, or use, the act of communication as a sign of favor that did not, in fact, exist. Moreover, the growing opposition to Somoza's rule within Nicaragua meant that the dictator might soon be replaced, and special care needed to be exercised to ensure that the administration did not alienate the moderate opposition forces that might hold the political balance in the coming transformation of the Nicaraguan regime. Brzezinski ordered Pastor to draft the letter Carter had asked for, clear it with the Department of State, and put whatever reservations he might have into a cover memo that would go with the draft to the president's desk.[26]

Pastor wrote his draft using straightforward and neutral language noting the specific commitments Somoza had recently made. He sent the draft to the Department of State, where it was reviewed by officials in the Human Rights Bureau, the Latin American Affairs Bureau, the Policy Planning Staff, and by the undersecretary for political affairs. Representatives from both Human Rights and Latin American Affairs, who were often at odds with each other over how to deal with the dictatorships in the hemisphere, were on this occasion in full agreement. They objected to the letter on much the same grounds that Pastor had identified. They were afraid that Somoza would use a personal communication from the president in a way that would be counterproductive. Moreover, Somoza did not have a good record of actually carrying out promised reforms, and the president's proposed letter might be premature.[27]

By the middle of 1978, the administration had regular procedures in place for handling policy disputes involving human rights.[28] The administration was required by law or policy to consider human rights progress in connection with aid, trade, and arms sales. In addition, human rights concerns were often raised in a variety of routine State Department transactions with nations throughout the world. Deputy Secretary of State Warren Christopher had been designated by Vance to screen, and wherever possible resolve, issues involving conflicts between human rights and other policies

26. Robert A. Pastor, *Condemned to Repetition: The United States and Nicaragua* (Princeton, 1987), 66–67.

27. Anthony Lake, *Somoza Falling: A Case Study in the Making of U.S. Foreign Policy* (Boston, 1989), 85.

28. Ibid., 25–45.

or goals in administration foreign policy. When a letter drafted in the NSC was criticized by the Human Rights and Latin American Affairs Bureaus, the issue was immediately referred to Christopher. It did not take him long to decide what to do.

The deputy secretary called Pastor to ask about the origins of the letter and was told that it had been drafted in response to a direct presidential request. Pastor did not tell Christopher about his own reservations concerning the wisdom of sending the letter to Somoza and left the deputy secretary with an easy decision to make. The president wanted to send a relatively innocuous communication to a Central American dictator telling him to keep up the good work (though, admittedly, he had not done very much good work) on human rights. It was standard practice for the administration to use both carrots and sticks in its effort to promote progress in respect for fundamental freedoms and movement toward democracy. This was a small carrot. Christopher sided with Carter, overruled his human rights and regional experts and sent the letter with some minor redrafting back to the White House. The State Department also recommended that delivery of the letter be held up for about a week while negotiations for the proposed visit to Nicaragua by the Inter-American Human Rights Commission were still under way.[29]

Brzezinski gave the draft and the delayed-delivery recommendation to Carter. He did not ask the president to review the reasons Pastor had summarized for not sending the letter at all. In the national security adviser's judgment this was not an issue that Carter needed to consider. After all, the president had already sent similar letters praising small steps in the right direction taken by Pinochet in Chile and Videla in Argentina, leaders with human rights records that were arguably worse than Somoza's.[30] In electing not to forward the Pastor arguments against sending the letter, Brzezinski was not making a major policy decision; he was simply protecting the president from having to make one more decision. Presidential time, even for a hard-working president like Carter, is always in short supply, and it was part of Brzezinski's job to make choices about what Carter should see and consider. He evidently did not believe that the president needed to give any more time to this letter than he already had. Moreover, Brzezinski may not

29. Ibid., 85.
30. Pastor, *Condemned to Repetition*, 67.

have wanted to challenge Christopher's decision when the administration was already being criticized for conflicts between the Department of State and the NSC, principally over policy toward the Soviet Union. Brzezinski had to choose carefully the occasions when he asked the president to overrule or reconsider a State Department recommendation. This was not one of them.[31]

When Carter received the draft letter he made a few minor changes to its tone, expressing "appreciation" for the positive steps where Pastor and the State Department had only expressed "interest" in them. He also added a phrase at the end of the letter praising "your announcement of these constructive actions" and deleted language that pointed out the difference between words and actions and diplomatically called on Somoza to follow through on his promises.[32] The president approved the recommendation that delivery of the letter be held up for a week, signed the revised draft, and put it in his out box. From the president's perspective that was the last he expected to hear about this minor matter.

Pastor, after reading the president's revisions, which had made the letter more personal and more complimentary, sent Brzezinski another memo on June 28 suggesting that Carter be advised about the reservations he and some of his colleagues in the State Department had about sending any communication to Somoza. "Our historical relationship with Somoza," Pastor wrote, "makes it very difficult for us to take any step which could be interpreted as supportive of Somoza without it antagonizing the democratic opposition in Nicaragua and our human rights supporters in the United States."[33] Pastor repeated his concern that Somoza frequently made political promises to divert or distract his opposition and then never carried them out. He volunteered to draft for the president a detailed analysis of the political situation in Nicaragua. Again, the national security adviser decided the issue was not worth Carter's time and attention. This buck stopped on Brzezinski's desk.

The letter was now in the hands of the Department of State for delivery

---

31. Lake, *Somoza Falling*, 86–87.

32. Undated draft letter to Anastasio Somoza Debayle with corrections in President Carter's handwriting. Copy provided by Robert Pastor.

33. Robert Pastor to Zbigniew Brzezinski, memorandum: "Nicaragua and the Somoza Letter," June 28, 1978. Copy provided by Robert Pastor. This memo is quoted with one minor error in Lake, *Somoza Falling*, 86.

to Somoza. The people who were not very enthusiastic about writing the letter in the first place were in no particular hurry in seeing that it reached its destination. Somoza would not receive his presidential letter until a month after Carter had decided to send it. The delay was a mixture of policy, procrastination, and procedure. The president had already approved a one-week delay while negotiations for a visit by a regional human rights monitoring group were completed. Additional delays occurred when the American ambassador in Managua raised the same concerns that Pastor and others had regarding presidential communications with Somoza. Ambassador Mauricio Solaun received a cable with the text of the president's letter on July 8; the letter itself was delivered to Managua in a diplomatic pouch that would not arrive for another nine days. In response to the cable, the ambassador requested permission from his superiors in Washington to relay the substance of Carter's message to Somoza without giving him the complete text. His request was received in the Department of State shortly before Solaun's next scheduled meeting with Somoza. Without contacting the White House, State Department officials authorized Solaun to use his discretion in this matter, and the ambassador restricted himself to an oral summary of the message, which he provided to Somoza on July 11.[34]

Pastor was surprised and angry to find out that in the middle of July the president's letter had still not been delivered. It was part of his job to monitor agency compliance with presidential policy in Latin America, and he told officials in the State Department that if they were not going to deliver Carter's letter they would have to persuade the president to change his mind. Secretary Vance was asked by some of the Latin American specialists in his department to approach the president about withdrawing the letter, allowing the ambassador's oral briefing to suffice. Vance, like Brzezinski before him, did not wish to reopen a minor Nicaraguan issue with Carter, and instead Solaun was told to inform Somoza that the letter was a private communication and should be treated accordingly.[35]

Somoza finally received his letter from Jimmy Carter on July 21 and immediately made plans to violate the confidentiality he had been asked to observe. Opposition to his rule had risen since the death of Chamorro at the beginning of the year. Strikes, demonstrations, street violence, and contin-

34. Lake, *Somoza Falling*, 87–88.
35. Pastor, *Condemned to Repetition*, 68.

ued success for the Sandinista guerrillas had all taken place after the assassination of the popular opposition leader. The positive steps that caught Carter's eye had been calculated to appease Somoza's critics at home and abroad without risking real reform. Now that he had Carter's endorsement of those steps in hand, Somoza asked for a private meeting with his most important regional enemy, Venezuelan president Carlos Pérez. The Venezuelan leader secretly supported the Sandinistas and publicly called for Somoza's resignation. When the two Latin American presidents met on an island off the coast of Venezuela, Somoza claimed that he enjoyed the support of President Carter. Pérez was unimpressed, had no desire to see the letter, and told Somoza that his policy would remain unchanged. The only solution to the problems in Nicaragua would be for Somoza to step down as president.

On the flight back to Managua, Somoza reports that he reread Carter's letter and realized that it was a trick. The president had mentioned the words "human rights" six times in the letter and "that was his vehicle for the destruction of me."[36] The letter, Somoza concluded, had been "designed to give us a false sense of security." In fact, "while praising my efforts to satisfy the United States, Mr. Carter was stepping up his attack against me and the government of Nicaragua."[37] Jimmy Carter was no fan of Anastasio Somoza and like Pérez hoped that there might be a way to bring about democratic reform in Nicaragua. But Somoza's conclusion that the president had intentionally given the dictator a false message of encouragement in order to get him to lower his guard is nonsense. In the summer of 1978, Nicaragua was not receiving much high-level attention in the White House. It was one of many nations on the long and complicated list of administration human rights concerns. The fact that Somoza may well have believed that the president's few words of praise were part of a plot against him shows how difficult it is for one leader to communicate with another. The next step in the story of the Somoza letter shows how hard it is for officials in Washington to do the same.

Thus far, the president's attempt to pat Somoza on the back for a few good deeds had done neither much good nor much harm. Somoza's failed attempt to use the letter with Pérez had convinced him that it had no value,

36. Anastasio Somoza, *Nicaragua Betrayed* (Boston, 1980), 146.
37. Ibid., 147.

and except for his secret meeting with the Venezuelan leader, Somoza had evidently kept his promise to keep the president's message confidential. On August 1, an article appeared on the front page of the *Washington Post* under the headline, "Carter Letter to Somoza Stirs Human-Rights Row." The article by John Goshko was apparently written on the basis of conversations with some of the officials in the State Department who had been opposed to sending a presidential message to Somoza. Goshko did not quote the text of the letter, which he had not seen, and reported only part of what went on in its preparation.[38] As a result, his article contained an incomplete and inaccurate account of what had transpired.

In the opening sentence of the article, the letter was described as "congratulating" Somoza for promises to improve human rights in Nicaragua, when that word had been carefully avoided in all the drafts prepared at NSC and State. In addition, the article said that the idea for the letter had originated with the NSC staff and that it had been sent despite State Department objections. Neither of those statements was correct. The idea was Carter's and the objections raised within the Department of State were resolved by the department's deputy secretary. Pastor's reservations had been relegated to two memos written to Brzezinski. In this case, there was no real dispute between the NSC and the State Department. In both institutions, mid-level staff members objected to the letter and their superiors approved it. The alleged dispute between NSC and State reported in the leak was more than inaccurate; it involved a kind of self-fulfilling prophecy. The major argument against sending the letter in the first place had been the fear that Somoza would publicize it and give a false impression that the United States actively supported his regime. Somoza did not give the letter to the press. Those who worried that he might did it for him.

In many ways, the leak was more important than the letter. It was widely disseminated and widely believed. Pérez, when he heard about the *Washington Post* story, was furious. He thought he had an understanding with Carter about how to deal with Nicaragua and was disappointed to learn that the letter Somoza had mentioned in their private meeting was complimentary to the Nicaraguan dictator.[39] President Carter was equally furious. He ordered the State Department to find and punish the source for the inaccu-

---

38. Pastor, *Condemned to Repetition*, 70.
39. Shirley Christian, *Nicaragua: Revolution in the Family* (New York, 1986), 68–69.

rate story. As usually occurs in such attempts, it was not possible to identify the persons who had spoken with the *Washington Post* reporter;[40] and the best that could be done was to issue a correction through the White House press office, which was printed in the back pages of the newspaper a few days later.[41]

The administration could not escape the false impression that it was giving Somoza more credit and more support than was actually the case. In the hills of Nicaragua, among the exiled leaders of the Somoza opposition, and in the capitals of Latin America the letter, as publicized by the *Post*, was probably seen as another example of American support for the Somoza family. In Washington, it led to heightened suspicion between the NSC staff and the Department of State, reducing the number of people who would be trusted to consider further steps in Nicaraguan policy. For Carter it was another example of bad news reporting getting in the way of the policies he wished to pursue. In his diary the day after the Goshko story appeared, the president noted that "the editorial policy of the *Washington Post* has been good. The news policy abominable."[42]

Conclusions

Neither of these letters belongs on the list of major foreign policy documents in the Carter presidency. They were both small steps in a long and complicated journey toward improved observance of human rights around the world. In isolation they are easily forgotten. The Somoza letter is not even mentioned in Carter's memoirs, and the letter to Sakharov receives only two sentences, one of which is misleading. Carter reports in *Keeping Faith* that Sakharov "had been detained by Soviet officials" and was writing to him about "his plight."[43] In fact, Sakharov had not been detained when he wrote his letter to the president (though he had been called in by the prosecutor before his letter to Carter was published in the *New York Times*). Sakharov's only personal request involved help in communicating with the

40. Pastor reports that some years later he learned from Goshko that the source was a "senior pro–human rights official in the Bureau of Inter-American Affairs." Pastor, *Condemned to Repetition*, 70. Lake adds that the leak occurred in a conversation at a social event and may have been inadvertent. Lake, *Somoza Falling*, 89.

41. "Somoza Letter Called Joint Effort," *Washington Post*, August 3, 1978, p. A17.

42. Jimmy Carter, quoted in Pastor, *Condemned to Repetition*, 69.

43. Jimmy Carter, *Keeping Faith: Memoirs of a President* (New York, 1982), 146.

West, and his letter dealt almost exclusively with the plight of others. Carter also says that he responded to Sakharov with "a pledge to promote human rights in the Soviet Union." This is true, but not precise. Carter's letter to Sakharov contains only a general statement about his support for human rights throughout the world and was drafted in language that would specifically avoid any direct reference to the Soviet Union.[44]

If neither of these letters gets much attention in Carter's memoirs, the opposite is true for their recipients. Both Sakharov and Somoza devote a whole chapter in their respective memoirs to the correspondence they received from Jimmy Carter. They each reprint the full text of what Carter wrote to them and speculate about the significance of the president's words. In this regard, Sakharov is, not surprisingly, more serious than Somoza. As we have seen, the Nicaraguan dictator, who at first attached great value to Carter's letter, later dismissed it as a ruse designed to encourage him to let down his guard. He never saw it for what it was, a simple and straightforward message endorsing and encouraging a few minor concessions made to the international demands for greater attention to human rights in Nicaragua. Somoza missed the point. The distorted leak in the *Washington Post* guaranteed that everyone else would do the same.

In the case of the Sakharov letter, the president's general message was more effectively conveyed. The consequences of that message were debatable. Critics of the administration's human rights campaign raised serious questions about whether direct communications between a president and a Soviet dissident would make matters worse or better for the cause of human rights in the Soviet Union and speculated that it would cause problems for subsequent arms control negotiations.[45] The crackdown that Sakharov was anticipating early in 1977 did, in fact, take place. Early in February 1977, Alexander Ginzburg was arrested; later that month Yuri Orlov was also taken into custody.[46] In mid-March Anatoly Shcharansky, another promi-

44. Sakharov notes the errors in Carter's memoirs and says that "Carter had either forgotten the contents of my letter . . . or had been mistakenly informed." Sakharov, *Memoirs*, 688.

45. Joseph Kraft, "The Kissinger Complex," *Washington Post*, February 15, 1977.

46. Ginzburg would later be released and allowed to leave the country as the result of Carter administration negotiations that the president followed very closely. Carter, *Keeping Faith*, 147.

nent member of the Helsinki Group, was seized.[47] At about the same time, a long-pending petition for a larger Moscow apartment for the Sakharov family ran into unexpected bureaucratic resistance, and a criminal investigation of Elena Bonner's daughter from a previous marriage, Tatyana Yankelevich, was initiated.[48] Somewhat later, while Carter was still in office, Sakharov was stripped of his national awards for scientific achievement and sent to an internal exile in Gorky, where he lived under house arrest.

All of this appeared to be Moscow's answer to Carter's human rights campaign, and indeed, critics of the president's policies toward human rights violations in the Soviet Union frequently argued that his efforts were counterproductive.[49] The president, they insisted, should have used conventional techniques of quiet diplomacy rather than writing personal letters to Soviet dissidents or making public statements about events in Moscow and Eastern Europe. In fact, Carter did use quiet diplomacy in dealing with Soviet officials and takes some pride in the fact that Jewish emigration from the Soviet Union, one of the most volatile human rights issues in U.S.-USSR relations, increased to record cold war levels during the first few years of his administration.[50] He also used public statements, like the Sakharov letter, and understood that there were risks in sending this kind of direct and open message to a Soviet dissident. There were risks in terms of maintaining good superpower relations and dangers that the crackdown, already under way when Sakharov wrote to the president, might be made worse by increased presidential attention. Carter remembers being aware of those trade-offs when the letter to Sakharov was being drafted and remembers deciding that the risks were worth taking for the opportunity to send a clear message expressing America's serious concern about the status of human rights in the Soviet Union.[51]

When Sakharov was asked by Western journalists about the same trade-offs, he emphatically rejected the proposition that things would have been

47. Shcharansky was another Soviet dissident whose fate Carter monitored. He discussed Shcharansky's arrest and trial with both Gromyko and Brezhnev. Carter, *Keeping Faith*, 220, 260.

48. Sakharov, *Memoirs*, 466–68.

49. See, for example, Townsend Hoopes, "The Double-Edged Sword of Human Rights," *Washington Post*, August 3, 1978.

50. Carter, *Keeping Faith*, 149.

51. Jimmy Carter interview by author, Atlanta, Ga., April 11, 1995.

better in the Soviet Union if the American president had been less outspoken about the violations of human rights in his country. "Repressions are our daily life," he told an ABC news correspondent about a month after receiving his presidential letter. "They existed under Nixon, under Ford, and both before and after Helsinki. The latest wave of repressions began during the first days of January—that is, before Carter took office."[52] The president's deputy assistant for national security affairs, David Aaron, makes the same point Sakharov does. Though the perception early in the Carter administration was that the president was going out of his way to "put a stick in the Russians' eye" on the subject of human rights, it was actually the other way around. The crackdown in the winter of 1976–77 presented the new administration with a challenge that Carter "clearly had to react to."[53] The correspondence with Sakharov was part of that reaction. Carter, Sakharov believed, had clearly done the right thing by answering his letter. Moreover, Sakharov was convinced of the president's sincerity and seriousness. Though he misunderstood what Carter had said in his helicopter interview, and remained confused on that subject years later, Sakharov fully supported the president's position on human rights.

> My critical remarks [in my memoirs] should not obscure my appreciation of Jimmy Carter's human rights policy. It may not always have been successful; that, after all, is fate. It's too early to judge the long-term consequences of his actions (and given our imperfect knowledge of the laws of history, we may never know them), but something, I am sure, will remain. As for his personal regard for me, I feel certain it is sincere, and not just politics.[54]

Carter's regard for Sakharov was indeed sincere. So was his desire to improve human rights in the Soviet Union and elsewhere in the world. Throughout his administration he used a combination of public statements and private diplomatic messages to bring attention to violations of human rights and to encourage movement toward greater respect for individual freedoms and democratic practices. His efforts to promote human rights in-

52. Lozansky, *Andrei Sakharov and Peace*, 213.
53. David Aaron, White House Staff exit interview, December 15, 1980, declassified June 15, 1994, White House Staff Exit Interviews, pp. 6–7, Carter Library.
54. Sakharov, *Memoirs*, 466.

volved a mixture of words, deeds, and symbols conveyed through diplomatic channels and the media. Very often the message in the media was not what the president intended it to be. That was clearly the case with his letter to Somoza, where a routine piece of modest encouragement was misread by its recipient and misrepresented in the *Washington Post*.

On other occasions subtleties in the president's human rights messages were lost on some recipients or missed all together. In the case of the Sakharov letter, the text of the president's message had been carefully drafted in general language that avoided any singling out of Soviet human rights violations.[55] The Kremlin leadership was not impressed by how the president's letter was worded and immediately objected to the fact that it had been sent. Even Carter remembers the picture of Sakharov holding his letter in front of the U.S. embassy better than he remembers what his own correspondence with the Soviet dissident actually said.[56]

Much the same thing happened when Carter dealt directly with the shah about the human rights problems in Iran, and part of what he wanted to say got lost in the transmission of a few powerful words and images. In Washington he had discussed human rights with the shah in private, in the Iranian capital he went public. His toast to the shah included an obvious reference to the subject of human rights in the quote he read from Saadi, the Iranian poet. The shah and the rest of the Iranians present got the message without any insult or complaint that Carter was interfering in the domestic affairs of their nation. The rest of the world was much more likely to hear only the president's remarks about Iran as an island of stability.

Carter was understandably accused of hypocrisy in his human rights policy toward Iran and other nations with which the United States had extensive business on a number of issues. Had he taken a very hard line against the shah—cutting off all military sales and personal contact with an important ally in a vital region—he would have been accused of excessive moralism and dangerous naïveté. Because he tried to deal with human rights in a serious fashion without ignoring other important foreign policy goals and international realities, he was almost always attacked by critics who wanted him to do more, or less, in any given instance.

55. Brzezinski made sure that this fact was clearly explained to James Reston. See "The Sakharov Letter," *New York Times*, February 20, 1977.

56. Carter, *Keeping Faith*, 146.

Of course, pleasing all the people all the time is a notoriously difficult task, and we should be suspicious of any chief executive who manages to carry it off. But in the people-pleasing department, human rights was an unusually divisive issue whenever the administration had to go from broadly popular general principles to the controversial complexities of particular cases. Carter was repeatedly criticized for his particular human rights efforts. For the most part, he took those criticisms in stride and went on to the next item on his human rights agenda. In major speeches, in meetings with foreign leaders, and in personal letters, he kept sending the same messages about the importance of democratic political processes and the protection of fundamental freedoms. He admits that assessing the effectiveness of these efforts is extremely difficult, as it surely is in the case of the two letters to Sakharov and Somoza. But, characteristically, he sees the positive side of the mixed results that his messages inevitably produced. Near the end of the chapter in his memoirs dealing with human rights he observes that

> it will always be impossible to measure how much was accomplished by our nation's policy when the units of measurement are not inches or pounds or dollars. The lifting of the human spirit, the revival of hope, the absence of fear, the release from prison, the end of torture, the reunion of a family, the newfound sense of human dignity—these are difficult to quantify, but I am certain that many people were able to experience them because the United States of America let it be known that we stood for freedom and justice for all people.[57]

For Jimmy Carter, the good results that occurred in at least some cases were sufficient justification for all the efforts, small and large, successful and unsuccessful, that went into his sustained human rights campaign.

57. Ibid., 150.

4

SPEAKING OUT
The Annapolis Address on U.S.-Soviet Relations

Late in May 1978, after completing a series of meetings with Soviet foreign minister Andrei Gromyko, Secretary of State Cyrus Vance sent a long personal memorandum to President Jimmy Carter urging him to give a major foreign policy address clarifying the state of relations between the United States and the Soviet Union.[1] There had been extensive criticism in the press during the spring of 1978 about differences between Vance and Brzezinski over U.S.-Soviet relations. Tensions were reportedly rising between those members of the administration who gave priority to the completion of a SALT II treaty and those who wanted a stronger American response to Soviet expansionism in Africa. The president needed to set the record straight, Vance argued, about how these issues were related and what precisely the administration expected in its dealing with the aging Kremlin rulers. After reading a particularly critical article in the *Washington Post* about the incoherence of his foreign policy, the president accepted Vance's advice.[2] He elected to make the speech recommended by his secretary of state at the United States Naval Academy, where he was already scheduled to deliver a June commencement address.

---

1. Cyrus Vance, *Hard Choices: Four Critical Years in Managing America's Foreign Policy* (New York, 1983), 102.
2. "Carter as Speechwriter: Limiting Split," *Washington Post*, June 8, 1978. The article that Carter read may have been Stephen Rosenfeld, "The Vance-Brzezinski Contest," *Washington Post*, June 2, 1978.

As diplomatic communication, the president's remarks at the Naval Academy succeeded in giving the Soviet leadership a harsh warning about the possibility that their actions in Africa and abuses of human rights at home could seriously undermine the détente and arms control agenda that both sides wanted to pursue. As an exercise in domestic public relations, the Annapolis speech failed to stem speculation about policy divisions between the State Department and the National Security Council staff. In fact, some observers read the president's speech at the Naval Academy as little more than an awkward combination of the basic Vance and Brzezinski soft- and hard-line positions on U.S. relations with the Soviet Union. "Two Different Speeches" was one of the headlines in the *Washington Post* on the day after the president spoke in Annapolis.[3]

A year later, in two articles published in successive issues of the *Atlantic*, Carter's former head speechwriter, James Fallows, confirmed what the *Washington Post* reporter had initially observed. The president, Fallows wrote, "assembled the [Annapolis] speech essentially by stapling Vance's memo to Brzezinski's without examining the tensions between them."[4] Talking to a group of scholars who were studying presidential rhetoric in 1979, Fallows was even more explicit. "What he [Carter] did, and this is a literal fact, is staple together the memo from Vance to the one from Brzezinski and that was his speech."[5] This anecdote about the haphazard production of the president's address for the Naval Academy graduation ceremonies has been frequently repeated.[6] The story of the stapled memos has been used by a number of scholars and commentators to illustrate both the inconsistency of Carter-era policy toward the Soviet Union and the inability of the administration to develop a coherent and effective rhetorical strategy.[7]

Fallows claims to have been an eyewitness to the stapling of the memos

3. "President Challenges Soviet Leaders: Two Different Speeches," *Washington Post*, June 8, 1978.

4. James Fallows, "The Passionless Presidency," *Atlantic Monthly*, May 1979, p. 43.

5. White Burkett Miller Center of Public Affairs, University of Virginia, "Rhetoric and Presidential Leadership," A Miller Center Research Document, March 1, 1979, p. 25.

6. For a recent and typical example, see Carol Gelderman, "All the President's Words," *Wilson Quarterly*, 19, no. 2 (spring 1995): 76. The secretary of state confirms the Fallows account, or at least refers to it, in his memoirs. Vance, *Hard Choices*, 102.

7. See, for instance, William F. Grover, *The President as Prisoner: A Structural Critique of the Carter and Reagan Years* (Albany, N.Y., 1989), 145, and Richard C. Thornton, *The Carter Years: Toward a New Global Order* (New York, 1991), 193.

and believes that his account of the origins of the Annapolis commencement address is accurate.[8] However, a careful reading of the files available at the Carter presidential library shows clearly that the Naval Academy address was not the product of an Oval Office stapler. The library files contain both a handwritten outline and a handwritten draft prepared by President Carter on the weekend before the Annapolis commencement. Though the president's first draft went through several revisions and eventually incorporated language proposed by a number of his advisers—including the secretary of state and the national security adviser—the final version is, in structure and content, largely what Carter planned to say from the outset.

The story of the Annapolis address and the anecdote it spawned involves a relatively important speech on U.S.-Soviet relations delivered at a time when there was widespread speculation about a major cleavage in the president's inner circle of foreign policy advisers. That would be sufficient reason to look carefully at what the president said and how he and his administration decided on the content of this particular presidential public statement. But because the origins of the Annapolis speech have been seriously misrepresented by an authoritative source who remains convinced of the essential accuracy of his version of events, there is even more reason to examine thoroughly the development of the Naval Academy address. Like so much else in the Carter presidency, understanding what went on in this instance requires careful attention to detail.

First Draft

Even before President Carter received the memorandum from Cyrus Vance and selected the topic for his Annapolis speech, it was clear that his scheduled appearance at the Naval Academy would be the occasion for a major event. The academy was Carter's alma mater, and he was its first graduate ever to serve as the nation's commander in chief. Two previous Democratic presidents, Woodrow Wilson and John Kennedy, had given commencement addresses to the naval midshipmen during their presidencies. Both addresses were regarded as major speeches when they were delivered and thus were likely points of comparison for Carter's remarks. Whatever the president chose to talk about in Annapolis, it could reasonably be expected that more than usual attention would be focused on his remarks there and more than normal preparation for the speech would be required.

8. James Fallows, letter to author, September 19, 1992.

According to the Carter speechwriters, the typical presidential address was written in about a week. One or two drafts were prepared by the speechwriters after the president, or a senior member of the administration, had given general instructions about the topic. Those drafts were reviewed by the relevant White House staff—the National Security Council in the case of speeches dealing with foreign policy topics—before a near final copy was given to Carter for his revisions and approval.[9] Much more than this was done in getting ready for the speaking commitment in Annapolis.

During April and May of 1978 the White House speechwriters solicited suggestions for themes, topics, and quotations from an unusually wide variety of people. Alex Haley, the popular author of *Roots*, observed that aside from native Americans, we are a nation of people who came to this country from across the seas. Some were immigrants, some were slaves, all "crossed oceans on a great flotilla of ships from other lands."[10] This nautical heritage, Haley suggested, could be used as the theme for the president's remarks to young naval officers. Sol Linowitz, the president's ambassador to the Panama Canal negotiations, wanted the speech to deal with peacemaking and the unique position occupied by the United States as the major promoter of peace in the Middle East, in Africa, and in Central America.[11] Lester Brown of the World Watch Institute suggested a speech that would emphasize the international implications of domestic issues, reviewing both the strengths of our society and our needs for the future.[12] Former secretary of state Dean Rusk urged the president to talk about the mundane aspects of international life that too often get overlooked in our tendency to focus on the crisis of the day. We should take note, Rusk proposed, of the large number of international treaties and agreements that are in full effect and contribute to global stability, the growing trade among nations, the free movement of people across international frontiers in most of the world, the common fight of all nations against diseases like smallpox, and the absence of fighting at most international borders.[13]

9. White Burkett Miller Center of Public Affairs, University of Virginia, Project on the Carter Presidency, Speechwriters Session, December 3–4, 1981, 45–52.

10. Jim Fallows to the President, memorandum, May 23, 1978, Office of Staff Secretary, President's Handwriting File, Box 89, Annapolis Speech 6/7/78 [1]: 6, Carter Library.

11. Ibid., 2.

12. Ibid., 3–4.

13. Ibid., 6–9.

Several of the people contacted by the speechwriters had ideas that were related to the theme eventually selected for the speech. There was good reason for their concerns about U.S.-Soviet relations in the spring of 1978. In the second year of the Carter administration, détente was in decline. The continuation of SALT II negotiations had gotten off to a rocky start with the deep-cut proposal of March 1977. By the middle of the following year, the strategic arms limitation talks were back on track, but increasingly controversial within the United States. The Committee on the Present Danger, formed in November 1976, just three days after Carter's electoral victory, was actively opposing the ratification of the SALT II treaty even though it was not yet fully written, let alone signed.[14] The criticisms from Paul Nitze and the other committee members went to the heart of the SALT process. The Soviets, they argued, were using arms control and détente to lull the West into a false sense of security while they continued the arms race and actively pursued a nuclear superiority that would be used for diplomatic advantage in future crisis confrontations. For many of the committee members and for the prominent arms control critics in the Congress, like Senator Henry Jackson, almost no agreement with the Soviet Union, and certainly not one based on a modification of the Vladivostok accords, would answer these criticisms. Any SALT agreement would have to overcome substantial political opposition and would inevitably involve the casting of controversial ratification votes in the Senate. After the passage of the Panama Canal treaties, getting two-thirds of the Senate to bite another treaty bullet would not be easy. But abandoning arms control negotiations with the Soviet Union was not an option for Carter, who continued to believe that reducing the dangers of nuclear war was possible and to make it one of his highest foreign policy priorities.

At the same time that the prospects for strategic arms limitation—the centerpiece of détente—worsened, other aspects of U.S.-Soviet relations were deteriorating. From his first days in office, Carter made a point of publicly criticizing violations of human rights in the Soviet Union and Eastern Europe, singling out for special attention Soviet suppression of internal political dissent. By the spring of 1978, there was little evidence that the Kremlin leadership had taken any of this unsolicited advice to heart. They

14. Dan Caldwell, *The Dynamics of Domestic Politics and Arms Control* (Columbia, S.C., 1991), 102.

remained wary of Carter's repeated public references to the treatment of individual dissidents and criticized Carter for his general statements about Soviet failure to comply with the Helsinki accords and other international agreements guaranteeing fundamental political and social rights. They regarded the human rights campaign of the Carter administration as an intentional American plan to discredit détente and an indirect way of slowing arms control negotiations.[15] In fact, Carter wanted progress in human rights as well as progress in arms control and was reluctant to choose between them. As international attention to Soviet domestic political practices put new pressures on the superpower relationship, old cold war concerns about Soviet expansionism were also revived.

In the Horn of Africa, the Soviets had abandoned their relationship with Somalia in favor of closer ties with Somalia's larger and strategically more important neighbor, Ethiopia. When long-standing territorial and tribal disputes between those two nations led to a Somalian invasion of the Ogaden region of Ethiopia in July 1977, the Soviets airlifted vast quantities of military supplies to assist their new Ethiopian friends. Cuban military advisers, already active in Angola and elsewhere in Africa, provided training and advice for the Ethiopian military. As the scale of the Soviet-Cuban assistance program became evident, members of the Carter administration, particularly Brzezinski, urged the president to come to Somalia's aid. Others, including Vance and Secretary of Defense Harold Brown, advised caution. In a bloody regional dispute in which Somalia was the aggressor and neither side had any meaningful respect for democratic values or human rights, Carter elected to stay out. He did, however, issue a series of public warnings to the Soviets beginning in the early weeks of 1978, stating that continued action of this sort would jeopardize other aspects of Soviet relations with the United States.[16] This was not the "linkage" of the Kissinger era, when movement in arms control negotiations was explicitly tied to progress in other areas of superpower concern. Instead, Carter articulated a kind of commonsense linkage. The Soviets needed to understand that ratification of SALT II or any other arms control agreement would be impossi-

15. For a review of Soviet reactions to Carter's human rights policies, see Raymond Garthoff, *Détente and Confrontation: American-Soviet Relations from Nixon to Reagan* (Washington, D.C., 1985), 563–76.

16. See for example Carter's statement on March 2, *Congressional Quarterly Weekly Report*, March 11, 1978, p. 658.

ble if American congressional and public suspicions of Soviet actions in Africa (or the actions of their Cuban surrogates) were seriously aroused. Linkage was not a policy for Carter, but it was a reality that Soviet leaders had to understand. When separatist rebels entered Zaire from camps in neighboring Angola, new sources of concern about Soviet-Cuban motives in Africa emerged. On June 1, the president received a briefing from the CIA on a new national intelligence estimate titled "Soviet Goals and Expectations in the Global Power Arena."[17] It is no wonder that the state of U.S. relations with the Soviet Union in the spring and summer 1978 was an obvious source of concern to many observers of American foreign policy, not just the secretary of state.

Among those who offered speech recommendations related to U.S.-Soviet relations were some of the nation's leading experts on international politics and some of the most prominent foreign policy makers from previous administrations. Averell Harriman urged Carter to press his human rights campaign against the Soviet leadership. Fifty years earlier, Harriman wrote, he had gone to see how a revolutionary philosophy was working in Russia. He found that the Soviet Union was a reactionary regime, not a revolutionary one, and that it was based on the "principle of the few dominating the many, a principle which makes an animal out of man, a principle man has been fighting against for centuries. We're on the *right* side of that fight," Harriman advised, "and that is what gives us our strength."[18] McGeorge Bundy thought that Carter should read two of Henry Kissinger's official statements on détente and define his own positions on U.S.-Soviet relations in terms of where he agreed with his predecessors and where he parted company with them.[19] George Kennan cabled four pages of suggestions from his vacation home in Norway and pointed out the dangers associated with a continuing ideological struggle between two powerful nations, each armed with weapons of mass destruction that were essentially irrelevant to any resolution of their ideological differences.[20] From Kennan's

17. Robert M. Gates, *From the Shadows: The Ultimate Insider's Story of Five Presidents and How They Won the Cold War* (New York, 1996), 74.

18. Jim Fallows to the President, memorandum, May 23, 1978, p. 2. Emphasis in original.

19. Ibid., 10. The speechwriters copied the Kissinger statements that Bundy mentioned, along with Kennedy's speech at the Naval Academy, and sent them to the Oval Office.

20. Rick Hertzberg, Jerry Doolittle, and Griffin Smith to the President, memorandum, May 26, 1978, Office of Staff Secretary, President's Handwriting File, Box 89, Annapolis Speech 6/7/78 [2], Carter Library.

point of view these dangers could be managed because it was clear in 1978 that no one wanted nuclear war.

> Everyone realizes, in the marxist countries as elsewhere, that there are no ideological victories to be won by the use of such weapons. In the fact that people do realize this we have something solid to build on, and there is no reason to suppose that by a combination of adequate strength on our side, of quiet self-restraint in the use of that strength, of a refusal to believe in the inevitability of war . . . we cannot eventually lead international society out into a more stable and hopeful state of affairs.[21]

Ernest May, the Harvard historian, pointed out that the late 1970s were much like the late 1950s, when excessive fear of Soviet military strength swept through American politics in the wake of the Sputnik satellite. May argued that the fears of Soviet power in both decades were unjustified and that the traditional sources of American power from the end of the nineteenth century on—material abundance and a highly educated population—remained the basic elements of our enduring international prominence.[22]

George Ball, too, was asked for his ideas about what the president might say to the graduating midshipmen. In response, he produced a fifteen-page draft for Carter's consideration, complete with overdone imagery about the ship of state and an upbeat summary of the sources of America's power in the world today. "We Americans have never been so strong . . . ," Ball wrote, "strong because of our economic power and strong because we are steadily developing a more just society. . . . Optimism, is, after all, the only self-respecting working hypothesis for Americans. It was optimism grounded on reality that made our country strong. It is that same well-grounded optimism that can lead us to fulfill the high purposes for which this country was founded."[23]

Still other contributors to the forthcoming speech were members of the

---

21. Ibid. Some of Kennan's language was used by the president in his draft of the speech and survived the various revisions.

22. Fallows to the President, memorandum, May 23, 1978, p. 11.

23. Rick Hertzberg to the President, memorandum, May 31, 1978, Office of Staff Secretary, President's Handwriting File, Box 89, Annapolis Speech 6/7/78 [1]: 15, Carter Library.

president's own administration. The presidential library files contain detailed outlines and suggested language from Stansfield Turner, the director of the CIA and another Naval Academy graduate; from Secretary of Defense Harold Brown; and from Chairman of the Joint Chiefs of Staff General George Brown.[24] The contributions and proposals from the president's two key foreign policy advisers, Vance and Brzezinski, which according to James Fallows constitute the heart of the speech, are hard to find. In one of the communications from the speechwriters to the president, reference is made to a memorandum about the speech from Vance,[25] but no copy of that memorandum is located in the files where all the other speech-related materials are stored. The files do contain an outline for the president's consideration drafted by Tony Lake, the State Department's director of policy planning and a frequent speechwriter for Secretary Vance.[26] Brzezinski, in his memoirs, disputes the claim that the speech was the product of conflicting memorandums prepared by himself and Vance and says that the speech was drafted by Carter and only later reviewed and revised by his senior foreign policy advisers.[27] There is, however, a short memo from Brzezinski to the president dated June 2, 1978, accompanied by five pages of proposed language for the speech.[28] Brzezinski's suggested language is heavily underlined, presumably by Carter, and includes a number of ideas and phrases that appear in the first and final drafts of the speech.

Neither the Lake outline nor the Brzezinski memo could be said to constitute half of the president's speech, and there is no evidence to suggest that they were quickly or carelessly stapled together in the drafting process. The

24. A full list of those who contributed ideas for the president's consideration, in addition to those already mentioned, would include Admiral Elmo Zumwalt, Arthur Goldberg, William Scranton, William Coleman, Tom Hughes, and Gordon Rule. Two of the president's speechwriters, Jerry Doolittle and Rick Hertzberg, also prepared an outline for the speech that includes a number of the points Carter elected to use in his own draft.

25. Jerry Doolittle and Rick Hertzberg to the President, memorandum, June 2, 1978, Office of Staff Secretary, President's Handwriting File, Box 89, Annapolis Speech 6/7/78 [2], Carter Library.

26. Fallows to the President, memorandum, May 23, 1978.

27. Zbigniew Brzezinski, *Power and Principle: Memoirs of a National Security Advisor 1977–1981* (New York, 1983), 320–21.

28. Z. Brzezinski to the President, memorandum: "Speech on U.S.-Soviet Relations," June 2, 1978, Office of the Staff Secretary, President's Handwriting File, Box 89, Annapolis Speech 6/7/78 [2], declassified 1/13/93, Carter Library.

Brzezinski memo and suggested language were evidently read carefully by Carter, but so was the large package of material prepared by the White House speechwriters with the eclectic suggestions reviewed above. The material of that package, like the Brzezinski memo, is heavily underlined and bears marginal notes in the president's handwriting. When Carter sat down to prepare his speech on U.S.-Soviet relations, he used ideas and language provided by many of the people, inside and outside his administration, who had been asked to contribute their ideas. Vance and Brzezinski had their most clearly documented impact on the speech only after the president had absorbed the suggestions he received from a wide array of formal and informal advisers, and only after he had written in his own words what he wanted to say.

At Camp David on the first weekend in June, Carter began working on his Annapolis speech by recording on a legal pad some of the points he wanted to make when he spoke to the new naval officers in the academy's graduating class.[29] Looked at alone, the president's list appears to have no order or logic, but when read alongside the written suggestions he received, the list is clearly the product of note taking that went on while the president read through the papers he had brought with him to Camp David. The recurrent theme in the items that attracted Carter's attention was the relative strength of the United States as compared to the Soviet Union. That comparison involved much more than just military power. Carter wanted to tell the naval midshipmen that the strengths of their society across a wide range of measures were substantial and that the growth of Soviet military forces, as dangerous as that growth might be, was ultimately no match for the power associated with American economic vitality, agricultural abundance, scientific knowledge, technological innovation, allied support, and longstanding commitment to democratic institutions and values.

In the margins of the president's list of points he wrote an outline for the speech. It was basically chronological. Carter planned to discuss the history of U.S.-Soviet relations during and after the Second World War, the current balance between the superpowers, and the prospects for the future. The last two parts of his outline would review the current conflicts between the two superpowers and the areas in which U.S. and Soviet interests remained

29. Untitled notes written in the president's hand, Office of the Staff Secretary, President's Handwriting File, Box 89, Annapolis Speech 6/7/78 [2], Carter Library.

compatible. Each of the major elements in Carter's outline was numbered, and the president apparently reread his own seven-page list of ideas, deciding which items would be included and assigning each one of them a number that corresponded to its expected place in the organization of the speech. The president then wrote, in longhand, thirty-six pages of speech text.[30]

He began by observing that the word "détente" was often misunderstood and by restating the standard administration position on linkage and the need for greater Soviet caution. A stable détente, he wrote, "to be supported by the American people, and to be a basis for widening the scope of cooperation must be truly reciprocal and not selective. Both nations must exercise restraint in troubled areas and in turbulent times." But even if both sides exercised restraint, Carter went on to say, "for a very long time, our relationship with the Soviet Union will be both cooperative and competitive."[31] The American people needed to understand both aspects of the relationship and avoid swings in the public mood from euphoria to hostility. The president's draft goes on to describe the sources of both cooperation and competition. In the nuclear age, both superpowers clearly want peace and relief from the anxiety that the other might be seeking strategic military advantage. Carter's prescription for continued strategic stability involved the maintenance of roughly equal military forces and cooperation in the negotiation of additional arms control agreements. Even with military forces in equilibrium and arms control negotiations under way, competition was bound to occur. As the new nations of the developing world struggled to achieve economic progress and political freedom, they were increasingly drawn to the example provided by the industrialized West. This trend posed a serious threat to the Soviet Union, which had once been considered the model for developing countries. In Carter's version of the competition between the United States and the Soviet Union for influence in the third world, the eventual victor was already decided.

The central message of Carter's draft—the overall strength of the United

30. Brzezinski reports in his memoirs that there were fifty-four paragraphs of presidential text in Carter's handwritten draft. Brzezinski, *Power and Principle*, 320. The correct number is fifty-eight.

31. Untitled speech drafted in the president's hand, Office of the Staff Secretary, President's Handwriting File, Box 89, Annapolis Speech 6/7/78 [1]: 2–3, Carter Library. He repeats his position on linkage later in the draft: 9–10. The language at the outset of the speech follows Brzezinski's suggestions in his June 2 memo.

States and democratic values as opposed to the Soviet Union and communism—was reinforced when the president reviewed the history of relations between the two nations after World War II and the elements of power on each side. Here he borrowed extensively from the suggestions he received from the members of his administration and the informal network of advisers contacted by his speechwriters. From Dean Rusk, he took note of the fact that our complicated governmental system is often seen as a source of weakness and division, when in fact the slow process of building solid consensus is part of what gives us the capacity for world leadership. From George Ball, he borrowed a description of America's pragmatic philosophy, which allows us to be flexible, to grow, and to resolve our own internal problems. Tony Lake's outline for the Annapolis speech ended with a list of attributes contributing to American international leadership. Almost all of them appear in Carter's draft, plus others that are found in the suggestions of Lester Brown, Stansfield Turner, and McGeorge Bundy.

The president's first draft of his Annapolis speech is neither original in content nor particularly elegant in formulation, but it does succeed in conveying a clear message about U.S.-Soviet relations. The relationship between the superpowers, Carter explains, is bound to be complicated and involve both conflict and common interest. In the long run, the United States will prevail in the contest with Soviet communism because our military strength is adequate to prevent war and because our social, economic, and political values are superior. The first draft of the speech has two basic messages for those in the United States who might be concerned about the state of superpower relations. The president offers reassurance to those afraid of a growing Soviet military menace, and explanation to those who may not have understood that SALT negotiations could proceed, for the time being, even as conflict in Africa intensified. The president's continuing desire for successful arms control negotiations and his growing concern about Soviet actions in the third world were later read respectively as the Vance and Brzezinski portions of the speech. Those two elements of the speech did, in fact, reflect the priorities of Carter's two principal foreign policy advisers, but they were not included as the result of some casual accommodation of the two positions. They were included from the outset because Carter wanted both a SALT II agreement and more moderate Soviet behavior in the third world. Moreover, the attention given to what the speech had to say about current issues involving arms control and Africa tended to miss

the larger optimistic message that the president also wanted to deliver—
that the United States was far more powerful than the Soviet Union and
was bound to prevail in any form of competition that might arise.

Revisions

When his draft was complete, Carter called an unusual Sunday evening
meeting of his senior foreign policy advisers and provided each person present with a copy of his handwritten speech in which the paragraphs had been
numbered in the margin. He invited their reactions to each paragraph in
turn. The meeting was attended by Vance, Brzezinski, Harold Brown,
Stansfield Turner, Hamilton Jordan, and Andrew Young.[32] The president
stayed for only part of the meeting, giving his advisers an opportunity to
discuss the draft in his absence. The changes incorporated as a result of
these deliberations were minor. Most were matters of style; a few softened
the edge of the message the president was sending to the Soviet leadership.
Where Carter had written, "The Soviet Union must be disabused of the
notion that military supremacy can either be attained or exploited," his advisers suggested a more balanced version that said, "Neither the U.S. nor
the Soviet Union should entertain the notion that military supremacy can
either be attained or politically exploited."[33] While the president had acknowledged in his draft the need for increased trade and scientific and cultural exchange with the Soviet Union, he had not said much about why
these kinds of cooperation were important. Stansfield Turner drafted a few
paragraphs that elaborated on this aspect of superpower relations.[34]

The only serious disagreement that apparently arose at the Sunday evening session involved the language that would be used in criticism of recent
Soviet actions in Africa.[35] Secretary Vance either volunteered or was appointed to prepare additional paragraphs on this subject.[36] Vance also con-

32. The Daily Diary of President Jimmy Carter, June 4, 1978, Camp David, Maryland,
6:32 P.M., Carter Library. An incomplete list of those attending the meeting appeared in
"Carter as Speechwriter: Limiting Split," *Washington Post*, June 8, 1978.

33. Changes were recorded on the president's handwritten draft, probably by Brzezinski,
and typed the following day. Draft —6/5/78, Office of the Staff Secretary, President's Handwriting File, Annapolis Speech 6/7/78 [2]: 4, Carter Library.

34. Ibid., insert A between pp. 9 and 10.

35. Untitled speech drafted in the president's hand, marginal note beside paragraph 28.

36. Draft—6/5/78, insert between pp. 20 and 21.

tributed new material on American values and human rights that expanded on points the president had made in his draft.[37] Given press reports about a deeply divided administration unable to develop a coherent policy toward the Soviet Union, there was very little dispute about what the president planned to say to the Naval Academy graduates.[38] Carter was reportedly surprised, and presumably satisfied, by the outcome of the meeting. Joking with his advisers, he reportedly told them that he had expected "some blood on the floor."[39]

The bloodless meeting was followed two days later by a final session to review the contents of the speech. This one, on the day before Carter went to Annapolis, was attended again by Vance, Brzezinski, Turner, and Jordan, but also included press secretary Jody Powell and the newly appointed assistant to the president for communications, Gerald Rafshoon.[40] Between the two meetings Brzezinski went over the draft produced on Sunday evening, including the inserts by Turner and Vance, and suggested more of his own changes. Again, almost all of Brzezinski's proposals at this stage were stylistic, including minor alterations in language and reordering of paragraphs. In a few places, particularly in the section dealing with the history of U.S.-Soviet relations in the post-war era, he elaborated on what Carter had written. Language Brzezinski drafted for the conclusion of the speech about cooperation between the United States and Soviet Union in fighting fascism during World War II was not, however, included in the updated draft prepared for the Tuesday meeting.

When the president's foreign policy and political advisers met on Tuesday to review a near-final version of Carter's speech, there was once again clear consensus about its content. A few repetitive paragraphs were deleted;

37. Ibid., insert between pp. 14 and 15.
38. Brzezinski, *Power and Principle*, 321.
39. "Behind Carter Annapolis Speech," *Washington Post*, June 11, 1978. No source is given for this quotation, though other facts in this story about the preparation of the speech are substantiated by the documents in the Carter Library.
40. The Daily Diary of President Jimmy Carter, June 6, 1978, The White House, 12:04 P.M. According to the notation on the front page of the 6/6/78 draft, a copy of the speech was also provided to Vice President Walter Mondale's assistant Richard Moe. See, Annapolis Speech 6/6/78—0720, Office of the Staff Secretary, President's Handwriting File, Box 89, Annapolis Speech 6/7/78 [2], Carter Library. Press reports say that the speech was also reviewed by Patrick Cadell. "Political Aides Lent a Hand for Foreign Policy Talk," *New York Times*, June 8, 1978.

a few word substitutions were made. Only one substantive addition was made to the speech by the president's advisers. That addition became the most frequently quoted passage of the president's remarks in Annapolis. At the end of the Tuesday draft, as a summary of what had been said throughout the speech, the following sentences were written at the bottom of the next to last page: "The Soviets can choose either confrontation or cooperation. The United States is adequately prepared to meet either choice."[41] These two sentences appear to be written in Brzezinski's hand, but since the national security adviser was the likely note taker at the Tuesday meeting, attended by principals only, it is not clear who suggested the additional language. Brzezinski reports that the sentences were added by Carter.[42] Though it was not a major change in the substance of the speech, the new sentences did put the challenge to the Soviet Union in sharper terms. In particular, by selecting the word "confrontation" instead of the more frequently used and less threatening term "competition," the president and his advisers were raising the rhetorical stakes in their message to the Kremlin leadership.

The Naval Academy speech went through one more round of revisions on the day before the president's trip to Annapolis. These revisions were probably done by the speechwriting staff. They included a final version of the humorous personal comments that the president would use at the beginning of the speech, another series of minor deletions and stylistic improvements, the correction of a statistic on Soviet defense spending, the shortening of a lengthy comparison of the Soviet and American navies, and the addition of a few concluding remarks aimed directly at the audience of graduating midshipmen. Once again, Carter reviewed this draft and made his own last-minute changes, none of which involved substantive matters.[43]

After the speech was typed in its final version, Carter made one more change. In a paragraph that read, "I am convinced that the people of the Soviet Union want peace. I cannot believe that their leaders could want war," he crossed out "their leaders" and inserted the pronoun "they," refer-

41. Ibid., 28.

42. Brzezinski, *Power and Principle*, 321.

43. Carter's handwriting is evident on this version of the speech, but some of the minor changes were made by someone else. Annapolis Speech 6/6/78, Office of the Staff Secretary, President's Handwriting File, Box 89, Annapolis Speech 6/7/78 [1], Carter Library.

ring to the Soviet people.[44] The discrepancy between what was written on the copy of the speech provided to the press and what the president actually said in person was noted by several reporters and believed to be a significant change, hinting that perhaps Carter thought that some Soviet leaders might want war.[45] More likely, the president noticed that the reference to Soviet leaders had been added by his speechwriters, or someone else, in the Tuesday afternoon draft and reverted to the formulation that had been used in earlier versions of the speech.

All in all, Jimmy Carter devoted a considerable amount of presidential time and attention to the Annapolis speech. He selected its theme, read almost a hundred pages of suggestions and briefing material collected by his speechwriters, outlined his own ideas, and wrote a first draft incorporating language from a variety of sources and some of his own formulations about the essential strengths of the United States in its struggle with the Soviet Union. The president then scheduled a series of meetings with his senior advisers, the first late on a Sunday evening, to discuss the draft he had prepared and their proposed revisions. On Monday and Tuesday, and again on Wednesday, just before the commencement address was delivered, he personally read and revised the latest version of the speech. He reportedly expected some dispute between Vance and Brzezinski, and may have thought that his preparation of a major administration statement on U.S.-Soviet relations would bring their differences to the fore. Instead, he found that both of his senior foreign policy advisers approved the description of cooperation and competition between the United States and the Soviet Union that he had written. In a reversal of roles, Vance drafted the portion of the speech criticizing Cuban and Soviet actions in Africa, while Brzezinski proposed conciliatory language about the wartime alliance that the cold war adversaries had once enjoyed. It must have been frustrating for the president to observe that the basic harmony he saw within his administration was reported in the media as continued division and that the speech he had so seriously worked on himself was eventually dismissed as a casual combination of memos written by his quarreling advisers. Tracing the development of these

44. President Jimmy Carter U.S. Naval Academy Commencement Speech, Wednesday, June 7, 1978, Office of the Staff Secretary, President's Handwriting File, Box 89, Annapolis Speech 6/7/78 [1]: 6, Carter Library.

45. "President Challenges Soviet Leaders," *Washington Post*, June 8, 1978.

false perceptions may actually be more important than detailing what happened in the preparation of the Annapolis speech.

Reactions

Beyond the Naval Academy graduates, there were two important audiences for Carter's comments on U.S.-Soviet relations in the summer of 1978—one was the community of attentive foreign policy observers who were increasingly convinced that the administration did not have a coherent strategy for dealing with the Soviet Union, the other was the Soviet leadership in Moscow. The Moscow reaction came within a few days of the president's remarks and was relatively easy to understand. In major articles carried by *Tass* and *Pravda*, Soviet officials responded directly to Carter's remarks at the Naval Academy. They accused the president of seeking to undermine détente and said that "a substantial part of the president's speech was devoted to fabrications concerning the Soviet Union and its system."[46] His speech was described as having "a smell of the malicious spirit of the Cold War," and was said to provide evidence that the administration was increasingly under the influence of the hard-line anti-Communist Zbigniew Brzezinski.[47] From Brzezinski's point of view, this was not an unsatisfactory response. The Soviets had obviously heard the displeasure expressed by the president regarding their actions at home and abroad and were likely to believe that Carter was serious when he raised the possibility of future confrontations.[48]

The reaction to the Annapolis speech in Washington was, perhaps not surprisingly, more mixed. Some commentators followed the line developed in the early newspaper reports about two different speeches. According to Evans and Novak, the Naval Academy speech was drafted by the president from "two memos—one State Department (soft), the other National Security Council (hard). Like ordering from a Chinese menu, the president was taking one from Column A, one from Column B."[49] As is common in such

46. "Moscow Replies: Carter's Policies Blocking Detente," *Washington Post*, June 8, 1978.

47. "Pravda Hits 'Cold War' Tone of Carter's Annapolis Speech," *Washington Post*, June 12, 1978.

48. Brzezinski, *Power and Principle*, 321–22.

49. Rowland Evans and Robert Novak, "The 'Divided President,' " *Washington Post*, June 14, 1978.

articles, Evans and Novak gave no sources for their account of how the speech was drafted. However, after their account was publicly endorsed by James Fallows, it became the dominant interpretation of the speech.

In June 1978 there were other complaints expressed by unidentified sources within the administration and without. One anonymous State Department official called the description of U.S. strength and Soviet ideological weakness "jingoism," while unnamed specialists in geopolitics reacted to the president's desire to see self-determination and majority rule in the Soviet Union, Eastern Europe, and China "with incredulity."[50] Looked at from the vantage point provided by the end of the cold war and the collapse of Communist regimes throughout the world, it is hard to find either jingoistic language in Carter's remarks or anything that merits an incredulous reaction. In general, critics of Carter's hard-line tone at Annapolis, whether they reacted to the speech in Moscow or in Washington, tended to dismiss the president's remarks as the misguided pronouncements of someone who did not understand how détente was to be conducted or evidence of Brzezinski's rising influence in a continuing struggle for control of the administration's foreign policy.[51]

Not all the commentary in the aftermath of the speech was negative. The editorial writers for the *New York Times* and the *Washington Post* gave the speech a favorable reading and focused attention on the realistic assessment of U.S.-Soviet relations that Carter provided. The Soviets needed to understand, the editorials argued, that in the complicated domestic politics of the American treaty-ratification process, the full range of their actions would be judged by the senators who controlled the fate of the emerging SALT II treaty.[52] Both papers praised Carter for providing the Soviets with a necessary warning. The editorial in the *Post* went on to say that the preparation of a coherent speech on U.S.-Soviet relations would not end the infighting within the Carter administration and that considerable presidential authority would be needed in order to rein in the divergent tendencies of Vance and Brzezinski. Both major national newspapers also published detailed,

50. "President Challenges Soviet Leaders."
51. "Carter on Soviet: An Ambiguous Message," *New York Times*, June 9, 1978.
52. "Mr. Carter on the Russians," *Washington Post*, June 8, 1978, and "From Linkage to Sausage," *New York Times*, June 8, 1978.

and largely accurate, accounts of how the speech had been drafted and the central role Carter had played in its preparation.[53] In the months and years that followed, those initial accounts would be obscured by Fallows's anecdote about the construction of the speech from contradictory Vance and Brzezinski memorandums. How did the truth about the Annapolis speech get lost?

To some degree, the truth about Carter's remarks to the Naval Academy graduates was never entirely lost. In addition to the newspaper analysis that appeared in the week following the Naval Academy commencement, Brzezinski gives an accurate summary of the preparation of the president's remarks in his memoirs. Brzezinski's description of the drafting process conforms with most of the documentary evidence in the Carter Library,[54] and though his version of events has been available since 1983, it has often been ignored. The Brzezinski account occupies only a few paragraphs in a lengthy memoir and is much less interesting than the Fallows version, with its vivid image of a hapless president stapling conflicting documents together and calling the result a speech. In the contest for public attention about a relatively minor event in the Carter presidency, the Fallows account invariably wins out. There are a number of reasons why this is so.

First of all, what Fallows said about the Annapolis speech conformed with the initial press reports about the bifurcated nature of the president's message. First impressions are important, and the speech was indeed trying to convey a two-part message. Moreover, Fallows's concurrence with the early press accounts came from an insider who was an eyewitness to the White House speechmaking process. Whatever it was he witnessed in this case is hard to reconcile with the documentary evidence. Though he worked on some of the early memos containing speech suggestions for the president, Fallows was apparently in California while the early drafting of the Annapolis speech took place.[55] Even if he had been in Washington, he might not have participated in the high-level meetings that reviewed the president's personal draft. None of the speechwriters attended those meet-

53. "Political Aides Lent a Hand for Foreign Policy Talk"; "Carter as Speechwriter: Limiting Split"; "Behind Carter Annapolis Speech."

54. Brzezinski, *Power and Principle*, 320–22.

55. Jim Fallows to the President, memorandum: "Memorandum to the President from Jim Fallows on Upcoming Speeches," May 17, 1978, Office of the Speechwriters, Box 26, Speech at Annapolis June 7, 1978, Carter Library.

ings. Fallows says that he vividly remembers seeing the president staple Vance and Brzezinski memos together in preparation for the Annapolis speech. He has not had an opportunity to review the evidence in the Carter Library and believes that the speechwriter files in the library are incomplete.[56]

One possible reconciliation of Fallows's account with the documentary evidence involves the Monday draft of the Annapolis speech, which has Brzezinski's handwritten notes in the margins and has inserts drafted by Vance and Turner. That document might have been given to Fallows by the president together with instructions to produce a polished final version of the speech, which the speechwriters did. To someone who had not attended the Sunday night meeting or read the president's handwritten draft, the typed version of the speech prepared on Monday might have appeared to be a combination of Vance and Brzezinski language. It is possible that Carter gave no indication that he was the principal author of the draft and paid no attention to what his speechwriters might have thought.[57]

Fallows's account of the Annapolis speech also acquired authority because it fit with a larger pattern that he observed throughout his service in the Carter campaign and administration. President Carter usually paid very little attention to the writing or delivery of speeches. During his political career, his most effective public presentations had been highly personal statements about his own life and beliefs. His Law Day address, given during his Georgia governorship, attracted national media attention, but was delivered extemporaneously and is more noteworthy for its compassionate appreciation of American political values than for its elegant language or logical argument. In the 1976 campaign, Carter's basic stump speech was a largely autobiographical account of his varied experiences as a naval officer, a farmer, a businessman, and a southern governor. It worked well in the early primary states, where Carter was an unknown, but did not impress sophisticated political observers. Before running for the presidency, Carter never had a speechwriting staff and had little experience working with professional writers. In the White House, he rarely gave sustained attention to

56. James Fallows, letter to author, September 19, 1992.

57. Fallows rejects this interpretation and offers a general warning to scholars who work in presidential libraries. "I ask that you consider the possibility that the archival record can create an air of spurious precision and completeness. . . . This, in its way, can be as misleading as personal anecdotes." James Fallows, letter to author, October 4, 1992.

the preparation of his public appearances and never had a senior assistant, like Kennedy's Theodore Sorensen, who was both a policy adviser and a writer of speeches. A president unusually inexperienced at speechwriting and more interested in policy accomplishments than public relations might well have combined two speech drafts without giving their contents adequate attention. What Fallows alleged about the Annapolis speech may have earned a place in the folklore about the Carter presidency because it made sense to political observers who were accustomed to expect very little from Carter's oratory.

But Fallows went further in his *Atlantic* articles. Not only was the president he described indifferent to the speechmaking arts, he was incapable, or unwilling, to think in terms of broad political principles or concepts. According to Fallows, Carter was the engineer who diligently approached each problem put before him, but failed to see the connections or the priorities among the issues he confronted. Carter was, in Fallows's phrase, the "passionless" president. It is difficult to think of Carter as passionless in connection with his desire to achieve arms control or improvement in human rights (or peace in the Middle East or justice for the people of Panama for that matter), but Fallows is right that Carter was reluctant to establish priorities and did not want to limit the scope of either his domestic or foreign policy agendas. At one point in the administration, Brzezinski attempted to do something about the president's tendency to do too much. The national security adviser made a list of the foreign policy initiatives, negotiations, and policy objectives that were being actively pursued and asked Carter to rank them and select the ones that were most important. Carter read the list and gave orders that he wanted everything on it to go forward. Carter was fond of lists. He was an unusually thorough individual, and he was ambitious about what he wanted to accomplish during his presidency. But it may be a mistake to say that his list-making tendency and his desire to accumulate a long list of achievements were synonymous with a failure to see or understand the connections between issues and the principles behind his foreign policy actions.

Conclusions

If James Fallows is right about the character of Carter's mind and his inability to conceptualize, then perhaps it does not matter that one of the anecdotes he uses to illustrate his point is inaccurate or incomplete. On the other hand, if he was wrong about the events surrounding the president's speech in Annapolis, perhaps the whole passionless presidency thesis needs to be reexamined. Fallows is not the author of the kind of kiss-and-tell White House biography that had a permanent place on the best-seller lists just before and after Ronald Reagan left office. He is a serious observer and responsible critic of the Carter presidency. He perceptively identifies some of the basic elements in Carter's operating style—his compulsive attention to detail, his ambition to succeed in a wide variety of initiatives, and his limitations as a communicator. But it may be a mistake to conclude that these elements in the president's makeup are derived from an absence of conceptual thought and commitment to overarching principles. In many ways, the Annapolis speech was a serious effort on Carter's part to articulate some of the policy connections and principles at the heart of U.S.-Soviet relations.

The connections between arms control and other aspects of détente were relatively clear in Carter's discussion of superpower relations in 1978. There was no reason, from the president's point of view, to expect that the dealings between the United States and the Soviet Union would be anything but complicated and contradictory. In fact, Carter criticized the American people for thinking otherwise and allowing the public mood to alternate between euphoria and despair. Détente would always be a matter of cooperation and competition. We had common interests in minimizing the dangers of nuclear war and fundamental differences in political values. There was no reason to rule out all arms control negotiations just because there was conflict in the third world. He did not mention it in his speech, but Carter might have pointed out that Nixon went to Moscow to sign SALT I at the same time that American military forces were mining the harbors of North Vietnam. Of course, at some point, as Carter acknowledged, Soviet actions at home or abroad could make it impossible to ratify a SALT II treaty. The Naval Academy address explicitly warned the Kremlin about this possibility. In the long run that warning was not effective. When Soviet troops invaded Afghanistan at the end of 1979, Carter withdrew the SALT II treaty from Senate consideration.

But beyond identifying the existence of an unavoidable linkage between Soviet actions and the prospects for arms control, Carter's Annapolis speech contained a more important message about U.S.-Soviet relations. The president's genuine commitments to human rights and democracy were the sort of overarching principles that Fallows found lamentably absent in Carter's presidency. Those principles shaped U.S.-Soviet relations for Carter, who was confident that in the long run the Soviet system would succumb to a global movement toward self-determination and respect for fundamental individual rights. This was a conviction that had been articulated at the outset of the cold war and one that Carter shared with his successor, Ronald Reagan. But instead of delivering repeated rhetorical assaults on the sins of the "evil empire," Carter was more inclined to express the positive side of the same message. His Annapolis speech, in all of its drafts, emphasized the superiority of democratic institutions and values. "Our philosophy is based on personal freedom, the most powerful of all ideas," he wrote in a passage that survived all revisions and reviews, "and our democratic way of life warrants admiration and emulation by other people."[58] From Carter's perspective, human rights and self-determination were first principles, not clichés. They came before other considerations and determined other aspects of American foreign policy. There could, and should, be U.S.-Soviet cooperation to reduce the dangers of nuclear war and the burdens of arms competition. A détente, if it was equally observed by both sides and prevented excessive competition in the third world, was desirable. But for Carter there was never an acceptance of realpolitik and the view that the Soviet Union was simply another great power equal to the United States in legitimacy and international standing. There were important matters of principle that separated the two superpowers and governed their dealings with each other.

But if it can be argued today that Carter did have some hierarchy in his foreign policy beliefs and did understand the connections between the objectives he was trying to accomplish in American dealings with the Soviet Union, that does not mean that the Annapolis speech was successful. It was not. It was one of the president's purposes to warn the Soviets about the consequences of their actions in the third world. Initially that message may have been received in the Kremlin, but after the invasion of Afghanistan, it was clear that Carter's warnings in Annapolis did not have lasting value. It had been one of the president's objectives to respond to the public perception of division among his foreign policy advisers. But his remarks at the Naval Academy about cooperation and confrontation were read from the outset in the context of those perceived divisions and did not alter public perceptions. In fact, the president's careful attention to the preparation of

58. Untitled speech drafted in the president's hand, 24.

his remarks was widely dismissed, and when the speech was characterized as a clumsy compromise of contradictory advice, that characterization stuck. Clearly Carter bears responsibility for the failure of the speech to accomplish what he set out to do.

It was probably not possible for any speech to end the speculation about a major division between Vance and Brzezinski. Such a division did, in fact, exist and was particularly evident in policy questions related to the Soviet Union. From Carter's perspective, though it may have been worth addressing what he regarded as exaggerated reports of divisions within his administration in what he would say at Annapolis, it was not worth doing much more about the problem. As far as the president was concerned, his two senior foreign policy advisers worked reasonably well together. Both were committed to human rights and promoting self-determination throughout the world. Both worked for the negotiation and ratification of a new Panama Canal treaty and for progress in the Middle East. Even on U.S.-Soviet relations, where real differences were present, both readily accepted the president's draft for the Annapolis speech. The differences in background and style that Vance and Brzezinski brought to the administration were useful to Carter, who learned from his national security adviser's facility for explanation and conceptualization and appreciated his secretary of state's experience and caution. Despite the public perception of a deeply divided administration in the management of foreign affairs, Carter never seriously considered firing either his secretary of state or his national security adviser. For the most part, he was pleased with their performance and not terribly concerned about public perceptions.

This may be the root of the problem that Fallows saw. Carter may not have lacked principles or passions, but he often demonstrated an impolitic indifference to matters of public relations. He was the unknown outsider when he entered the stage of national politics in 1976, and to many observers he remained a mysterious politician throughout his four years in Washington. The American people, and even some members of his administration, may not have fully known what Carter wanted in relations with the Soviet Union or in other important foreign policy issues. He did not seek out labels or slogans to summarize or advertise his positions. In the absence of a clear public perception about where the president stood, the differences between Vance and Brzezinski, in style and in substance, had an exaggerated significance to a press and public attempting to define an administration that would not define itself.

In the summer of 1978, at about the time that the Annapolis speech was given, Gerald Rafshoon, the president's publicist during the 1976 campaign, took a full-time position on the White House staff. He assumed responsibility for the speechwriting office and for the development of a more positive image for the president and the administration. But Rafshoon's addition to the White House staff could not alter Carter's character. Fundamentally, Jimmy Carter was a president more concerned with public policy than with public perception. Like other presidents who served before and after his term in office, he wanted both arms control with the Soviet Union and the prevention of Soviet expansion in the third world, but unlike other presidents, he was unwilling to present himself or his policies in simplified terms. The administration never described America's relations with the Soviet Union in language comparable to Nixon's vision of a "new structure of peace" or Reagan's attack on the "evil empire." Carter's policies were complicated, so was the president who pursued them, so was his speech to the Naval Academy graduates.

5

THE ESSENCE OF INDECISION
The Neutron Bomb Controversy

It began with a clerical error. An unclassified congressional document mistakenly included brief references to a secret program to develop a new warhead for some of the American short-range Lance missiles stationed in central Europe. It became a sensational media story, a matter of debate between the president and Congress, and a major issue in the NATO alliance. When it started, neither President Carter nor any of the senior members of his White House staff had given serious attention to the minor program for the development of an enhanced-radiation warhead (ERW) that was misnamed the neutron bomb in the national and international press.[1] In terms of budget impact or policy-maker interest, the ERW was not even a blip on the national security radar scope until it became a media storm that could not be ignored. When it was over, the ERW program was neither canceled outright nor fully approved for production and deployment. The issue came out of nowhere in the summer of 1977, sparked passionate debate, was never fully resolved, and returned to a kind of policy limbo ten months later.

In the process, Jimmy Carter's reputation for indecisiveness was rein-

1. On June 9, 1977, Brzezinski wrote a memo to his defense specialist on the NSC staff, Victor Utgoff, asking him to find out if the press reports he had been reading about the neutron bomb were accurate. White House Central File, Subject File, Defense, Carter Library.

forced, and alliance relations, particularly those between the United States and West Germany, were badly strained. These results do not, however, tell the full story of what went on behind the scenes and what less desirable alternatives may have been avoided. In some ways, Carter was not indecisive about the neutron bomb and, after determining what he wanted to do about ERWs, maintained a consistent position against significant domestic and international pressure. Alliance relations were damaged by the controversy, but America's European allies were arguably well served by the final resolution of the central issue. The alliance nations did appear to be giving in to Soviet pressure and propaganda, but they lost a weapon of marginal military value and avoided substantial domestic political pitfalls that would have accompanied the deployment of the controversial warheads. In the end, a determined president was widely portrayed as indecisive, and NATO leaders, who were never enthusiastic about the new weapon, were bitterly disappointed when they were not forced to accept it. All of this makes for a complicated story that reveals some important things about President Carter, about the role of the media in the conduct of American foreign policy, and about recurring problems related to American alliance leadership in the nuclear age.

Out of Nowhere

On June 6, 1977, the *Washington Post* published a front-page story announcing that funds for the development of a "neutron killer warhead" were buried in the 1978 budget for the Energy Research and Development Administration (ERDA), one of the new federal organizations that replaced the old Atomic Energy Commission.[2] The story was based on a congressional committee report that inadvertently included testimony about an enhanced-radiation warhead for the short-range Lance missile.[3] ERW technology had been talked about by strategists and weapons designers for decades, but the program to develop warheads based on this technology had not been approved until the Ford administration. The decision to build new short-range-missile nuclear warheads for European deployment was important to

2. Walter Pincus, "Neutron Killer Warhead Buried in ERDA Budget," *Washington Post,* June 6, 1977, p. 1.
3. The story did not mention that enhanced-radiation technology was also being developed for artillery shells intended for deployment in Europe.

military planners because the existing warheads assigned to NATO forces were old, unreliable, and inaccurate. The design and construction of new ones would provide an opportunity to correct a number of defects in the existing arsenal that were probably more important than the utilization of enhanced-radiation technology. In 1977, the existence of a program for the development of new nuclear warheads for the European theater was still classified and should not have been mentioned in a document made available to the press.

In a typical Washington leak, disgruntled participants in a contentious policy-making process release inside information to influence a decision or punish opponents in a bureaucratic battle. The *Washington Post* story by Walter Pincus was not an example of major plumbing problems in our nation's capital. The brief reference to ERW in the committee document was more like an accidental drip than an intentional leak. It happened to be noticed by an alert and knowledgeable reporter. Pincus was a former aide to Senator Stuart Symington and someone who understood the classified issues and political dynamics surrounding Pentagon plans to modernize tactical nuclear weapons in Europe. Earlier in the decade, Symington had taken a leading role as a congressional critic of the modernization of NATO's tactical nuclear arsenal.[4] As a journalist, Pincus took a similar position.[5] His June 6, 1977, story introduced the term *neutron bomb* and suggested that important decisions about a new and controversial weapon that killed people but saved property were being hidden to prevent careful public scrutiny. In fact, enhanced-radiation warheads, which did involve neutron radiation but were never intended to be used as bombs carried by aircraft, were neither new nor particularly controversial before the publication of the *Washington Post* article.

The idea of designing enhanced-radiation warheads that reduced the blast and heat effects of nuclear explosions and increased the amount of energy released in the form of immediately lethal levels of radiation was an old one that had been under consideration by government scientists for over twenty years.[6] The first public discussions of enhanced-radiation weapons

4. Ivo H. Daalder, *The Nature and Practice of Flexible Response* (New York, 1991), 140.

5. Walter Pincus, "A New Generation of Weaponry—Why More Nukes?" *The New Republic*, February 9, 1974, and "Nukes Nobody Needs," *The New Republic,* April 20, 1974.

6. Fred M. Kaplan, "Enhanced-Radiation Weapons," in *Arms Control and the Arms Race:*

occurred in 1959, when supporters of the concept played a minor role in debates over test-ban negotiations. At that time, it was argued that any limitations on testing should be delayed pending the development of new, and more humane, "clean" nuclear weapons.[7] The clean weapons were neutron bombs.

Serious consideration of enhanced-radiation weaponry was, however, abandoned in the early 1960s and not revived until the middle of the next decade. In 1975, Secretary of Defense James Schlesinger called for the modernization of America's aging tactical nuclear arsenal in Europe, including the introduction of ERWs, as part of a larger program to address growing Soviet military capabilities. The replacement of the older tactical nuclear weapons in Europe had been discussed in a number of NATO forums for some time when Schlesinger made his recommendations.[8] In 1976, President Ford signed legislation funding ERDA research and development for ERWs intended for deployment on Lance missiles and for use in nuclear artillery shells.

In the original *Washington Post* story, and in those that followed, the media dramatized the unique features and moral implications of neutron bombs. Headlines announced the arrival of "killer warheads," and articles provided detailed descriptions of the medical consequences of exposure to high levels of neutron radiation. An NBC news broadcast on June 17, 1977, showed graphic footage of what happens to monkeys exposed to lethal radiation. A few days later, Pincus wrote a story about the public reaction to the broadcast.[9] These accounts fed an emotional response to the proposed ERW technology and left the public with a misleading picture of neutron warheads that was never corrected. Later, a Soviet propaganda campaign against the new weapons reinforced the first and false impressions that sen-

---

Readings from Scientific American (New York, 1985), 164. This article was originally published in the May 1978 *Scientific American*.

7. Sherri L. Wasserman, *The Neutron Bomb Controversy: A Study in Alliance Politics* (New York, 1983), 24–27.

8. Daalder, *The Nature and Practice of Flexible Response*, 143–48.

9. David Whitman, "The Press and the Neutron Bomb," in *How the Press Affects Federal Policy Making: Six Case Studies*, by Martin Linsky et al. (New York, 1986), 157. Whitman's account is a detailed and valuable case study of the role of the press in the neutron bomb issue. Another comprehensive case study of the issue can be found in Vincent A. Auger, *The Dynamics of Foreign Policy Analysis: The Carter Administration and the Neutron Bomb* (Lanham, Md., 1996).

sationalized press coverage had created. President Carter is probably correct when he suggests in his memoirs that the neutron bomb was one of the "least understood issues I had to face as President."[10]

Enhanced-radiation warheads were exactly what their proper name implied. They were nuclear weapons which produced all the usual consequences of nuclear weapons—an enormous explosion, a shock wave, a brilliant light, intense heat, dangerous forms of radiation and fallout. The new warhead designs being developed by ERDA would, however, have significantly reduced the amount of energy released as blast and heat while increasing the area around the explosion saturated with high levels of radiation. Detonated at a higher altitude with a smaller blast than many existing tactical nuclear weapons, the new warheads would do far less damage to buildings and local terrain and reduce the volume of radioactive fallout. A typical fission explosion will unleash 5 percent of its energy as prompt radiation; fusion reactions are more flexible, and can theoretically be made to give off 80 percent of their power in that form. The ERWs actually considered in the 1970s would have involved a combination of fission and fusion reactions and would have released 30 percent of their energy as prompt radiation.[11] This change in the characteristics of the explosive effects did not mean that a wholly new weapon was being brought into existence. A scientist reviewing neutron-warhead technology in the May 1978 *Scientific American* reported that "the enhanced-radiation warhead promises to be neither the collateral-damage-free weapon that its supporters see nor the 'ultimate capitalist weapon' (destroying only people, not property) that many people in peace groups fear."[12]

The attractiveness of ERWs for NATO military planners was their anticipated ability to disable Warsaw Pact armored and mechanized infantry divisions engaged in a large-scale invasion of Western Europe without completely destroying the populated territory that NATO was attempting to defend. Such a weapon could more easily be used against the large conventional forces available to the Soviet Union in central Europe and thereby make deterrence more credible. That was the basic argument in favor of ERWs. There was, however, considerable debate about whether or not

10. Jimmy Carter, *Keeping Faith: Memoirs of a President* (New York, 1982), 225.
11. Kaplan, "Enhanced-Radiation Weapons," 166–67.
12. Ibid., 167.

ERWs would actually accomplish this objective. The extent to which neutron radiation would successfully incapacitate the crews of Soviet tanks, and the numbers and yields of neutron weapons that would be needed in theoretical tactical nuclear exchanges in Europe, remained controversial questions in the community of strategic experts. As a result, there was never any consensus about the precise levels of collateral damage that could be expected from the use of ERWs.[13] Some experts claimed dramatic reductions in that damage; others predicted no significant change. All such speculations depended, of course, on what kinds of Soviet retaliations might take place in response to a NATO decision to use ERWs and whether the Soviets would develop their own neutron warheads or respond to their use with existing tactical nuclear weapons. Ironically, this uncertainty within the technical and strategic communities had little effect on the general public debate. Because the media portrait of the neutron bomb exaggerated its novel features and implied that the differences between existing nuclear warheads and their proposed ERW replacements were matters of kind rather than degree, the political debate about the neutron bomb was distorted from the outset.

The debate was further distorted because any discussion of tactical nuclear weapons in Europe touched raw nerves in the Atlantic alliance and raised troublesome questions about NATO's nuclear doctrine. European attitudes toward nuclear weaponry, and particularly the attitudes of West Germans, who occupied the front line in any anticipated combat with Warsaw Pact forces, had always been deeply ambivalent. The tactical nuclear weapons deployed in Europe from the mid-1950s were there for important military reasons. They were needed to compensate for Soviet superiorities in many measures of conventional military power. They were also there for symbolic reasons. The deployment of American nuclear arms on NATO's front line was a promise that the United States would be directly involved, with its most sensitive arms, in any military conflict with the Soviet Union.

That promise was, of course, a two-edged sword, or perhaps a two-tipped bomb. It reassured Europe of a continuing American military commitment that would hopefully deter Soviet aggression, but it also involved the NATO nations in all of the risks and dangers connected with threat-

13. See for instance the arguments of Herbert Scoville, "A New Weapon to Think (and Worry) About," *New York Times*, July 12, 1977.

ened nuclear warfare on European soil. As the American tactical nuclear weapons sent to NATO in the 1950s got older and more outdated and as the Soviet conventional military threat became more powerful, military pressure to replace the existing nuclear arsenal with newer and more effective weapons grew. Addressing that military need could not be accomplished, however, without also addressing the politically sensitive role of American nuclear weapons in Europe's defense. The European members of NATO seemed to be simultaneously afraid of being dragged into a superpower nuclear war they did not want and being abandoned by an America unwilling to live up to its nuclear guarantees.[14] Maintaining a credible NATO nuclear deterrent was a sensitive business that raised difficult questions, questions that tended to produce ambivalent answers.

The first reaction of the Carter administration to the neutron bomb issue was also ambivalent. After the *Washington Post* stories attracted broad public attention in the United States and in Europe, Carter instructed the Defense Department to provide him with a detailed report on why enhanced-radiation weaponry was needed. In the meantime, he asked Congress to provide standby funding for ERWs that would allow the president to make a final decision about the production and deployment of the new warheads later in the year. He asked Congress, in other words, for a blank check, or at least an undated check. The president might, or might not, fill in the blanks after reviewing the military case for ERWs. As media and public uproar about the new weapon grew, this request was difficult for Congress to grant.

On Capitol Hill

Members of the House and Senate, like the president and his senior advisers, were caught off guard by the sudden publicity given to enhanced-radiation warheads in the summer of 1977. Before the media took up the neutron bomb issue, funding for the ERW program had no serious opposition on Capitol Hill. After it became a public issue, continued approval for the development of ERWs was won by narrow margins and only after Congress imposed its own conditions on presidential action. Carter's request to fund

14. Michael Mandelbaum, *The Nuclear Revolution: International Politics Before and After Hiroshima* (Cambridge, Eng., 1981), 140–76. See also Michael Howard, "Reassurance and Deterrence: Western Defense in the 1980s," *Foreign Affairs* 61, no. 2 (winter 1982–83).

ERWs for 1978 before any final decisions about their production had been made was accepted in the House of Representatives but was nearly blocked in the Senate.

In June 1977, the House committees with jurisdiction over weapons research and development had already approved the 1978 appropriation for ERDA, which included the ERW program. That legislation was on its way to the floor when Walter Pincus wrote his first story. Acting about a week later, the House debated the neutron bomb, but approved ERDA's full 1978 appropriation. In the Senate the same legislation had a more hostile reception. Mark Hatfield, a Republican member of the Senate Appropriations Committee, made a concerted effort to block Carter's open-ended request for ERW funding. At a closed session of the committee, Hatfield offered an amendment to the ERDA bill deleting all expenditures for the Lance-missile ERW. His proposal lost on a 10–10 tie vote, but was reintroduced on the Senate floor. In a rare closed session on July 1, the full Senate discussed enhanced-radiation weaponry but took no action. After two and half hours of secret debate, the Senate returned to open session and took up a Hatfield proposal to delete funding for ERWs. His arguments against the ERW were both substantive and procedural.

Substantively, Hatfield criticized the proposition that neutron warheads would enhance deterrence by creating a credible threat against Soviet armored divisions. Deterrence was based, Hatfield argued, on the horrors of nuclear war and legitimate fears that any use of tactical nuclear weapons could escalate to all out strategic nuclear warfare, with all of the horrific consequences that would entail. In the senator's opinion, neutron bombs would blur the distinction between conventional and nuclear weapons and create new dangers in Europe by offering false expectations that limited nuclear warfare might be possible. Because of their consequences for NATO's nuclear defense, enhanced-radiation weapons were too important to be approved without an extensive debate about their strategic implications. Hatfield and other Senate critics of the ERW program felt rushed by Carter's request for the funding of a weapon system that the president had not yet approved. They looked for some procedural device to force the administration to take a definite position or at least reserve the right of the legislature to reconsider the issue after Carter had made up his mind.

John Stennis, chairman of the Senate Armed Services Committee and a member of Appropriations, tried to satisfy Hatfield's concerns by offering an amendment to his outright deletion of funding for the ERW. The Stennis substitute called for a temporary suspension of spending on the program until the administration had provided Congress with an arms control impact statement for the Lance ERW and a presidential certification that neutron warheads were in the national interest. The Stennis amendment, which would have given Carter more or less what he wanted, passed by a one-vote margin, 43–42. It was not, however, satisfactory to Hatfield. The senator from Oregon blocked a final vote on ERDA legislation with a filibuster that lasted until the Senate adjourned for its Fourth of July recess.

When senators returned to Washington, the ERDA appropriation was still on the floor and Hatfield's objections were still under debate. Part of the problem with the ERDA bill was alleviated when the administration finally produced the arms control impact statement required by law. The decision to mandate such statements was supposed to ensure that new weapons were considered in an arms control context before they were funded for research and development. The classified impact statement for enhanced-radiation artillery shells had been delivered to the Congress by the Ford administration without controversy before the neutron bomb issue became public. No statement had been prepared for the new Lance-missile warhead. When it was finally sent to the Senate, it gave very little guidance to senators. The statement acknowledged that the new Lance-missile warheads with their reduced collateral damage would enhance deterrence, but admitted that they might make actual use and the crossing of the nuclear threshold more likely. In any case, the test of any weapon's deterrent value was lodged in Soviet perceptions, which are always "difficult to analyze." The conclusion of the statement was that the proposed weapons system "has no arms control advantages" and only a "marginally negative" impact on ongoing negotiations involving a comprehensive nuclear test ban and mutual and balanced force reductions in Europe.[15]

After the administration delivered the late arms control impact statement, Hatfield's amendment to delete ERW funding lost by a vote of 38 to 58. Edward Kennedy then proposed a single-house legislative veto of the president's final decision, which also lost, but on a much closer vote. Oppo-

15. For a copy of the complete statement text and excerpts from the Senate debate, see Robert J. Pranger and Roger P. Labrie, eds., *Nuclear Strategy and National Security: Points of View* (Washington, D.C., 1977), 333–68.

sition to ERWs on both votes came from liberal Democrats and a few Republicans. A compromise position put forward by the two party leaders, Senators Robert Byrd and Howard Baker, giving Congress forty-five days following a presidential ERW-production decision to veto the president's action by concurrent resolution, received broad support. The ERDA appropriation bill, with the leadership endorsed two-house legislative veto provision, was approved by the Senate on July 13. The House of Representatives accepted the Senate version of the bill, and ERDA funding for ERWs was approved for 1978.

Throughout the Senate deliberations, Carter's position on ERWs remained ambiguous. In a letter he wrote to Senator Stennis on July 11, the president said that his final decision would not be made until the Pentagon had provided him with the information he requested, but he added that his current judgment was that enhanced-radiation weapons were in the national interest. While he indicated a tentative agreement with the military argument in favor of ERWs, Carter also tried to alleviate fears that the introduction of neutron warheads would make tactical nuclear war in Europe more likely. To Stennis, he gave assurance that any decision to use nuclear arms in Europe would be a presidential decision of the highest order. For Carter, there was no reason to believe that that decision would be any easier with ERWs than it would be without them. At a press conference, Carter admitted that he had given no consideration to ERWs before the media took up the issue. He furthermore argued that NATO's conventional forces were adequate to deter a Soviet invasion of Western Europe without resort to nuclear weapons of any kind.[16]

These statements about the importance of the decision to use nuclear weapons in Europe and the belief that conventional arms alone could defend NATO should have been taken as indicators of Carter's reluctance to attribute much importance to the ERW program and his genuine ambivalence about the need for enhanced-radiation weapons. But that may not have been the way they were interpreted at the time. Coming as they did when the president was trying to win congressional approval for standby funding, his statements about European nuclear issues could easily have been misread as support for ERW technology intended to promote the legislative prospects for the ERDA appropriation.

16. "Senate Backs Carter on Neutron Warhead," *Congressional Quarterly Weekly Report*, July 16, 1977, p. 1481.

In the end, the president got the appropriation he wanted but only after making public statements that suggested he was leaning toward deployment. He failed to tell the nation or the Congress enough about his own personal reservations concerning ERWs. He had equal difficulty communicating those reservations to our NATO allies and to his own staff.

In the White House and Across the Atlantic

The Defense Department report requested by President Carter was completed on August 15. It argued in favor of ERWs on the familiar grounds that modernization of the aging European stockpile of tactical nuclear weapons was essential and that enhanced-radiation technology would be effective against Soviet tank forces and would, therefore, strengthen European deterrence. At the weekly meeting of Carter's senior foreign policy advisers two days later, Vance, Brown, and Brzezinski agreed to push forward with alliance consultations that they expected would lead to eventual deployment of neutron warheads.[17] On this issue, there was no difference between the secretary of state and the national security adviser, who both understood the sensitivity of nuclear issues in the NATO alliance and readily accepted the Pentagon preference for ERW deployment. Later that day, they reported their recommendation to the president, who, according to Brzezinski's journal, showed some reluctance to deal with the issue. The president, Brzezinski reports, "did not wish the world to think of him as an ogre and we agreed that we will press the Europeans to show greater interest in having the bomb and therefore willingness to absorb some of the political flak or we will use European disinterest as a basis for a negative decision."[18]

This was the core of Carter's position on the neutron bomb. He did not like the new warheads, and he did not want to be associated with their creation. But if they were needed, and nearly all of his senior military and foreign policy advisers endorsed the proposition that ERWs would enhance NATO's deterrent ability, he was prepared to approve their production and deployment. The president had only one proviso. Our European allies would have to openly agree to the deployment of the new warheads, and

17. Zbigniew Brzezinski, *Power and Principle: Memoirs of the National Security Advisor 1977–1981* (New York, 1983), 302.
18. Ibid.

thus share responsibility for what would clearly be a controversial move. If that condition was met, Carter would go ahead with the ERW program. If it was not, he would cancel. That is what Carter told Brzezinski in the summer of 1977; he reiterated the same conditions seven months later, after extensive alliance deliberations. It may have been his position all along. Unfortunately for the president, it was not precisely the position that either our European allies or his own administration would eventually recommend.

Efforts to enlist European public commitments to the deployment of the neutron bomb met with little success in the summer and fall of 1977. The public uproar that nearly led to congressional cancellation of the ERW program in July had its parallel in Europe, where opposition to the neutron bomb was on the rise. Neither the NATO defense ministers, who gathered in Bari, Italy, in October, nor the alliance's Nuclear Planning Group, which met in December, were able to agree on a final alliance policy for ERWs. Administration officials attending these meetings and conducting additional alliance consultations during the fall gave balanced presentations outlining the advantages and disadvantages of neutron warhead deployment and asked for European reaction.[19] Privately, NATO leaders wanted the United States to proceed unilaterally with production of neutron warheads and to seek support for their deployment at a later date.[20] But this was precisely what Carter had ruled out in his instructions to Brzezinski.

Publicly, several NATO members were equivocating or moving toward open opposition to ERWs. Inconclusive debates took place in the Dutch and West German parliaments during the fall of 1977, and public protests against neutron warheads were held in a number of European capitals. When Helmut Schmidt's Social Democratic Party met for its party conference in November, a resolution was passed calling on the federal government to work toward an alliance policy that would not require the stationing of neutron weapons on Federal Republic territory. Schmidt pledged himself to support the party position.[21]

The neutron bomb was not the only security issue facing Europe, and

19. "Draft 2/17/81," p. 8, Zbigniew Brzezinski Collection, Box 34, Folder "NSC Accomplishments Enhanced Radiation Weapons: 2/81," Carter Library.

20. For evidence about Schmidt's private views, see David S. Yost and Thomas C. Glad, "West German Party Politics and Theater Nuclear Modernization Since 1977," *Armed Forces and Society* 8, no. 4 (summer 1982): 532.

21. Ibid., 533.

for Schmidt, it was far from the most important. A month before the SDP conference, Schmidt spoke to an international audience about European security in an era of superpower strategic arms limitation. The German prime minister told the members of the International Institute for Strategic Studies (IISS) in London that the continuing SALT negotiations between the United States and the Soviet Union, which were taking the superpowers toward equal and perhaps smaller strategic nuclear arsenals, would "inevitably impair the security of the West European members of the alliance" if concomitant imbalances in Europe were not addressed.[22] If the United States no longer maintained strategic nuclear superiority, the deterrent value of its pledge to defend NATO against any Soviet attack might be weakened. If at the same time that strategic equality was written into SALT II treaty language, the Soviets built and deployed new shorter-range nuclear delivery systems not covered by the provisions of strategic arms limitation, the American guarantee to NATO's defense would be further weakened. The principal weapon of concern to Schmidt was the Soviet Union's new mobile SS-20, a modern intermediate-range missile with multiple warheads that had no NATO counterpart.

Schmidt was serious about the European security problems that might emerge from a successful SALT process, but he was in a weak domestic political position to do very much about it. He led a left-of-center political party in a coalition government that was committed to a continuation of détente with the Soviet Union and improved relations with East Germany. The left wing of his own party would have preferred to cut defense spending and reallocate the savings to domestic needs. After his speech to the IISS, Schmidt became the leading European politician to express serious concern about the SS-20 and the growing Soviet nuclear capabilities in Europe. He would naturally have been expected to be an advocate of the neutron bomb, and was in private, but he could not do so openly without causing dissension in his own political party. James Callaghan, prime minister and leader of the British Labour Party, was in a similar political position. Many responsible European military and political leaders wanted the neutron bomb for all the same reasons that Carter's senior defense and foreign policy advisers wanted it, but there were real domestic political costs to any

22. Helmut Schmidt, "The 1977 Alastair Buchan Memorial Lecture," *Survival*, January–February 1978, 4.

social democratic or labor party leader who openly took responsibility for the deployment of a new and controversial nuclear weapon.

Throughout the unsuccessful alliance consultations on the neutron bomb a barrage of media reports kept the issue in the public eye. Between June 1977 and April 1978, there were 84 stories about the neutron bomb in the *Washington Post*, 113 in the *New York Times*, and 47 in the London *Times*. In the *Frankfurter Allgemeine*, there were at least 28 front-page stories dealing with the issue. In Europe, there was also an extremely pervasive Soviet propaganda campaign, which outdid even the Western media in its portrayal of the neutron bomb as a wholly new and morally offensive addition to the world's nuclear arsenals. From June 1977 until the end of the year, *Pravda* carried a regular column on its foreign policy page with the title "No to the Neutron Bomb," a slogan which many West European peace groups adopted. During the last two weeks of July and the beginning of August 1977, 13 percent of all Soviet overseas radio broadcasts were devoted to anti-neutron bomb items.[23] At the end of the year, Brezhnev publicly offered a joint East-West renunciation of ERW technology and threatened to develop a Soviet version of the neutron bomb if the United States failed to accept his offer.[24]

In January of 1978 the Carter administration responded to the growing Soviet propaganda campaign with its own covert effort to influence European public opinion. Late in the month, Leslie Gelb, the director of politico-military affairs in the State Department, and George Vest, the assistant secretary for European affairs, wrote a memo titled "Covert Action to Counter International Anti Neutron Bomb Forum." They proposed that the administration use its intelligence agency personnel in Europe to encourage the publication of favorable news stories about enhanced-radiation technology. Their suggestion was supported by Vance, Brzezinski, and Stansfield Turner and once implemented apparently led to some improvement in the climate of European public opinion.[25] Nevertheless, large-scale public dem-

23. Clive Rose, *Campaigns Against Western Defense: NATO's Adversaries and Critics* (New York, 1985), 108–10.

24. "Brezhnev Offer on the Neutron Bomb Accompanied by Threat," *Times* (London), December 24, 1977.

25. Whitman, "The Press and the Neutron Bomb," 180–83. This was not technically a covert operation. Leslie Gelb recalls that "our use of the word 'covert' in the memo simply meant using agency people in Europe to energize Europeans to write and speak up publicly in favor of deploying the neutron bomb." Leslie Gelb, letter to author, May 11, 1995.

onstrations against the neutron bomb were organized throughout the early months of 1978 and put political pressure on Schmidt and others who were being asked by the United States to endorse deployment of the new warheads.

In deference to European political sensitivities, members of the Carter administration began to move toward a compromise on ERWs. At a Special Coordinating Committee (SCC) meeting in November of 1977, Brzezinski pushed for a new round of consultations with our European allies that would soften the bad news of accepting neutron weapons by including a proposal to restrain ERW deployment in exchange for Soviet restraint in the deployment of their SS-20 missiles. In other words, the United States would proceed with production of the neutron warheads, plan for their deployment in Europe, and use the production period to negotiate with the Soviets. The actual deployment of the controversial warheads would take place only if those arms control negotiations failed.

ERWs and the SS-20 were hardly comparable weapon systems, and the prospects for any productive arms control agreement that involved only these new systems were uncertain. But combining a production decision with an arms control initiative would, in all likelihood, have reduced the growing domestic resistance to ERWs in Western Europe. The idea for an arms control component in ERW decision making originated with the West Germans, who preferred to link ERWs to the issues under discussion at the Mutual and Balanced Force Reduction (MBFR) negotiations.[26] It would have been logical to discuss ERWs at the same table where Soviet conventional forces were under consideration, but the MBFR talks involved complicated coordination between the United States and the other NATO nations, had been going on for some time, and showed little prospect for progress. The SS-20 may not have been a comparable weapon, but it was a new Soviet system and could have been discussed in a new set of bilateral negotiations between the United States and the Soviet Union.[27]

The November proposal for an arms control component in the ERW decision was approved in the SCC and by the president before it was duly

26. Some U.S. government officials also favored trading neutron bombs for Soviet tank force reductions in Europe, but that option did not prevail. "Draft 2/17/81."

27. Skeptics may have wondered why the Soviets would agree to give up a weapon system they were already deploying in exchange for limitations on a system not yet in production.

incorporated into alliance consultations. Though Carter approved this policy modification, he may not have realized that the delay in deployment of ERWs to allow for arms control negotiations would encourage the reluctant Europeans to also delay their formal deployment decisions and avoid immediate responsibility for the expected U.S. decision to produce the new warheads.

At a February 1978 meeting of NATO ambassadors in Brussels, Leslie Gelb officially put forward a proposal to include ERWs in new arms control negotiations. This new American position in the alliance consultations corresponded with the official position of the West German Federal Security Council and resolutions passed by the Dutch parliament, but did not fully meet the concerns of most European leaders. In Britain, the Labour government, while willing to accept deployment of ERWs on British soil, was less than enthusiastic about the prospect of carrying out that decision. In the Netherlands, opposition forces were gaining momentum, making any deployment of ERWs there highly unlikely. In West Germany, Schmidt was insisting that at least one other non-nuclear Continental European power accept deployment of ERWs before he could support their eventual deployment in his country. That was as far as the West German government was willing, or politically able, to go.

By the middle of March, it was apparent that the kind of European commitment to ERWs that Carter had originally asked Brzezinski to secure was not to be had. Even a partial European commitment to the neutron bomb was in trouble. Early in March, after the Dutch defense minister resigned in protest over the ERW issue, the Dutch parliament voted by a large majority to oppose any production of the new weapon, with or without arms control negotiations. Time appeared to be running out for a coordinated NATO decision on the issue, and after months of headlines, Soviet and American propaganda campaigns, and alliance consultations, the costs associated with not going forward with the new system were substantial.

On March 18, Vance, Brown, and Brzezinski sent Carter a memo outlining the final resolution of the neutron bomb controversy.[28] The United States would make a decision to produce the new warheads, followed by an offer to negotiate with the Soviet Union. If the Soviets were willing to forgo deployments of SS-20s, the administration would halt production of neu-

---

28. Brzezinski, *Power and Principle*, 304.

tron warheads. The alliance as a whole, rather than particular European countries, would endorse the deployment of ERWs in two years, if, by that time, the arms control initiative had failed. There would be no explicit statement about where the weapons might eventually be deployed, and the level of participation in the NATO decision would vary depending on the political sensitivities of individual NATO governments. Plans to announce the policy outlined by Carter's national security team were already going on within the alliance when the March 18 memo was written. A trial run for the new policy was to take place at a meeting of the North Atlantic Council later in March. At the last minute the president abruptly derailed those plans.

A Final Indecision

President Carter took the neutron bomb memorandum from his senior national security advisers with him on a brief vacation to St. Simons, Georgia, after the hard-fought vote on the first Panama Canal treaty. When he read it, he was, to put it mildly, displeased. Over the weekend he ordered a cancellation of the forthcoming public announcement of NATO's neutron bomb decision even though those plans were fully in motion and known to many people in the defense and foreign policy bureaucracies in Washington, Brussels, and the major European capitals. Writing in his diary, he noted that "my cautionary words to them [foreign policy advisers] since last summer have pretty well been ignored, and I was aggravated."[29] Aggravation was not a typical reaction for Carter, who, in general, enjoyed making the hard choices in his administration and rarely showed discomfort with foreign policy decisions, even those that were clearly controversial and politically damaging. Considerable attention has been given to whom the president may have spoken to during his March weekend vacation. Charles Kirbo was his fishing partner. None of the senior foreign policy or political advisers made the trip, though the president is reported in the press to have talked about the issue with Hamilton Jordan, Jody Powell, and Andrew Young.[30] Of the three, Young was known to be a critic of the new weapon,[31] and presumed to have been influential in supporting the president's decision

29. Carter, *Keeping Faith*, 227.
30. "Furor over the Neutron Bomb," *Newsweek*, April 17, 1978, p. 38.
31. "Young Criticizes Neutron Bomb," *Washington Post*, July 14, 1977.

to cancel the North Atlantic Council announcement. In fact, the official records of the president's schedule and telephone log do not indicate any conversations with Powell, Jordan, or Young during his weekend at St. Simons.[32]

When Carter returned to Washington Monday evening, he met with Secretary Vance briefly in the Oval Office and later that night talked with both Vance and Brzezinski in the national security adviser's office.[33] Brzezinski recorded in his journal that "I don't think that I have ever seen the President quite as troubled and pained by any decision item. At one point he said: 'I wish I had never heard of this weapon.' "[34] Carter insisted that additional consultations be carried out and that explicit statements of support for eventual deployment of ERWs be sought from Callaghan and from Schmidt before he would consider any production decision. His advisers uniformly objected to the president's proposed course of action and insisted that the allies had gone as far as they could, and that given the extensive consultations which had already taken place, it was impossible for the United States to back out of a production commitment without appearing to be inconsistent, weak, and willing to surrender to Soviet propaganda. Jody Powell was worried about giving new fuel to those who accused the president of indecision and about the political problems that would arise for any Democrat in the White House who failed to demonstrate strength on a high-profile issue related to national defense.[35] Brzezinski was particularly vigorous in opposing the president's position, and later, in a private conversation with Vance and his press secretary, Hodding Carter, called the possible cancellation of ERWs "the worst Presidential decision of the first fourteen months," an assessment which was shortly leaked to the press.[36]

At this point the president faced a classic policy-making dilemma—the high costs of changing course once a decision has acquired momentum within the bureaucracies of the American government and, in this case,

32. Presidential Diary and Appointments, March 18, 19, 1978, Carter Library. The closest contact with Andrew Young recorded in the official record is on March 16, when Young and several foreign visitors had a brief meeting with the president in the White House.

33. Ibid.

34. Brzezinski, *Power and Principle*, 304.

35. Jody Powell, telephone interview by author, March 14, 1995.

36. Brzezinski, *Power and Principle*, 305. The quotation appeared in a *Newsweek* cover story on the neutron bomb in April.

within the processes of consultation developed by the Atlantic alliance. By the time Carter refocused his attention on the neutron bomb issue, the essential compromise position—postponed deployment to allow an arms control initiative—was considered a done deal in Washington offices and foreign capitals, even though no public announcement of the compromise had yet been made. Stopping that announcement was bound to have negative consequences for the president's political reputation. Vance, Brzezinski, and Brown, as well as the president's personal political advisers, were fully aware that a change of course on the ERW issue, even if it involved bringing the policy back to the president's original preference, would result in media commentary about the weakness and indecision of the president and his administration. Jimmy Carter was not usually persuaded by arguments involving the promotion or protection of his reputation. He wanted to do what he thought was right on this and almost every other issue, but in this case he was clearly told that doing what he thought was right would carry a high political price.

The next week saw some intensive internal debates among Carter and his senior advisers. The president, who sarcastically praised Brzezinski for his persistency in this matter, did not give ground.[37] During the same period in March there was also an intensive effort to keep the president's position on ERWs out of the press, since premature publicity would have disrupted the efforts to change Carter's mind or plan for an orderly cancellation announcement. Given the large number of officials in Washington and Europe who knew about the abrupt withdrawal of the carefully crafted North Atlantic Council statements on the neutron bomb, it is surprising that there were no major leaks in the immediate aftermath of Carter's return from St. Simons.

On March 27, just before leaving on an overseas trip to Africa and Latin America, Carter informed his staff that barring any changes in European willingness to publicly accept deployment, he would cancel ERWs. Deputy Secretary of State Warren Christopher was dispatched to London and to Bonn for a final round of talks with British and German officials. His instructions were to explore any last-minute changes in allied willingness to explicitly support deployment and, in the absence of such support, to discuss procedures for publicly announcing ERW cancellation. Immediately there-

37. Brzezinski, *Power and Principle*, 305.

after, West Germany's foreign minister, Hans-Dietrich Genscher, made a quick trip to Washington to consult with Carter on the same issues. When Christopher met with Schmidt in his home, the German leader spoke in an icily calm voice that failed to disguise his anger and frustration. Schmidt was apparently "stunned by Carter's decision" and found it incredible that the leader of the Western alliance would even contemplate cancellation of a controversial policy initiative that had gone this far.[38] Nevertheless, Schmidt refused to go beyond his established formula of accepting deployment only after arms control opportunities had been explored and only in conjunction with some other non-nuclear Continental NATO member—a condition that remained nearly impossible to meet.

While these last-minute consultations took place, the efforts to keep a lid on the neutron bomb story broke down, and press reports about the internal disputes between Carter and his senior foreign policy advisers made a successful resolution of Carter's differences with Schmidt and other European leaders even more difficult to achieve. On April 4, the day after the president returned from overseas and the day before Genscher began his meetings in Washington, the *New York Times* ran a front-page story by Richard Burt under the headline: "Aides Report Carter Bans Neutron Bomb: Some Seek Reversal."[39] The story provided an accurate account of Carter's plans to announce cancellation unless he received unlikely public commitments for deployment from London and Bonn. It also discussed the resistance to Carter's ERW position among the administration's senior foreign policy makers. The story was denied by the president, his press secretary, and officials at the Departments of Defense and State on the narrow ground that no final and official decision had yet been made. Premature revelation that cancellation was likely guaranteed that there would be no graceful way out of the ERW mess and added to the distrust and tensions in America's relations with its NATO allies.

In domestic politics the press reports about a pending neutron bomb cancellation brought forth a flood of congressional criticism. Leading Demo-

38. Christopher was accompanied by George Vest when he met with Schmidt. It was Vest who supplied the description of Schmidt's response to the deputy secretary. George Vest, telephone interview by author, April 18, 1995.

39. For detailed discussion of the *New York Times* article and speculation about its source and impact, see Wasserman, *The Neutron Bomb Controversy*, 120–21, and Whitman, "The Press and the Neutron Bomb," 190–95.

crats, including Senate majority leader Byrd and others who had worked hard to win approval for ERW funding the previous summer, urged the president to go forward with production of the new warheads. Byrd argued that a unilateral American cancellation would appear to be a surrender to the Soviet Union and would reduce the chances for Senate ratification of SALT II. Senators Charles Percy and Sam Nunn, respected Republican and Democratic members of the Foreign Relations and Armed Services committees, made public criticisms of the pending cancellation.[40] Newspaper commentary lambasted the administration for its inability to pursue a consistent policy and used the neutron bomb example as proof that the president, after nearly a year and a half in the White House, still did not know how Washington and the world worked.[41]

The final, and official, administration position on ERWs was announced on April 7, 1978. It was a decision to defer, rather than cancel, ERWs with a vague threat that further decisions about enhanced-radiation weaponry would be based on Soviet restraint in conventional and nuclear deployments in Europe. New warheads for the Lance missile were to be designed so that conversion to ERW technology at a later date could easily be accommodated. Research on ERW components would continue. Given what had proceeded, and the extent of the press coverage of internal administration decision making, this public announcement was widely seen as merely a face-saving substitute for outright cancellation. It turned out to be a bit more than that. Carter's inclination, as he indicated to Brzezinski early in May, was to leave the neutron bomb in limbo and not push for its eventual production.[42] But research and development did continue, and in August of 1981 President Reagan issued a unilateral American order to produce ERWs without any commitments concerning deployment. The weapons were built but never sent to Europe.

There was widespread media criticism of both the April 7 decision and

40. Wasserman, *The Neutron Bomb Controversy*, 123–24.

41. "The Mishandled Bomb," *New York Times*, April 6, 1978.

42. In a May 3 memo to the president, Brzezinski outlined three options for the implementation of the April 7 announcement. They were (1) prefer production, (2) prefer non-production, and (3) genuinely contingent on Soviet restraint. The president selected option 2. Zbigniew Brzezinski to the President, memorandum: "Enhanced Radiation Weapons," May 3, 1978, Zbigniew Brzezinski Collection, Box 22, Folder "Defense-Enhanced Radiation Warhead [3/78–8/78]," Carter Library.

the way the administration had handled the issue. Even Walter Pincus shamelessly joined the chorus of critics complaining about how Carter had responded to the crisis in alliance relations that his own reporting had helped to create.[43]

Following Carter's announced deferral of ERW production, the West German Bundestag debated the issue and narrowly endorsed the American decision. According to Brzezinski, Carter gave instructions after the April announcement that there were to be no recriminations, in statements on or off the record, against the United States' NATO allies. He particularly wanted to spare the West Germans from any criticism for their refusal to share public responsibility for the ERW decision. The president would take the blame himself.[44]

Conclusions

In the neutron bomb controversy, appearances and realities were often confused and distorted. Like a child walking past a wall of fun house mirrors, the same subject seemed to take on radically different shapes and sizes depending on the curves and contours of the surfaces from which it was viewed. For many in the press and public who automatically opposed the enhanced-radiation warhead, it was an entirely new and dangerously revolutionary development in the horrors of modern war. For the military specialists and nuclear strategists who recommended its production and deployment, the neutron bomb was a rather modest addition to NATO's large and varied nuclear arsenal. For students of the complicated and controversial relations between the United States and the Western European nations in matters of nuclear policy, it was a symbol of America's continued commitment to the alliance and a reminder of the substantial risks associated with a nuclear defense of NATO. Political leaders in Europe and the United States were invariably caught between experts who saw the new warheads and artillery shells as sensible and responsible improvements to alliance defensive capabilities and vocal critics in the press and parties of the left who saw the same weapons as immoral and reckless provocations to nuclear war. These two pictures, like two mirrors on a wall, stood side by side and could not easily be brought together.

43. Whitman, "The Press and the Neutron Bomb," 203–204.
44. Brzezinski, *Power and Principle*, 306.

The neutron bomb was the kind of issue for which politicians might have been well advised to choose up sides rather than seek a middle position. Yet both Carter and prominent leaders in the NATO alliance were reluctant to take a clear position for or against ERWs. The Europeans wanted the weapons, but without much of the controversy that would inevitably accompany them. Carter was predisposed against the new weapons, but was willing to go along with the recommendations of his defense and foreign policy experts if European leaders would take some of the responsibility they were trying to avoid. Across the Atlantic and within Washington, there were extensive consultations on matters related to the neutron bomb, but not enough effective communication of the president's reluctance to go ahead or the European preference for unilateral American action. Participants tended to see the issue in their own mirror and often failed to understand how it must have looked for others.

If perceptions of the character and importance of neutron bombs were often distorted, so were perceptions of how decisions were made within the Carter administration. From the outside the movement toward a neutron bomb decision makes Jimmy Carter look indecisive and weak. First he asked for money for ERWs without saying whether he would build them. When prospects for funding legislation became uncertain in the Senate, he gave assurances that producing ERWs would probably be in the national interest. When he finally said yes to the new warheads, it was a conditional yes that required political support from our principal NATO allies. When that support was not forthcoming, his advisers moved toward a compromise position without presidential objection. Just as that compromise was being prepared for public presentation, Carter backed off and insisted on his original formula of shared NATO responsibility in production and deployment decisions. The final rounds of alliance consultations were painful and embarrassing for all concerned and produced a vague threat to the Soviets and an indefinite postponement of production decisions about the new weapon system. That is the picture we see from the outside looking in.

But there is another way to view the same series of events. Looked at from within the administration, the president's position on ERWs appears to be reasonably consistent from August 1977 on. He agreed to go along with the neutron bomb if his proviso about allied support could be met. In March 1978, when Carter reasserted that position, he was anything but indecisive and weak. He was strong-willed, even bullheaded, in insisting that his original instructions be faithfully and fully carried out. In doing so, he went against the nearly unanimous advice of his senior advisers and accepted the substantial costs in domestic political reputation and alliance cohesion that clearly went along with his position.

Though it might be argued that Carter's position on ERWs remained fundamentally unchanged throughout the controversy, the public impression at that time, and since, has remained one of indecision and inept policy making. There are a number of reasons why a stubborn and consistent president gave the impression of being just the opposite. First of all, there was the nature of the president's position. It was genuinely ambivalent. Carter refused to take an absolute moral position against ERWs, though he did not like them; and he refused to cancel their production as long as the Pentagon and his foreign policy advisers insisted that they were important. Instead, he said at the outset and at the end of deliberations that he would approve the production of neutron warheads if the Europeans met his conditions and were willing to share the political burden of the unpopular decision. The Europeans, and particularly the West Germans, never met those conditions, and Carter refused to go it alone in making a production decision.

Despite this consistency, it was easy to portray Carter's position as indecisive, because his position on the ERW issue was not the same as that of his subordinates. Vance, Brown, and Brzezinski, all of whom had more experience than Carter with European nuclear issues, were willing to be flexible and vague about the details of an eventual deployment of ERWs in order to accommodate the domestic political realities of the United States' European allies. Carter was not. He failed, however, to make his position fully clear until late in the day to the public, to allied leaders, or even to his own staff. The administration did not, therefore, speak with one voice.

In mid-March 1978, Vance and Brzezinski—who were in full agreement on this issue—found themselves opposed by a determined president. Both Vance and Brzezinski admit that they sensed Carter's early discomfort with the neutron bomb, but neither believed that he would refuse to accept the March 1978 compromise position. Vance says that he was busy with other issues, particularly SALT, and never gave much time or attention to ERWs.[45] Brzezinski, who took a more active role in pushing for a resolution

45. Cyrus Vance, *Hard Choices: Four Critical Years in Managing America's Foreign Policy* (New York, 1983), 95.

of the matter, assumes more responsibility for misjudging the extent of Carter's doubts and for taking the alliance consultations beyond Carter's instructions. "In retrospect, it is obvious to me that Vance, Brown and I misread the President's intentions, and underestimated Schmidt's intransigence."[46] Brown has not published his memoirs, but presumably bears considerable responsibility for a decision that was being pressed by his department. The secretary of defense was also the most senior member of the administration with detailed knowledge about ERW technology when the first Pincus story appeared. An early effort to counter the exaggerations in the initial media coverage by a high-level official might have produced a less sensationalized public reaction to the new weapons.[47] Carter's major failing in the handling of the issue was his inability to impress upon his subordinates the need to follow fully and carefully his policy preferences on ERWs. Carter was not an indecisive leader in the neutron issue, but neither was he an effective one.

One issue in evaluating Carter's performance requires special attention. How did President Carter, renowned for his attention to detail, let his subordinates take the neutron bomb negotiations so far afield from what he wanted and expected? Like Vance, Carter was extremely busy with other issues, particularly the Senate ratification of the Panama Canal treaties, during the early months of 1978 when the compromise position on ERWs was developed in consultations with West Germany and other NATO members.[48] The president, even in the midst of his efforts to win ratification of the Panama Canal treaties, must have read reports about those consultations. He would have had no objection to the introduction of an arms control component to the forthcoming ERW decision, but might have missed the fact that the proposed two-year arms control delay was partially designed to allow the Europeans to escape immediate responsibility for deployment of the new weapons. Alternatively, he might have been following

46. Brzezinski, *Power and Principle*, 306.

47. Whitman speculates that this might have helped and reports that some in the Pentagon thought it best that the secretary ignore the Pincus story with the mistaken expectation that the absence of an official response would make the issue fade faster. Whitman, "The Press and the Neutron Bomb," 154–57.

48. Carter provides a long list of domestic and foreign policy issues he was trying to deal with at the same time he was deeply committed to the Panama ratification battle. The list does not include any mention of the neutron bomb negotiations. Carter, *Keeping Faith*, 171.

the progress of NATO negotiations carefully, and elected not to intervene when the U.S. position became more flexible than he wanted because he expected the negotiations to fail in any case.[49]

More than a busy schedule or an expectation of failure may, however, have been involved. As we have seen, Brzezinski reports that Carter had an aversion to dealing with the neutron bomb issue—an aversion that was unusual for a president who seemed to relish making hard, and often unpopular, foreign policy decisions. That aversion, rooted in Carter's deeply felt desire to reduce nuclear dangers rather than add to them, may have been so powerful that it distracted him from the kind of detailed monitoring he normally gave to important issues.

The president's resistance to ERWs was, in part, a reflection of his moral reservations about neutron warheads and his genuine desire to be associated with reductions in the dangers of nuclear war and the costs of the arms race. But his hesitancy to proceed with any production of neutron warheads may also have coincided with an accurate assessment of the difficulties that would accompany their deployment. President Carter did not want to waste money on a weapon that would never be stationed where it was most needed. Such a waste is exactly what happened in the Reagan administration. In 1978, judging whether or not neutron weapons would eventually be deployed in Europe was not an easy task.

From the beginning neutron bombs were magnets for bad publicity and fuel for political forces opposed to all nuclear weapons. As the issue developed, it became clear that the political aspects of ERW production and deployment were far more important than any military advantages they might have provided. The president's personal ambivalence to ERWs was widely shared in Europe, where public apprehension was apparently growing in strength early in 1978. It cannot be conclusively stated that the proposed course of action outlined in the March 18 memo from Vance, Brown, and Brzezinski would have led to the successful deployment of ERWs or to better alliance relations. It could equally have led to an earlier emergence of the European anti-nuclear mass movements witnessed in the early 1980s. In many ways neutron warheads would have been a much better issue for

49. This was suggested as a possibility by Brzezinski. Zbigniew Brzezinski, interview by author, February 17, 1995.

those movements than either cruise or Pershing II missiles. ERWs were not a response to Soviet nuclear deployments; they were clearly intended to be used very early in any European conventional war; and, of course, they did more of their killing with radiation. As a result, they were far more objectionable to European public opinion than the longer-range missiles that would counter the SS-20s.

Carter may have paid a high political price for his decision to postpone production of the neutron bomb, but a decision to proceed would also have had its costs, and those costs might have been even higher. There is no evidence to suggest that Carter was making these kinds of long-range political calculations. But his gut reaction to the neutron bomb may have been more in tune with emerging European public opinion than the more experienced and sophisticated reactions of his senior foreign policy advisers.

There is another aspect of Carter's position worth considering. His consistent refusal to force the new weapons on the alliance may well reflect a serious commitment to trilateralism and to a more mature alliance system based on genuine cooperation and an equitable distribution of alliance burdens. Though critics of the Carter administration tend to describe the Trilateral Commission as a sinister conspiracy or a job placement service for out-of-work foreign policy experts, it was actually an organization with a serious mission—the improvement of relations among the United States, Japan, and Europe based on greater understanding and respect for an emerging multipolar world. The commission was also Carter's first introduction to foreign affairs, and he may well have taken to heart the message that the United States needed to treat its major military and economic partners in a new and more equal fashion. In 1982, speaking with a group of political scientists, Carter explained his thinking about the neutron bomb issue:

> Habitually, historically might be a better word, the NATO alliance had worked on a premise that the military leaders would decide on a new weapon or a new strategy. The United States would take the public onus for their proposal and would, in effect go ahead with enough momentum so that some of the weaker European countries could do it ostensibly with reluctance, but under pressure from the United States. I thought that was ill-advised. . . . I didn't want the United

States to develop a weapon and then force it on the Europeans. I thought that time had passed.[50]

Unfortunately for Carter, taking a "trilateral" approach to nuclear decision making in NATO—against the advice of other former commission members Brzezinski, Vance, and Brown—did not automatically lead to a new era of better alliance relations. It did lead to greater care in dealing with these sensitive matters.

When it became clear that some NATO response to the Soviet deployment of SS-20 missiles was needed, a series of private alliance consultations produced the December 1979 two-track decision—scheduling the deployment of cruise and Pershing II missiles while simultaneously offering to conduct arms control negotiations with the Soviets on intermediate-range systems. Though the Reagan administration would have the task of implementing these policies, and would encounter many obstacles in doing so, the groundwork done in 1979 produced a united NATO front that held, against extensive public protest, a revived Soviet propaganda campaign, interalliance disputes over East-West trade and responses to the invasion of Afghanistan, and a temporary breakdown of all arms control negotiations with the Soviet Union. The eventual deployment of cruise and Pershing II missiles, and the subsequent INF Treaty, may well be the most significant legacies of the neutron bomb controversy.

There are additional legacies of perhaps broader importance for American foreign policy and for the NATO alliance. One of these involves the role of the media.[51] From the beginning this was a media-driven issue. It came to the fore because of a newspaper article, and the public response to the "killer warhead" was shaped by the early and misleading press coverage it received. Throughout the public commentary on the neutron bomb, it retained the name that Walter Pincus gave it along with the description of the new weapon as one that killed people and left buildings intact.[52] The name

---

50. White Burkett Miller Center of Public Affairs, University of Virginia, Project on the Carter Presidency, President Carter Session, November 29, 1982, p. 34.

51. For a detailed review of media coverage on this issue, see Whitman, "The Press and the Neutron Bomb," 145–216.

52. The Pentagon eventually tried, without much success, to get people to call the weapon the "reduced-blast warhead." The ombudsman for the *Washington Post* did succeed in convincing his editors and writers to drop the phrase "killer warhead," on the sensible grounds that warheads that kill are not exactly newsworthy. If the Pentagon ever developed

was wrong and the description was a gross oversimplification. Throughout the decision making, all the major administration moves were widely, though not always accurately, reported in the press. At critical stages in alliance deliberations and internal administration decision making, news reports about what was allegedly going on interfered with clear thinking and careful planning of the next policy step.

After the initial *Washington Post* stories, media interest in ERWs never really faded. As a result, there was constant competition among the major newspapers, magazines, and networks to stay on top of the story and to uncover the latest evidence of internal decision making. A parallel interest on the part of the European news media made it very difficult to conduct private consultations within the alliance. The neutron bomb issue illustrates all the classic problems of open diplomacy. Private deliberations became public headlines. Personal judgments became media gossip. And all the news reports, even those that were sensationalized or inaccurate, tended to have equal status with official government statements. An open administration in an open society conducting its relations with democratic allies is in constant danger of the kinds of problems that plagued the resolution of the neutron warhead issue. Because the issue was unanticipated and its full dimensions were originally underestimated, these natural problems were exacerbated.

It remains to be explained why the public and the media paid as much attention as they did to the neutron bomb issue. As a research or procurement budget item, neutron warheads were relatively insignificant.[53] As a modernization of existing nuclear forces, they were far less important than the subsequent modernization decisions involving cruise and Pershing II missiles. After leaving office and before the end of the cold war, Harold Brown suggested that short-range tactical nuclear weapons in Europe be eliminated altogether. They had marginal military value and were too vulnerable to preemptive attack to be worth keeping.[54]

Despite their questionable military significance, neutron warheads were

---

a warhead that did not kill, *that* should be put in the headlines. Whitman, "The Press and the Neutron Bomb," 162, 175.

53. According to one estimate, the total cost of the ERW program would have been between two billion and four billion dollars. Alton Frye, "Low Fuse on the Neutron Bomb," *Foreign Policy* no. 31 (summer 1978).

54. Harold Brown, *Thinking About National Security: Defense and Foreign Policy in a Dangerous World* (Boulder, Colo., 1983), 110.

the focus of widespread public concern. Something about a weapon that killed with radiation (even if it also killed with its reduced blast and heat) touched presidential and public consciences. Throughout the nuclear age the subject of radiation has been the source of intense, sometimes exaggerated, public fears and the focal point of much of the moral outrage engendered by nuclear weapons.[55] A silent and invisible force that attacks the body like a poison and leads to both immediate and long-term illnesses, producing some of its effects in future generations, is the stuff of which nuclear protest is easily made. The neutron bomb, like the environmental consequences of atmospheric nuclear testing, sparked a public outcry and made a minor military decision into a major political issue.

Finally, the fact that the weapons were intended for deployment in Europe guaranteed additional controversy. The permanent, and somewhat inconsistent, European cold war fears that nuclear weapons would be used in Europeans' own territory, leading to massive death and destruction, or not used, making possible another European conventional war and a different sort of death and destruction, complicated any decision making connected with ERWs. European nuclear security concerns were always difficult to satisfy. Presidents in the 1950s and 1960s were never able to convince Charles de Gaulle that France could depend on an American nuclear guarantee; and when President Kennedy tried to share nuclear responsibilities within the NATO alliance by proposing the creation of a multinational nuclear-equipped military force, his efforts failed.

Europe's split personality on nuclear issues was easily diagnosed, but difficult to cure. This may be because the Europeans during the cold war had a great deal to be split about. Though all nations in the nuclear age have reason to feel insecure, the front-line European states during the extended confrontation between NATO and the Warsaw Pact were more justified than the rest. They would have been the battlefield in a tactical or limited nuclear exchange or in a protracted conventional conflict that did not become a nuclear war. However remote the prospects for either of those alternatives may have been, they could not be eliminated, and the practical consequence, at least for the democracies in Europe, was powerful public sensitivity to all things nuclear. Dealing with that sensitivity was one of the most difficult issues faced by the cold war presidents. It was especially difficult for Jimmy Carter.

55. Mandelbaum, *The Nuclear Revolution*, 23–50.

6

ADVICE AND CONSENT
Senator DeConcini and the Panama Canal Treaties

At about the same time that the neutron bomb issue was reaching the point of final presidential decision, or indecision, the Senate was preparing to vote on the ratification of two new treaties that would completely alter the relationship between the United States and the small Central American nation of Panama. However difficult American dealings with Europeans may have been in the resolution of a controversial nuclear-alliance issue, there may well have been times when President Carter would have preferred meeting with a room full of angry NATO diplomats to meeting with one filled with U.S. senators still undecided about how they would vote on the Panama Canal treaties. In the final analysis, the Europeans, angry or not, would have to accept any reasonable nuclear policies dictated by an American president. Senators were, however, another matter. The Constitution gave them the task of providing advice and consent before any treaty negotiated by the chief executive could go into effect. In carrying out that task, senators were free to defy their nation's leader (and their party's leader, for that matter) if they so wished. One-third of their number, plus one, could undo more than a decade of negotiations by two Republican and two Democratic administrations working to produce an equitable resolution of long-standing differences between the United States and Panama.

Even a senator who voted with the administration on the canal issue could try the president's patience, aggravate the people of Panama, and nearly destroy the treaties.

The Treaties

In the 1976 presidential campaign the future of the Panama Canal was a major issue for Republicans and a controversy that Carter tried to avoid. American control over the canal, and the zone on either side of it, had been granted to the United States in perpetuity in a 1903 treaty negotiated under suspicious circumstances and forced on the newly independent nation of Panama. Three-quarters of a century later, the 1903 agreement was a source of mild embarrassment for American diplomats and deep resentment for the Panamanian people. In a world community that frowned on colonialism, and neo-colonialism, the treaty relationship between the United States and Panama was outdated; and the canal itself was highly vulnerable to acts of terrorism or sabotage that might someday be used by individuals, groups, or governments opposed to the permanent American presence in Panama.

Negotiations for a new treaty had begun in the Johnson administration after serious riots in and around the Canal Zone occurred in 1964. Those negotiations continued, off and on, under Nixon and Ford and appeared to be nearing completion when Secretary of State Henry Kissinger and Panamanian foreign minister Juan Tack agreed to a set of principles to be used in the drafting of a new treaty, which would transfer the canal and zone to Panama while protecting American security interests in the free movement of commercial and military vessels through the waterway. Those principles were effectively attacked by Ronald Reagan in his bid to take the Republican nomination away from the unelected Gerald Ford. The governor of California got cheers from his audiences in 1976 whenever he reminded them that we built the canal, "we paid for it, it's ours, and we should tell [the Panamanian leaders] Torrijos and company that we are going to keep it."[1]

Carter had no political incentive to get in the middle of a heated battle between Republican presidential candidates and was, in any case, somewhat surprised by the intensity of feeling this issue seemed to engender.[2] As a candidate he made only a few inconclusive statements about the future of the Panama Canal.[3] After the election, however, he quickly decided to pur-

1. Jules Witcover, *Marathon: The Pursuit of the Presidency, 1972–1976* (New York, 1977), 402.

2. Jimmy Carter, *Keeping Faith: Memoirs of a President*, (New York, 1982), 154–55.

3. He told one reporter that he "would not relinquish practical control of the Panama Canal Zone anytime in the foreseeable future," but he also endorsed the Kissinger-Tack

sue a treaty based on the Kissinger-Tack framework and made the negotiations with Panama the subject of his first administration-wide foreign policy review. Once he had studied the issue carefully, President Carter wanted to rectify the injustices in the U.S.-Panamanian relationship, even though there was a clear recognition from the outset that any new treaty with Panama would be politically controversial.[4] Such rectification, if it could be accomplished, would send a positive message to our Latin American neighbors, and to small nations throughout the world, that the United States was prepared to be forthright about past errors and fair in its international dealings in the future. Moreover, rewriting the relationship between the United States and Panama was the single best way to guarantee the long-term security of the canal in an age of rising nationalism in Central America. According to Brzezinski, the Panama Canal treaties for Jimmy Carter "represented the ideal fusion of morality and politics; he was doing something good for peace, responding to the passionate desires of a small nation, and yet helping the long-range U.S. national interest."[5]

Carter appointed Sol Linowitz, a businessman and expert on Latin American affairs, to join the senior American diplomat Ellsworth Bunker in negotiations with Panama. He instructed them to write a new treaty that would be "generous, fair and appropriate."[6] Roughly six months later, the negotiators had produced draft language for two new treaties. One, the Panama Canal Treaty, dealt in detail with the gradual transfer of control over the canal and zone to the Panamanians; the other agreement, officially titled the Treaty Concerning the Permanent Neutrality and Operation of the Panama Canal, assured international access to the waterway after it was transferred to Panama and recognized a continuing American interest in the commercial traffic and warships that used it.

The two treaties reflected the principal concerns of the two nations. For Panama, the essential element in the bargain was the renunciation of the

---

principles, which were incorporated into the 1976 Democratic Party platform. Sol M. Linowitz, *The Making of a Public Man: A Memoir* (Boston, 1985), 149.

4. Carter, *Keeping Faith*, 155. Among others, the First Lady advised Carter to postpone the Panama Canal until his second term. Rosalynn Carter, *First Lady from Plains* (New York, 1984), 155–56.

5. Zbigniew Brzezinski, *Power and Principle: Memoirs of the National Security Advisor 1977–1981* (New York, 1983), 137.

6. Linowitz, *The Making of a Public Man*, 152.

1903 treaty and the establishment of clear Panamanian control over the canal and zone. For the United States, there had to be a Panamanian acceptance of legitimate American involvement in the security of the canal before and after its transfer to Panama. Balancing these two somewhat contradictory positions required some delicate diplomacy. Absolute and arbitrary Panamanian control over the canal threatened vital American economic and military interests; permanent American rights with regard to its operation and safety offended Panamanian national dignity. The two sides reached agreement by compromising and avoiding the use of too much threatening or offensive language in the two treaties.

The announcement of the completed negotiations and the elaborately staged Washington signing ceremony, attended by most of the Western Hemisphere heads of state (though not by Anastasio Somoza), failed to win widespread public support for the new agreements. The applause line from Ronald Reagan's unsuccessful presidential campaign was still winning applause a year later and was typical of the rhetoric being used by conservative political organizations actively raising money and mobilizing citizens for a massive national campaign against the treaties. Though the new agreements were supported by former presidents Nixon and Ford and by Latin American and foreign policy experts in both political parties, they were never enthusiastically embraced by the American people.[7] Most citizens did not care very much about the future of the canal; and those who did care tended to have a passionate and patriotic reaction against surrendering a symbol of American greatness to a tiny Central American nation. In the same month that the treaty negotiations were completed, the administration's congressional liaison staff counted 11 senators opposed to the treaties and another 19 likely to vote against them.[8] Those were dangerously high numbers, only 4 votes away from the number needed to block ratification.

In the months that preceded and followed the final stage of negotiations with Panama, the administration organized its own national campaign to win support for the controversial treaties. Hamilton Jordan and his assis-

7. For a detailed review of public opinion on the Panama Canal issue, see George D. Moffett, *The Limits of Victory: The Ratification of the Panama Canal Treaties* (Ithaca, N.Y., 1985), 112–37.

8. The rest of the count was 33 positive, 24 leaning positive, and 13 undecided. Memorandum by Bob Thompson, 8/30/77, Staff Office Files, Chief of Staff (Jordan), Box 36, File "Panama Canal Treaty, 8/77 [2]," Carter Library.

tants in the White House prepared a strategic plan for the anticipated ratification battle.[9] The plan had a variety of elements. The president was to give televised speeches about the importance of establishing a new relationship with Panama. Those speeches, along with the media coverage of the Washington signing ceremony, would hopefully win some support for the treaties from the majority of citizens who were still largely uninformed about the issue. While waiting for public opinion to move in a favorable direction, senators would be encouraged to take trips to Panama, see the canal and zone for themselves, and hold their own private conversations with General Torrijos. Elaborate White House briefings would be held for community leaders in states whose senators had not yet announced how they would vote on the treaties.[10] Senior members of the administration, including the president, would speak at those briefings and lobby members of the Senate directly. A committee of prominent national figures, including conservative treaty supporters like William F. Buckley, Jr., and John Wayne, would be organized and encouraged to work for ratification. Administration officials at all ranks would be asked to accept speaking engagements wherever they could explain the treaties.[11] A particularly effective lobbying technique involved working with those American businesses that would be adversely affected if violence in Panama led to even a temporary closing of the canal.[12]

All of this activity helped to keep the ratification prospects for the treaties

9. For a sample of the detailed planning, see Hamilton Jordan to the President, memorandum: "Memorandum for the President from Hamilton Jordan," June 29, 1977, Staff Offices, Chief of Staff (Jordan), Box 34, File "Foreign Policy Issues—Work Plan, 6/77," Carter Library.

10. The ten states targeted in August 1977 were Tennessee, Georgia, Kentucky, Oklahoma, Florida, Pennsylvania, Arizona, Montana, New Hampshire, and New Mexico. Hamilton Jordan to President Carter, memorandum: "Status Report on Panama Canal Treaties," August 21, 1977, Staff Offices, Chief of Staff (Jordan), Box 36, File "Panama Canal Treaty, 8/77 [1]," Carter Library.

11. By one estimate, there were more than 1,500 personal appearances made by administration treaty supporters around the country. William L. Furlong and Margaret E. Scranton, *The Dynamics of Foreign Policymaking: The President, the Congress, and the 1977 Panama Canal Treaties* (Boulder, Colo., 1984), 141.

12. Landon Butler, Hamilton Jordan's assistant, played a significant role in developing the business-community strategy for treaty ratification. For a complete description of the White House efforts to win ratification, see Moffett, *The Limits of Victory*.

alive, but even with the carefully orchestrated efforts at public persuasion and legislative lobbying by the president and the senior members of his administration, Senate approval of the resolutions of ratification for the two treaties was by no means a sure thing. The knowledge that the treaties were opposed by a significant segment of the population, the high volume of mail and phone calls that treaty opponents were able to generate, and the anti-treaty advertising campaigns that were being financed by organizations like the American Conservative Union, made every member of the Senate wary of the forthcoming votes.

A crucial element in the administration strategy was making sure that the majority and minority leaders in the Senate, Robert Byrd of West Virginia and Howard Baker of Tennessee, would support the treaties and work for their ratification. Both senators held their judgment in reserve in the early months following the completion of negotiations and eventually decided that they would support the treaties if clarifying language could be added to the neutrality treaty—the first of the two agreements to come before the Senate. The need for such language became apparent when Panamanian officials trying to convince their citizens to vote in favor of the treaties in a plebiscite made public statements containing unacceptably narrow interpretations of American rights with regard to the military use and defense of the canal.

In a hastily scheduled meeting in Washington between Carter and General Omar Torrijos in mid-October 1977, the two national leaders prepared a statement interpreting the neutrality treaty in a much more balanced fashion than was evident in many of the unilateral statements made by Panamanian politicians. The joint Carter-Torrijos understanding issued on October 14, and later used as the basis for leadership amendments in the ratification process, repeated the basic compromise in the negotiations. It restated the right of both nations to defend the canal in clear language: "each of the two countries shall, in accordance with their respective constitutional processes, defend the Canal against any threat to the regime of neutrality, and consequently shall have the right to act against any aggression or threat directed against the Canal or against the peaceful transit of vessels through the Canal." The same statement also said that the American right to defend the canal against aggression or threat "does not mean, nor shall it be interpreted as, a right of intervention of the United States in the internal affairs of Panama. Any United States action will be directed at insuring that the Canal will remain open, secure and accessible, and it shall never be directed against the territorial integrity or political independence of Panama."[13]

There was an obvious tension between these two statements and an intentional ambiguity in the combination of them. The United States, under the neutrality treaty, would have the right to defend the canal against both "aggression," which implied the use of force by some nation or party outside Panama, and against any "threat" to the canal's operation, which was a much more open-ended term. Moreover, the United States could take action in connection with this provision of the treaty independently and through its own constitutional processes. That was the guarantee of permanent American involvement in the defense of the canal that the United States insisted on in the negotiations. It was combined in the Carter-Torrijos understanding, and the subsequent leadership amendments, with the reassurance that the United States would not use its legitimate rights to defend the canal in order to interfere in the internal affairs of Panama. That was the recognition of Panamanian sovereignty that Panama found fundamental.

What Carter and Torrijos agreed to, and what Baker and Byrd inserted into the neutrality treaty as their clarification of it, was not really new. It was a restatement of the core compromise between the two nations. That compromise included potentially contradictory American commitments to defend the canal against any future "threat" without violating Panama's "territorial integrity" or "political independence." It was obvious that if the threat to the canal came from within Panama, the United States might very well end up failing to fully respect Panamanian independence. The history of American foreign policy in Central America made the use of U.S. military forces to protect American interests in that part of the world a distinct possibility. That reality was clearly understood in Panama City and in Washington, but it could not be plainly stated in a document that any popular Panamanian leader could be expected to sign. A bit of ambiguity about the extent of America's rights to defend the canal was the best that diplomacy could produce.

That ambiguity satisfied both Panamanian and American negotiators. It

---

13. The joint statement also clarified that American warships in cases of national emergency would receive expedited passage through the canal. For the full text of the statement, see *Department of State Bulletin*, November 7, 1977, p. 631.

satisfied the leaders of the two nations. It satisfied the people of Panama, who voted to approve the treaties in their plebiscite a few weeks after the Carter-Torrijos statement was issued. It satisfied the two Senate party leaders who incorporated the Carter-Torrijos language into their amendments to the first of the two treaties to come up for ratification. Unfortunately, it did not satisfy the junior senator from Arizona.

The Undecided DeConcini

Dennis DeConcini was thirty-nine years old when he was elected to the Senate in the same year that Jimmy Carter was elected to the presidency. He had been a lawyer and prosecutor in Tucson for many years and a member of a politically active family in the state. He ran for the Senate as a moderate Democrat and won, even though Arizona went for Gerald Ford in the presidential polling. In fact, he won his race in 1976 by a much larger margin than Jimmy Carter won his on the national ticket.[14] In his early months on Capitol Hill, Senator DeConcini was noted for his intelligence and serious manner, but was not expected to steal the limelight from other newly elected senators in 1976, like the millionaires Howard Metzenbaum and John Heinz, the former Rhodes scholar and Indianapolis mayor Richard Lugar, the controversial college professor Samuel Hayakawa, who made a national reputation by criticizing student protesters, or the flamboyant Daniel Patrick Moynihan, already well known from his service to Democratic and Republican presidents.

DeConcini's vote for the Panama treaties might have been easily secured if the senior senator from Arizona, Barry Goldwater, had chosen to vote for them. In the summer of 1977, as the negotiations with Panama were nearing completion, the vote-counters in the White House classified Goldwater, along with Baker and a few other Republicans, as among those inclined to support the treaties.[15] Goldwater remained undeclared on the canal issue for some time after the negotiations were completed, but eventually announced that he would vote against both treaties.[16] That left DeConcini without po-

14. He beat his Republican opponent for an open seat in the Senate by 54 percent to 43 percent.

15. Jordan to the President, memorandum, June 29, 1977.

16. William J. Jorden says Goldwater made his announcement against the treaties in September 1977, William J. Jorden, *Panama Odyssey* (Austin, Texas, 1984), 532. Moffett says February 1978, Moffett, *The Limits of Victory*, 97.

litical cover in a conservative state where the new treaties were clearly un-popular. Some polls showed as many as 70 percent of the citizens of Arizona opposed to the treaties, and the mail arriving in DeConcini's office early in the ratification process was running 20 to 1 against the agreements.[17]

In November of 1977, Senator DeConcini sent President Carter a letter describing the results of polling in the western states on the question of the Panama Canal. He noted that even after several months of administration public relations efforts, a large majority of the people in Arizona, and in the other mountain states, were opposed to the treaties. The letter was an-swered twice, first by Hamilton Jordan, and later by Frank Moore, the head of the White House congressional liaison office. Moore passed along some more favorable national polling data and argued that when pollsters gave their respondents more information about the Panama agreements, the level of support tended to rise.[18] That answer gave little comfort to the Arizona Democrat, who remained on the administration's short list of undecided senators circulated early in December.[19]

Later that month DeConcini made his trip to Panama to see the canal and talk with Panamanian officials. He was not part of one of the large del-egations that had accompanied Byrd and Baker on their trips earlier in the fall or the bipartisan group from the Foreign Relations Committee. Instead, DeConcini went to Panama with a smaller group of colleagues in what ap-pears to have been the senatorial off season. He made the trip with his wife, mother, and younger brother. It happened that the DeConcini family was touring the canal and zone at the same time that Hamilton Jordan was meeting with Torrijos. Jordan had come to Panama to reassure the general that President Carter was still committed to the treaties and had placed the

17. Charles Kelly, "Most in State Know Little About Canal Pacts, but 70% Oppose Them," *Arizona Republic*, April 13, 1978. This and subsequent Arizona newspaper articles noted in this chapter can be found in the Senator Dennis DeConcini Papers, clippings scrap-books 1977–1978, Special Collections, University of Arizona Library, Tuscon, Ariz.

18. Hamilton Jordan to Dennis DeConcini, November 21, 1977, and Frank Moore to Dennis DeConcini, November 30, 1977, White House Central File, Subject File, Foreign Affairs, Box F018, File FO3-1/Panama Canal, Carter Library.

19. In addition to DeConcini, the other undecided Democrats were Lloyd Bentsen, Rob-ert Byrd, Thomas McIntyre, and Edward Zorinsky. Douglas Bennett, Jr., Robert Beckel, and Robert Thompson to Hamilton Jordan and Frank Moore, memorandum, December 1, 1977, White House Central File, Subject File, Foreign Affairs, Box FO15, File FO3-1/Pan-ama Canal 11/1/77–1/20/81, Carter Library.

ratification of them at the top of his agenda for the coming new year. As a result of the Jordan visit, the American ambassador to Panama did not pay much attention to DeConcini. "Fully occupied with the president's top assistant," wrote William J. Jorden, "I had less time than I wished to spend with the new arrival from Phoenix. There was no way that anyone could know that the mild-mannered young man would, three months later, do more to endanger the work of thirteen years of painstaking diplomacy than anyone else."[20]

When DeConcini met for two hours with Torrijos, he raised the delicate matter of what would happen if the canal were to be closed as a result of some future political upheaval or labor union dispute in Panama. The Panamanian leader responded that the United States would be free to intervene "if you come in at my request and on our side."[21] That was not the kind of answer that would reassure DeConcini or other Americans worried about internal threats to the canal's security, but it was a clear indication that DeConcini's question touched raw nerves in Panama. In most of his conversations with American senators, Torrijos was reportedly careful, charming, and charismatic. Those conversations, particularly with Byrd and Baker, played a key role in moving important legislators toward approval of the treaties.[22] Torrijos was evidently less tactful in his exchanges with a little-known and newly elected senator.

At the end of January 1978, the Senate Foreign Relations Committee completed its hearings on the Panama Canal treaties and sent them to the Senate floor with a favorable endorsement. The substantial majority in support of the treaties on the committee did not, however, reflect the sentiments of the Senate as a whole, where the 67 votes needed for ratification had not yet been found. The floor debate began in the second week of February. It lasted for more than a month and would, for the first time in Senate history, be broadcast without interruption or editing on National Public Radio. Rebroadcast with translation into Spanish allowed the people of Panama as well to hear the treaty deliberations. What was intended as an

20. Jorden, *Panama Odyssey,* 500.

21. General Omar Torrijos Herrera, quoted in Moffett, *The Limits of Victory,* 97.

22. White Burkett Miller Center of Public Affairs, University of Virginia, Project on the Carter Presidency, Robert Beckel Session, November 13, 1981, p. 15.

experiment in public education and a step toward the openness that would eventually lead to televised coverage of the House and Senate on C-Span was not altogether successful. To an American audience, the debate was often dull and tedious, with extended discussions of obscure procedural issues, apparently senseless quorum calls when there was no one readily available to address the small number of senators actually present for the debate, and nearly endless repetition of the basic arguments for and against the agreements.

To a Panamanian audience, the tedium was broken by treaty opponents who repeatedly and bluntly berated Panama's government, leaders, and citizens. There were frequent statements made about the lack of Panamanian competence to operate the canal in the future, the absence of stability in the Panamanian government, the alleged involvement of members of the Torrijos family in drug trafficking, the suspected ties between Torrijos and Castro, and the likelihood that the Panamanian people rather than moving toward greater democracy would eventually find themselves governed by a dictator much worse than General Torrijos. The general reportedly smashed several radios while listening to the Senate debate. In public, however, he and most other Panamanian government officials remained silent during the long and often painful broadcasts.[23]

Much of the Senate deliberation was devoted to proposed amendments to the neutrality treaty or amendments to the resolution of ratification for the treaty, which was technically the legislative business before the chamber. Amendments to the treaty itself would normally have required the concurrence of the Panamanian government and perhaps a second plebiscite by the Panamanian people to approve revisions to the official treaty language. Given the long and difficult negotiating history that had produced the two treaties, any reopening of the negotiations carried serious risks that the agreements reached in 1977 would be lost. In the end, only one set of changes to language in the text of the neutrality treaty was approved by the Senate. Those changes were in the leadership amendments introduced by Senators Byrd and Baker incorporating portions of the Carter-Torrijos understanding of October 14 into the body of the treaty. Because that language had been approved by Torrijos and was known to the Panamanian people

23. Jorden, *Panama Odyssey,* 521.

before they voted in their ratification process, it was determined that those changes would not require renegotiation or reconsideration in Panama.[24]

Amendments to the resolution of ratification—referred to as conditions, reservations, or understandings—usually involved Senate interpretations of treaty language, requirements for administration action, or statements of policy not covered in the agreements. These amendments, indirectly attached to the treaties, were binding under American and international law and would be delivered to Panama in the formal exchange of final treaty documents at the end of a successful ratification process. Conditions, reservations, and understandings (which had particular meanings to the Clerk of the Senate, but were used interchangeably, along with the word *amendment,* in the media and by many senators) did not necessarily require renegotiation or further approval in Panama. It was, however, clearly understood by treaty opponents in the Senate that if they could pass amendments unacceptable to Panama, whether they involved changes to treaty language or attachments to the resolutions of ratification, those unacceptable amendments would kill the treaties. Therefore, much of the floor debate involved "killer" amendments that the senators managing the resolutions of ratification, Frank Church and Paul Sarbanes (both Democrats on the Foreign Relations Committee), worked to defeat with simple majorities. The hard part for the floor managers and for the administration lobbyists was finding the two-thirds majority that would be needed for passage of the final amended resolutions of ratification.

Building that coalition of sixty-seven positive votes on two unpopular treaties involved a wide variety of lobbying techniques beyond the activities outlined in Jordan's original strategic plan. During the Senate debate, President Carter was actively engaged in the lobbying process and kept a notebook on his White House desk with regularly updated information about how each senator was expected to vote and what administration contacts with that senator had already taken place.[25] There were numerous phone

24. There was some confusion on this point. When it was proposed that the leadership language be added as a new free-standing article at the end of the treaty, the Panamanians objected, saying that such a change would require a new plebiscite. They had less objection to several additions to exiting articles using the Carter-Torrijos language. This confusion was an indication of communication problems between Senate supporters and Panamanian officials that continued throughout the ratification process. Jorden, *Panama Odyssey,* 506–509.

25. Carter, *Keeping Faith,* 164.

calls by the president to senators in both political parties and White House meetings with senators and the members of the House of Representatives, which would later have to pass legislation implementing the treaties. Particular attention was, of course, given to the undeclared senators, and some of the standard colloquial phrases used to characterize legislative-executive relations—arm-twisting, ego massaging, and horse-trading—could appropriately be applied to what was going on.

Carter mentions in his memoirs that he approved a desalination plant in Oklahoma that was important to Senator Henry Bellmon without ever knowing if that minor budget decision influenced the senator's eventual commitment to vote for the treaties. He made sure that Senator James Sasser of Tennessee was invited to a White House country music concert where "Tom T. Hall, Loretta Lynn, Conway Twitty, Larry Gatlin, and Charlie Daniels proved to be a lot of help to me and Panama."[26] He even took time to read a textbook on semantics that Senator Hayakawa had written when he was a Berkeley college professor and said, not altogether honestly, that he would enjoy meeting with the California senator on a regular basis to discuss administration foreign policy.[27] On March 14, the day before the first vote, the president had his secretaries of state and defense, former secretary of state Henry Kissinger, the generals and admirals on the Joint Chiefs of Staff, Hamilton Jordan, the vice president, Frank Moore, and the rest of the congressional liaison staff spend the entire day on Capitol Hill talking with individual senators. Rosalynn Carter called the wives of Senators Paul Hatfield of Montana and Edward Zorinsky of Nebraska to ask them if they could help to persuade their husbands to vote for the treaties, and in a slightly comic exchange of missed appointments and phone calls the president tried to speak directly with Senator Zorinsky during the last few days of Senate debate on the neutrality treaty.[28]

There were, of course, limits to how much special attention or explicit trading could go on before administration officials and senators would become embarrassed by accusations that votes were being bought and sold on a major foreign policy issue facing the nation. At one point in the ratification process, Senator James Abourezk of South Dakota, who voted with the

---

26. Ibid., 172–76.
27. Ibid., 177.
28. Ibid., 171.

administration on both treaties, tried to get a major change in energy policy and administration support for House and Senate rule changes that would open up conference committee procedures on energy legislation. Administration officials could not do anything about congressional rules and refused to make a significant change in the energy legislation they were promoting.[29] The White House did, however, announce plans to purchase $250 million worth of surplus copper for the national strategic stockpile, a move which gave a boost to a hard-hit mining industry in a number of western states, including Arizona.[30] Senator Herman Talmadge of Georgia got some last-minute support for some farm policy legislation that he was hoping to get through the Agriculture Committee, though President Carter believes that Talmadge's vote for the treaties was actually motivated by his desire to make sure that a fellow Georgian, and the first ever to serve in the White House, did not suffer a major political defeat.[31] For a time during the ratification battle, Senator Moynihan complained that he had hurt the state of New York by announcing his intention to vote for the treaties too early in the process, while Senator Dole, a consistent opponent of the agreements, joked that he was holding out for a new naval base in Kansas.[32]

A different, and perhaps more legitimate, kind of bargaining was also going on in the early months of 1978. A number of senators, including Dennis DeConcini, wanted administration support for amendments to the treaties, or to the resolutions of ratification, that would demonstrate to their constituents that they had been important players in the advice-and-consent process and had made their decision to vote for the treaties only after the agreements had been improved. These "improvements" needed to be sufficiently substantive to justify the controversial votes that the legislators were being asked to make, but not substantive enough to trigger renegotiation or outright Panamanian renunciation of the agreements. The administration

29. Ibid., 175.

30. There were press reports that this government purchase of copper was important in DeConcini's vote for the canal treaties, but DeConcini vigorously denied a connection and accurately pointed out that the whole Arizona legislative delegation, from Goldwater to Mo Udall, was lobbying for aid to copper miners in 1977. Charles Pine, "Sen. DeConcini Says No Deals Were Made," *Yuma Daily Sun,* May 2, 1978.

31. Jorden, *Panama Odyssey,* 530; and Carter, *Keeping Faith,* 170.

32. Thomas M. Franck and Edward Weisband, *Foreign Policy by Congress* (New York, 1979), 278.

might be able to accept a few "wounding" amendments, but had to avoid the "killer" variety. Sometimes it was hard to tell the difference.

DeConcini's Condition

DeConcini and his staff had a number of ideas for improvements to the neutrality treaty that the senator might sponsor. For a time, the negotiations between DeConcini and the administration focused on whether he would be allowed to offer an administration-approved amendment to the treaty text, like the leadership amendments that Baker and Byrd sponsored, or whether he would have to settle for an amendment to the resolution of ratification. When the State Department resisted any changes to treaty language beyond the leadership amendments for fear that new negotiations or voting in Panama would go badly, DeConcini insisted on introducing a serious amendment to the resolution of ratification for the neutrality treaty.

One idea he had been discussing for some time involved a subject not fully addressed in the treaties. Under the Panama Canal Treaty, all U.S. military facilities in Panama were to be turned over to the Panamanians prior to the end of the century; under the treaty concerning neutrality, the United States would have responsibilities and rights to defend the canal after all of those American bases had been abandoned. Those responsibilities would obviously be easier to fulfill if there was a continuing U.S. military presence near the canal, but the removal of U.S. forces from Panama was also an important aspect of the Panamanian effort to reestablish full control over its own territory. Several of the killer amendments proposed by treaty opponents Jesse Helms and James Allen dealt with this issue and included unacceptable extensions of a U.S. military presence in Panama. DeConcini considered an amendment to extend limited U.S. basing rights in Panama for a five-year period at the beginning of the twenty-first century, but that too was likely to be rejected by Panamanians and would, in any case, only have postponed the required American military departure from Panama. A different version of the same idea was also discussed. An amendment to the resolution of ratification might stipulate that nothing in the two treaties would prohibit the United States and Panama from reaching a future mutual arrangement about the stationing of U.S. forces in Panama. That modest clarification was eventually sponsored jointly by Senators Nunn and Talmadge, two Georgia legislators who, like DeConcini, wanted to be associated with an improvement to the agreements.

DeConcini supported the Nunn-Talmadge amendment and introduced another amendment that changed the formula for U.S. payments to Panama in the event that revenues from operation of the canal fell below expectations prior to the transfer. He also supported changes in the provisions regarding the possible construction of a second canal in Central America. None of these changes attracted much attention in Panama or in the United States, and Senator DeConcini is now remembered for an amendment to the resolution of ratification that dealt with a much more sensitive subject.

As the first Senate vote approached, DeConcini pushed for a clarification of the intentionally vague language about what the United States would be permitted to do if the canal were ever threatened by internal political upheavals. He wanted to state plainly that American troops could be sent into Panama to reopen the canal if it were closed by labor unrest, student riots, or other internal political disruptions. This was the concern he had raised with Torrijos in Panama when the Panamanian general dismissively suggested that American interventions in such cases could only take place at his invitation and when American troops were fighting on his side. A general American right to defend the canal already existed in the treaty language and the leadership amendments giving the United States the ability to respond, in accordance with its own "constitutional processes," to any "threat" posed to the canal. But that right had been combined with an explicit American promise not to use any treaty provisions as an excuse for intervention in the internal affairs of Panama and had been carefully worded to minimize offense to Panamanian nationalism that would naturally accompany any acknowledgment of an American right to take independent military action on Panamanian territory. On this, one of the most cautiously phrased compromises in the agreements, Senator DeConcini wished to make his mark.

On February 9, the day after floor debate began, DeConcini, together with Senator Wendell Ford of Kentucky, submitted an amendment to the neutrality treaty. It was one of many submitted by senators hostile and sympathetic to the agreements that might or might not be called up for debate on the floor.[33] In its first version, the DeConcini amendment said that "if the Canal is closed, or its operations are interfered with, the United States

33. In all, 192 amendments were filed and 88 were voted on during the course of ratification.

of America shall have the right to take such steps as it deems necessary to reopen the Canal or restore the operations of the Canal, as the case may be."[34] That language might have been more acceptable to Panama than some of the subsequent versions that DeConcini put forward on this issue, but because it was intended to be an amendment to the neutrality treaty, it failed to win administration endorsement.

When the senator agreed to attach his amendment to the resolution of ratification, the central issue became how that amendment would be worded. Administration negotiations with Senator DeConcini were handled primarily by Deputy Secretary of State Warren Christopher, who had been designated by Secretary Vance to serve as the senior department official in the most sensitive congressional liaison matters related to the treaties. During the week before the first scheduled Senate vote, Christopher, along with Vice President Mondale and members of the congressional liaison staff, met repeatedly with DeConcini and other undecided senators on Capitol Hill.[35] At that time, DeConcini was still insisting on an extension of U.S. basing rights in Panama and on language that would specify what would happen if the "threat" to the canal turned out to come from internal Panamanian political events. Christopher did not reject the possibility of an amendment dealing with internal threats to the canal, but did ask if he could take a few days to redraft what DeConcini was proposing on the possible use of U.S. military force in Panama.[36]

In the revised Christopher version, all the specific references to strikes and civil unrest in Panama were deleted, as was a prepositional phrase about the use of military force "in Panama." DeConcini accepted some of the Christopher deletions, but when he was advised by his staff that the State Department changes amounted to a "gutting" of his amendment, the senator decided that he would have to retain his prepositional phrase.[37] The

34. DeConcini amendment, quoted in Jorden, *Panama Odyssey,* 520.

35. Jorden reports that the meeting took place on March 9. Jorden, *Panama Odyssey,* 530–31. Moffett says the meeting was on Friday, March 10. Moffett, *The Limits of Victory,* 98. There may well have been meetings on both days, in preparation for and as follow-up to DeConcini's meeting on the afternoon of the 9th with President Carter.

36. Ambassador Jorden criticizes Christopher for failing to attack DeConcini's proposals frontally and for not telling him that "if he persisted in his arrogant approach, the treaties were going to fail and the consequences . . . would be laid directly on his doorstep." Jorden, *Panama Odyssey,* 533.

37. Moffett, *The Limits of Victory,* 98.

amendment, technically a condition to the resolution of ratification when it was finally brought to the Senate floor, said that "if the Canal is closed, or its operations are interfered with, the United States of America and the Republic of Panama shall each independently have the right to take such steps as it deems necessary in accordance with its constitutional processes, including the use of military force in Panama, to reopen the Canal or restore the operations of the Canal, as the case may be."[38] In subsequent conversations on the day before the first Senate vote, Christopher again tried to get DeConcini to drop the phrase "in Panama" from his pending condition, but the senator refused.[39]

It may be hard this far removed from the events in March of 1978 to fully grasp how this single prepositional phrase came to acquire major diplomatic significance. The canal was, after all, located "in Panama," and the already accepted treaty language, which included a U.S. right to defend the canal against any threat, logically meant that American military forces might be called upon to defend the canal in the country in which it was physically located. Moreover, a realistic assessment of the power relationship between the two countries and a mere cursory review of the history of American foreign policy in Central America suggested that the United States could, and probably would, use force to protect its national interests in the region.

In a White House meeting with political leaders in the fall of 1977, Brzezinski had been blunt on this subject. Asked what the United States would do if, after the year 2000, a Panamanian government arbitrarily announced that the canal was being closed for repairs, the national security adviser promptly replied that the United States would go in and announce that the Panamanian government was being closed for repairs.[40] It was, of course, one thing to say that in a private White House meeting and quite another to incorporate that idea in formal treaty language. The neutrality treaty, with the leadership amendments, allowed for such American action, but DeConcini wanted to say so in plainer language.

That language was offensive to Panamanians. Moreover, it came up at the end of weeks of vituperative Senate debate. After repeated insults to their nation, Panamanians may have been even less willing to accept plain

38. *Department of State Bulletin,* vol. 78, no. 2014 (May 1978), p. 53.
39. Jorden, *Panama Odyssey,* 545.
40. Brzezinski, *Power and Principle,* 156.

speaking about the realities of international politics in the hemisphere than they were at other times. Near the end of a long and painful public debate, the Panamanians were primed for an explosion, and Senator DeConcini was playing with matches.

In addition to his meetings with Deputy Secretary Christopher, DeConcini had two highly publicized meetings in the White House with President Carter. At the first, on March 9, the president asked the senator to abandon his demands to sponsor an administration-endorsed amendment to the treaty language.[41] At the second, on March 15, the day before the Senate was to vote on the neutrality treaty, DeConcini asked for administration support for his condition involving the possible use of American military forces in Panama. President Carter reportedly turned to Christopher and asked if the administration could live with that language. The deputy secretary replied that it would cause some problems in Panama, "but nothing we can't handle."[42] The president then endorsed the amendment and accepted the senator's promise to vote for the neutrality treaty.

Carter reports in his memoirs that at the time of his first meeting with DeConcini, on March 9, he did not fully understand how difficult the senator's language on using U.S. military force in Panama would turn out to be.[43] He may have heard more on that subject before his second meeting with DeConcini, but even if he did realize how offensive this language would be in Panama, he also understood that on the day before the first Senate vote the sixty-seven supporters for ratification had not yet been secured. In a memo from Frank Moore about the second scheduled presidential meeting with DeConcini, the director of the congressional liaison staff was unequivocal. "Without Senator DeConcini we cannot win."[44]

Even with DeConcini, the fate of the treaties was uncertain. On the weekend before his second meeting with the Arizona senator, Carter began

41. Bob Thompson memorandum to Frank Moore, "Additional Talking Points for Senator DeConcini," March 9, 1978; President's Diary and Appointments, March 9, 1978; Carter Library.

42. Warren Christopher, quoted in *Newsweek,* April 24, 1978, p. 27.

43. Carter, *Keeping Faith,* 169–70. Moffett quotes this passage about the president's thinking on the 9th as if it remained his thinking on the 15th. Moffett, *The Limits of Victory,* 100.

44. Frank Moore to the President, memorandum: "Meeting with Senator DeConcini," March 14, 1978; President's Diary and Appointments, March 15, 1978; Carter Library.

calling a list of senators who were declared opponents to the treaties, including Barry Goldwater, hoping to convince one or two of them to change at the last minute with the argument that the reputation of the country and the institution of the presidency would be in serious jeopardy if the treaties were lost.[45] At the time Carter met with DeConcini on March 15, there were reportedly two other undecided senators explicitly tying their votes to administration approval of the senator's condition.[46] That meant that a six-vote swing was in the balance when Carter asked Christopher if the De-Concini language was acceptable. At that point, saying no to DeConcini meant losing the treaties; saying yes meant only that the administration still had a chance for victory. All of this put the president in a weak bargaining position, and it is not clear whether Christopher's judgment that the administration could handle the DeConcini language was an underestimation of the problems that the amendment would create in Panama or an accurate estimate of the negligible prospects for ratification without a concession to the senator from Arizona. It was probably a bit of both.[47]

During the last week of desperate negotiations on Capitol Hill, the Panamanian ambassador to the United States, Gabriel Lewis, and the U.S. ambassador to Panama, William Jorden, were both sending signals that the DeConcini amendment would not be acceptable in Panama.[48] Torrijos was furious about the DeConcini language and began talking about going on national radio and television to denounce the changes being introduced by the Senate, call for a new plebiscite, and recommend rejection of the revised treaties. There were also reports that passage of the DeConcini condition and their denunciation in Panama could cause new riots in Panama, much larger than those that took place in 1964, and provide evidence of exactly

45. Carter, *Keeping Faith,* 171.

46. Paul Hatfield, the newly appointed senator from Montana, said on the Senate floor that his vote would depend on passage of the DeConcini condition, and Kaneaster Hodges of Nebraska may have been in the same position.

47. Jorden, reporting on the basis of interviews with Christopher after the fact, argues that the deputy secretary may have misread the messages being sent to Washington from Panama City, confusing the embassy advice on future negotiated military bases in Panama (which the ambassador reported might be acceptable) and the embassy conclusion on the DeConcini condition (namely, that it would be rejected in Panama). Jorden, *Panama Odyssey,* 540.

48. Jorden, *Panama Odyssey,* 537–38.

the kind of political instability that treaty opponents had predicted and that DeConcini had been trying to address.[49]

As this information reached the White House, both Hamilton Jordan and President Carter called General Torrijos and made personal appeals for more time to deal with the consequences of the DeConcini condition. Jordan, who had developed a close personal relationship with the Panamanian leader, was reportedly crucial in persuading him to postpone any public denunciations of DeConcini.[50] Carter, before calling Torrijos, sent him an urgent written message just after he concluded his March 15 meeting with DeConcini. The president acknowledged that "the long public discussion of the Treaties in the United States has involved difficulties for you and your country"—an understatement—and warned that just prior to the vote the Senate "will almost certainly attach a number of reservations, conditions or understandings reflecting certain of its concerns. We have made every effort and have been successful to date in ensuring that these will be consistent with the general purposes of our two countries as parties to the Treaty. I hope you will examine them in this light."[51] This was rather diplomatic language for describing the DeConcini condition and requesting Panamanian patience in considering it. Torrijos replied on the same day in less guarded language. He agreed to wait until both treaties were ratified before judging the significance of the Senate amendments to the resolutions of ratification but warned that "the Panamanian people would not accept words, improperly placed commas, or ambiguous phrases which have as purpose or meaning the occupation in perpetuity disguised as neutrality or an intervention in its internal affairs." The letter praised Carter's "high morality and honesty" and expressed faith that the "men of integrity and righteousness of your Senate" would do the right thing.[52]

In the White House, even after the meeting with DeConcini and the communications with Torrijos, there remained some question about whether there would be enough senators willing to do the right thing. The

49. Ibid., 542.

50. Project on the Carter Presidency, Robert Beckel Session, 16. Jorden believes it was Carter's call that was crucial in the Torrijos decision not to make public denunciations of the DeConcini condition. Jorden, *Panama Odyssey,* 544.

51. Jimmy Carter to General Omar Torrijos, March 15, 1978, Moffett Collection, Box 6, File "Congressional," Carter Library.

52. Ibid.

uncertainty about the final vote count meant that it was nearly impossible to respond to the belated recognition that the DeConcini language was producing a crisis in Panama. An attempt to add an additional amendment to the resolution of ratification which would reiterate America's commitment to non-intervention and partially offset the DeConcini condition failed. Senate leaders advised the administration against such an amendment on the grounds that the coalition of treaty supporters was far too fragile to sustain any last-minute changes in floor strategy.[53] If DeConcini's amendment created problems in Panama, those problems would have to be addressed in the debate over the second treaty.

And so the stage was set for the final round of reservations, conditions, and understandings and then the vote on the amended resolution of ratification. As the names of senators were called in alphabetical order, Senator Byrd withheld his vote so that he could cast the sixty-seventh and decisive yea near the end of the tally. As the count in favor of ratification became clear, Senator Howard Cannon, listed in most predictions as a treaty opponent, chose to vote for the agreements as a courtesy to his fellow senators. With Cannon's sixty-eighth vote, no single senator could be pointed out in forthcoming elections as the one responsible for passage of the controversial agreement.[54]

The reception in the White House was a muted sense of triumph. Victory against long odds had been achieved, but only a partial victory. The second treaty still needed ratification, and the negative reaction in Panama was almost as serious as the diplomats in Washington and Panama City had warned. Protests were held outside the U.S. embassy, and President Carter was hung in effigy in the Panamanian capital. Torrijos did not publicly denounce the treaties, but early in April his government informed the member states of the United Nations that the DeConcini condition was a violation of the UN Charter and the treaty creating the Organization of American States. Both of those documents contained clear non-intervention clauses. As the Senate moved toward a vote on the Panama Canal Treaty, attention was focused on efforts to strengthen the existing language on non-intervention in the two agreements. Of course, this had to be done without alienating Dennis DeConcini or any of the other senators who had voted for the first treaty.

53. Moffett, *The Limits of Victory,* 100.
54. Franck and Weisband, *Foreign Policy by Congress,* 281.

Senator Abourezk was still worried about energy legislation; Senator Hayakawa was displeased with the general direction of Carter foreign policy and the handling of the neutron bomb issue; and a new group of senators, including the unexpected administration supporter Senator Cannon, wanted their own amendments to the second resolution of ratification in order to put a personal stamp on the treaty process. Liberal senators, who had been in favor of the treaties all along, were expressing sympathy for the Panamanian protests against DeConcini's interventionist language, and moderates like Howard Baker were surprised by the level of Panamanian discontent against the Arizona senator's contribution to the neutrality treaty debate. All of these legislative concerns had to be carefully addressed, but they were secondary to the ongoing negotiations with DeConcini.

On March 22, 1978, the president sent letters to all the senators who had voted for the neutrality agreement. They were identical form letters, and to make them more personal, Carter added a handwritten note at the bottom of each one usually praising the leadership, courage, and statesmanship that a particular senator had shown on this issue or recalling some incident in the long ratification process. The notes varied from letter to letter and suggest that the president gave some time and attention to make sure that they would be read as genuine expressions of his appreciation. The letter to Senator DeConcini was the only one out of sixty-eight to which President Carter did not add a personal note.[55] He may not have known exactly what to say to the junior senator from Arizona who had both saved and endangered the treaties.

In the period just before and immediately after the first treaty vote, DeConcini became a national media celebrity and the target for much of the intense emotional reaction that the canal treaties tended to generate. For a few weeks he was a guest on the important weekly news programs and gave interviews to the network anchors. On one visit to Arizona he held a meeting with constituents in which journalists and camera crew members outnumbered the Arizona citizens.[56] But while his sponsorship of the most controversial amendment to the neutrality agreement was attracting national attention, it did not do much to help with treaty opponents in his home

55. White House Central File, Subject File, Foreign Affairs, Box FO19, Folder "FO3-1/ Panama Canal 3/22/78–4/4/78," Carter Library.

56. "Sen. DeConcini Visits Valley," *Casa Grande Dispatch,* March 31, 1978.

state. They began organizing a recall campaign almost immediately after the first treaty vote and flooded his office with mail and phone calls criticizing his decision to support the treaties. Some of the phone calls included death threats.[57] In Washington, treaty supporters were almost as critical of DeConcini as the treaty opponents were. The *Washington Post* printed two negative editorials, calling the Arizona senator a "lightweight" who was "ludicrous and irresponsible and hopelessly out of his depth."[58] The editors of *Newsweek* headlined their DeConcini story "Dennis the Menace."[59] The junior senator from Arizona seemed to deal reasonably well with the attention and pressures his new notoriety was producing, though he did complain at one point that "I can't go to Panama and I can't go home."[60] It was lonely in the limelight.

As the extent of opposition to the DeConcini amendment in Panama became apparent, Robert Pastor, the Latin American specialist on the National Security Council, wrote Brzezinski a memo warning that some senators were beginning to believe that the Panamanians wanted to scuttle the treaties, when in fact all that Torrijos wanted was some language in the second ratification "which makes a self-evident point: that the treaties are consistent with the U.N. and the O.A.S. Charter." Pastor proposed that Carter call DeConcini, explain that the Panamanians were clearly misinterpreting his condition which the senator had never intended as a violation of the UN or OAS charters, and suggest that DeConcini sponsor a reiteration of our non-intervention commitment.[61] When Pastor's memo was forwarded to Hamilton Jordan, Jordan sent Brzezinski a brief handwritten reply saying that a meeting between the president and DeConcini was being planned and that the administration was already proceeding along the lines that Pastor suggested. Nevertheless, Jordan added, the situation "is very precarious—like it or not, DeConcini holds the fate of the treaties in his hands."[62]

57. "DeConcini Death Threats," *Tempe Daily News,* April 19, 1978.

58. Editorials, *Washington Post,* April 9, 13, 1978.

59. *Newsweek,* April 24, 1978, pp. 28–29.

60. "DeConcini Caught in Middle Over His Canal Treaty Vote," *Tucson Daily Citizen,* March 31, 1978.

61. Robert Pastor to Zbigniew Brzezinski, memorandum: "Getting the Panama Debate Back on Track," April 10, 1978, White House Central File, Subject File, Box FO19, Folder "FO3-1/Panama Canal 4/5/78–4/27/78," Carter Library.

62. Ibid., handwritten note on cover sheet.

The scheduled meeting between DeConcini and President Carter did not take place. It was canceled when the senator and Christopher failed to agree on non-intervention language that could be added to the second resolution of ratification to temper Panamanian complaints about the original DeConcini amendment. As the vote on the second treaty approached, the principal negotiations with the Arizona senator were done by Senate leaders rather than administration officials. Senator Byrd and other senior senators worked on the wording for an amendment to the second resolution of ratification that would satisfy both the Panamanians and DeConcini. In these negotiations the Panamanian government was represented by its own well-connected American negotiator, William D. Rogers, a friend of Ambassador Lewis and a former State Department official with extensive Latin American experience. In this process DeConcini's Senate colleagues reportedly put considerable pressure on him to compromise. According to a memo prepared for the president on March 20 by the congressional liaison team, "Senator DeConcini has hurt himself badly with his colleagues. Many see his amendment as pure political opportunism on an issue where the stakes are dangerously high."[63] Pressure on DeConcini was also coming from labor leaders in Arizona, who had supported his 1976 election.[64] The combination of public and private pressures convinced DeConcini to accept a watering down of his original contribution to the ratification debate. He made public statements that he had never intended his condition to the neutrality treaty to establish an American right to intervene in Panama, that he had never used the word "intervention," and that the new amendment generally restating America's commitment to the principle of non-intervention would receive his support.[65]

The vote on the second treaty took place on April 18, and though there were apprehensions about possible defections, it turned out to be identical to the vote on the first, 68–32. All of the senators, including DeConcini, who supported the Neutrality Treaty also voted for the Panama Canal Treaty. The DeConcini condition was balanced by an amendment to the resolution

63. Frank Moore, Bob Beckel, Bob Thompson to the President, memorandum: "Re: Panama Treaty—Status," March 20, 1978, George D. Moffett Collection, Box 6, File "Congressional," Carter Library.

64. Roger Hedges, "With Vote, DeConcini Hopes for Some Peace," *Tucson Daily Citizen,* April 18, 1978.

65. Diane Johnsen, "Rift Healed on Canal Pact," *Arizona Daily Star,* April 18, 1978.

of ratification for the Panama Canal Treaty which repeated the American commitment not to intervene in the "internal affairs of Panama" or interfere with "its political independence or sovereign integrity" in the course of defending the canal.[66] It could be argued that neither DeConcini's amendment nor the one designed to balance it made a significant addition to the negotiated treaty language. Neither amendment made some future intervention by the United States in Panama, such as the one that occurred in the Bush administration, more or less likely. Together they focused attention on the compromise at the core of the agreements and helped to demonstrate how fragile the treaties were in both of the nations that made them.

Conclusions

For President Carter, ratification of the Panama Canal treaties was one of the most daunting tasks he faced during his four years in office. At a press conference on March 17, the day before the first Senate vote, he called the ratification effort the "most difficult political problem that I have ever faced." The assembled reporters laughed when he went on to say that "I think I would almost equate it with the difficulty of being elected President."[67] For a presidential candidate who entered the 1976 race with no national base, limited financial resources, and negligible name recognition, that comparison, even if it was partly in jest, was telling.

The successful ratification of the two new agreements between Panama and the United States was a remarkable political accomplishment. Sixty-eight senators voted for treaties that were strongly opposed by a significant portion of their constituents; and those constituents clearly demonstrated that they were well organized, politically active, and willing to make Panama an issue in the next election. Though some public opinion polls showed that treaty opponents were in the minority nationwide, they were a vocal and vociferous minority of the sort that professional politicians customarily respect. There was no comparable organizational clout or public passion among the citizens who supported the treaties. As a result, voting for the Panama Canal resolutions of ratification was known to be politically dan-

66. Resolution of Ratification for the Panama Canal Treaty, quoted in "Senate Backs Turning Over Canal to Panama," *Congressional Quarterly Review,* April 22, 1978, p. 952.

67. *Public Papers of the Presidents of the United States, Jimmy Carter 1978* (Washington, D.C., 1979), 520.

gerous. John F. Kennedy's popular 1957 book, *Profiles in Courage*, described a number of occasions in the history of the Congress when individual legislators took principled but unpopular stands. There are many such cases, but far fewer instances where two-thirds of the Senate membership simultaneously took substantial political risks in voting for a controversial treaty ratification.[68]

The senators who took those risks were persuaded to do so by a very elaborate legislative lobbying campaign. That campaign, coordinated by a White House task force, included the series of Washington briefings for business and community leaders from states that were crucial in the hoped-for Senate coalition. Those briefings did not involve the president going over the heads of his legislative enemies. Instead, they were a way for the administration to help their friends on Capitol Hill by offering coveted invitations to the White House for the influential supporters of a particular member of the Senate. The briefing sessions were so successful that they became a regular part of administration efforts to promote both domestic and foreign policy initiatives. Anne Wexler's Office of Public Liaison in the White House institutionalized this practice, which has been used in subsequent administrations.

The targeting of the businesses that would be hurt if the canal were ever closed was also an extremely effective technique for putting pressure on reluctant senators. It was widely understood in Washington that defending the canal against a hostile Panamanian population would be a very costly and complicated mission. The Pentagon estimated that it would take 100,000 troops to carry out such a defense and that even a force that large might not be able to prevent all acts of sabotage or terrorism. As a result, there was a real possibility that killing the treaties in the Senate would unleash the kind of government-sponsored or government-condoned attacks on the canal that would have closed it. Torrijos confirmed those fears in some of the comments he made after the ratification of the second treaty.[69] In other words, the kind of domestic threats to the canal that Senator De-Concini was concerned about were very real possibilities. But ironically, the

68. Of the twenty senators who voted for ratification and were up for reelection in 1978, only seven were elected to another term. Even in 1980, treaty supporters were defeated in large numbers, and of course Ronald Reagan (and not Howard Baker or Gerald Ford) won the Republican nomination and went on to defeat Jimmy Carter.

69. Jorden, *Panama Odyssey*, 623–26.

best defense against such attacks was to be found in completing the negotiations that began under President Johnson and removing from U.S.-Panamanian relations the major grievance that had produced tensions between the two nations for decades. As George Moffett has pointed out, the whole canal debate was complicated by the fact that the best way for the United States to defend the canal was to give it away.[70] That argument was counterintuitive, difficult to explain, and could, in any case, not be given extensive publicity without providing some fuel for the treaty opponents.

Senator DeConcini's decision to highlight the problems surrounding American defense of the canal against Panamanian domestic disruptions very nearly created an example of the kind of disruption he thought was inadequately provided for in the negotiated treaty language. His insistence on plain language regarding the use of American military might "in Panama" nearly led to a Panamanian rejection of the treaties.

The Carter administration dealings with DeConcini were (after the successes with Baker and Byrd) arguably the most important in the long legislative liaison effort to win ratification. Part of their importance was a reflection of the sensitive nature of the language that DeConcini wished to use. But it was also a matter of timing. As Richard Fenno has argued, legislative decision making is typically sequential and the last legislators to make up their minds on a close vote naturally receive attention out of proportion to their status as one member of the majority or minority position on a particular piece of legislation.[71] Senator DeConcini became the majority maker on the Panama Canal issue, and when it was clear that he held that position he had every incentive to seek presidential meetings, national publicity, and a change to the treaties that would placate some of the treaty opponents in his state.[72]

Critics have claimed that it would have been better for the president to take a lower profile in the ratification battle and depend more on the Senate leadership to build his coalition. Senator Byrd is reported to have said that he had several additional votes he could have called on if they were absolutely necessary for ratification of the Neutrality Treaty, including that of

70. Moffett, *The Limits of Victory,* 41.

71. Richard F. Fenno, Jr., "Observation, Context, and Sequence in the Study of Politics," *American Political Science Review* 80, no. 1 (March 1986), 3–15.

72. Later in his career, DeConcini was undecided and then a majority maker in President Clinton's controversial budget proposals of 1993.

his West Virginia colleague, Senator Jennings Randolph, who voted against the agreements.[73] With those votes and his position as majority leader, Byrd might have been able to put more pressure on DeConcini than could the president.[74] Robert Beckel, the chief congressional liaison staff member for the White House Panama campaign, is convinced that DeConcini was holding most of the cards in the final round of negotiations and that without DeConcini there would have been no two-thirds majority.[75] Byrd may have had a different style of dealing with a junior colleague and some special institutional carrots and sticks he could have used, but the fundamental political dynamics would not have changed if Byrd had done the final stage of negotiations on the DeConcini condition. The treaties were unpopular in Arizona, and DeConcini would not have hurt his political career if he had walked away from talks with Carter or Byrd and announced that he would vote against them. In fact, his highly publicized role in the buildup to the first Senate vote did not win wide praise in his home state, and treaty opponents were more active and vocal in their criticisms after his vote in favor of the neutrality treaty. Because he made up his mind so late in the process, and at a time when the outcome was clearly in the balance, he was in a good position to make substantial demands from the president, or from the majority leader, and could in either case have positioned himself as the author of the most consequential of the amendments to the first resolution of ratification.

Initially, the full measure of the consequences that DeConcini's condition would produce in Panama was missed by both the administration and the Senate leadership. Ambassador Jorden faults the administration for not maintaining a regular system of prompt consultation between Washington and Panama City to make sure that problems in Panama were quickly made known to the administration negotiators on Capitol Hill.[76] The ambassador may be right that such a system would have helped Christopher, but in the final week before the first Senate vote the deputy secretary of state

73. I. M. Destler, "Treaty Troubles: Versailles in Reverse," *Foreign Policy,* no. 33 (winter 1978–79), 59–60. On the status of Randolph's vote, see Jorden, *Panama Odyssey,* 554.

74. Franck and Weisband, *Foreign Policy by Congress,* 281, and Jorden, *Panama Odyssey,* 532.

75. Project on the Carter Presidency, Robert Beckel Session, 16. See also Franck and Weisband, *Foreign Policy by Congress,* 279.

76. Jorden, *Panama Odyssey,* 538.

was handling a variety of sensitive issues with a number of senators and working with the assumption that he needed to satisfy most of the undecided senators in order to produce a two-thirds vote.

President Carter was operating under the same constraints. Events were moving quickly, and victory was never certain or likely enough to give him much leverage in his two meetings with DeConcini. In the end, the president and his senior adviser, Hamilton Jordan, had more influence with Torrijos than with DeConcini and managed to persuade the Panamanian leader to accept a considerable insult to his nationalist pride. In the final analysis, Torrijos trusted the administration to do what it could to repair the damage DeConcini was doing. The Panamanian leader reportedly said after his phone conversation with President Carter on March 15 that the president was a "good man" and that he would wait to see what Carter would do to moderate the DeConcini condition.[77] That confidence in President Carter from another, very different, national leader bought the time needed to produce a satisfactory resolution of the issue.

Carter's ability to win the confidence of Anwar Sadat produced an even more important international breakthrough in the months that followed the ratification of the Panama Canal treaties.

77. Ibid., 544.

7

SHUTTLE DIPLOMACY
President Carter in the Middle East

On the long list of foreign policy goals that Jimmy Carter brought with him to the Oval Office, few would demand more of his time, energy, and ingenuity than the effort to bring peace to the Middle East. In that effort there would be two episodes of intense presidential involvement—the thirteen days at Camp David in September of 1978 and the president's personal diplomatic mission to Cairo and Jerusalem in March of 1979. On both occasions there were substantial risks of failure, which the president understood when he elected to involve himself directly in high-level negotiations. Through persistence, mastery of detail, a special relationship with Anwar Sadat, and a clear sense of what was possible, President Carter was successful in both negotiations. Surprisingly, those successes earned relatively little, if any, domestic political advantage. The president's standing in the polls rose after the Camp David negotiations, but the rise was short-lived; and when he traveled to the Middle East to complete the peace treaty between Egypt and Israel, there was no significant change in his public standing in the aftermath of this remarkable achievement. The reward President Carter received for his personal diplomacy in the Middle East was the knowledge that at least one of Israel's longtime enemies was willing to sign a treaty reducing the danger of war in a region that had seen nearly constant conflict and tension for three decades. Perhaps that was reward enough.

Up and Down the Mountain

The administration began its planning for Middle East policy with a typically ambitious and comprehensive strategy. When Secretary of State Vance made his initial round of visits to Middle East capitals at the end of his first month in office, he invited the leaders of Israel, Egypt, Jordan, Syria, Lebanon, and Saudi Arabia to attend a Geneva conference that would address the full range of issues in the region.

The conference to be co-chaired by the United States and the Soviet Union would have considered steps to implement the fundamental formula for peace in the Middle East that had been established in UN Resolution 242, passed by the Security Council after the dramatic Israeli military victories in the 1967 war. That formula could be stated in a deceptively simple three-word slogan: "land for peace." Israel would withdraw from territory taken in 1967 if Israel's neighbors would accept Israeli sovereignty, territorial integrity, political independence, and right to exist within secure and recognized boundaries. But the simple version of the 242 formula disguised some devilishly difficult problems.

The territories taken in 1967 varied in strategic significance, demographic makeup, and political sensitivity. For Israel, returning the large and sparsely populated Sinai desert to Egypt would be one thing, but giving up the militarily important Golan Heights quite another. The final fate of the other occupied territories was even more controversial and complicated. The simple formula of land for peace glossed over enormous problems connected with the Palestinians living on the West Bank, in Gaza, and as refugees elsewhere in the Middle East. Should the West Bank and Gaza be returned to the countries from which they were taken in 1967, or should the people living there be given some opportunity to decide their own political destinies? What role would Palestinians who had once lived in Israel, or in the occupied territories, and now lived abroad play in determining the future of their former places of residence? The United Nations General Assembly in another resolution had declared that all Palestinian refugees had the right to return to their homes or receive compensation for their lost property. But if those Palestinian homes were to become a homeland, it would mean that other nations would have to surrender territorial claims in order to create a new sovereign power in an already volatile region. For most Israelis, there could be no "secure" borders for their nation if an armed Palestinian state was located on the other side of any of those borders. Of course, an unarmed Palestinian population would have its own legitimate security concerns. For these difficult issues even to be discussed, there was the additional problem of determining who would represent the Palestinians. Would it be Jordan, Egypt, a coalition of Arab states, the PLO (which was still unwilling to accept the existence of a Jewish state in the Middle East and, for that reason, had no formal diplomatic communications with either Israel or the United States), or some new representatives selected by organizations or processes not yet in existence?

Even if these obstacles could be overcome, there was the further problem that for a growing number of Israelis certain land could never be traded for peace. The city of Jerusalem was the declared capital of the state of Israel, though the United States and most other countries did not recognize that designation. In addition, the new and growing Israeli settlements near Jerusalem and elsewhere on the West Bank had religious, military, and political importance that would make it extremely difficult for Israel even to talk about placing them under any form of Arab administration. The election of Prime Minister Menachem Begin, the head of Israel's Likud Party, in the fifth month of Carter's presidency, appeared to make all of these problems more difficult to address. Likud leaders had long been more wary of the peace process than their Labor Party counterparts and were committed to permanent possession of Jerusalem and settlement expansion on the West Bank.

The difficulties in dealing with these problems at a Geneva conference chaired by the two cold war rivals would have been substantial and caused considerable anxiety in Israel and within the American Jewish community. Nevertheless, Carter and his senior foreign policy advisers believed that the time had come to go beyond the Kissinger approach of step-by-step negotiations.[1] No one was quite sure what could, or would, happen if all the Middle East diplomatic issues—territorial, political, and military—were placed on the same negotiating table, but it seemed worth a try. And given the growing importance of Middle East oil to the international economy, suc-

1. In an influential Brookings study published in 1975 one of the conclusions was that "the time has come to begin the process of negotiating such a [comprehensive] settlement among the parties, either at a general conference or at more informal multilateral meetings." Brookings Middle East Study Group, *Toward Peace in the Middle East* (Washington, D.C., 1975), 1. Brzezinski was a member of the study group.

cessful peace negotiations offered the additional payoff of greater global economic stability.

The planning for a new Geneva conference occupied the Middle East experts in the Carter administration during their first year in office and was at the top of the agenda when many of the Arab and Israeli political leaders came to Washington to meet the new president. Though the reconvening of a Geneva conference was officially called for in a joint U.S.-Soviet statement issued on October 1, 1977, the planning for such a conference was quickly overshadowed by the dramatic news that Anwar Sadat would visit Jerusalem. For a time, the administration, and the rest of the world, tried to catch up with the Egyptian leader's imaginative initiative and its significance for the prospects of peace in the Middle East.

Sadat followed his trip to Jerusalem with an invitation to the Israelis and representatives from Arab states to come to Cairo for a meeting that would pave the way for Geneva, or obviate the need for a full-scale international conference. It quickly became apparent, however, that Sadat was the only major leader in the Arab world who was serious about conducting negotiations with Israel. As he was increasingly criticized by, and isolated from, his Arab neighbors and the Soviet Union, Sadat was drawn closer to President Carter and the United States. Eventually, the American president set aside his plans for a Geneva conference and emerged as the active mediator helping Sadat and Begin reach a settlement in their negotiations for a separate peace between Egypt and Israel. When the momentum that Sadat had set in motion began to slow, President Carter invited both Sadat and Begin to join him at the presidential retreat named for Dwight Eisenhower's grandson and Richard Nixon's son-in-law.

The story of what went on at Camp David has been vividly told by President Carter and others who were intimately involved.[2] In general, the commentators on the Camp David negotiations give the president credit for realizing earlier than others that a separate peace between Israel and Egypt was both possible and desirable, and that Sadat would be willing to accept much less progress in the resolution of the Palestinian issues and the future

2. Jimmy Carter, *Keeping Faith: Memoirs of a President* (New York, 1982), 319–403; William B. Quandt, *Camp David: Peacemaking and Politics* (Washington, D.C., 1986); Moshe Dayan, *Breakthrough: A Personal Account of the Egypt-Israel Peace Negotiations* (New York, 1981).

of the West Bank and Gaza than he had publicly demanded. In many ways, that was the key to Carter's Camp David triumph. He saw where the negotiations were likely to go; he made an accurate assessment of Sadat's flexibility and courage; and he persevered in the effort to convert those insights into an agreement.[3]

The Camp David negotiations, expected to take a few days, ended up lasting almost two weeks and had their own dramatic steps forward and backward on the road to peace. Both Sadat and Begin threatened to leave the presidential retreat without reaching any agreement, and Carter demonstrated considerable diplomatic skill in making sure that the negotiations kept going. Moreover, the president played a central role in the private meetings with Sadat and Begin and personally drafted key passages of the emerging agreements. When the Camp David talks ended, there was a commitment to finalize a peace treaty between Israel and Egypt with the Sinai to be fully returned to Egypt in exchange for the establishment of normal diplomatic relations. Israeli airbases in the Sinai would be relocated with American assistance, and the border regions between the two countries would be demilitarized and monitored by international observers. The final fate of the small Israeli settlements in the Sinai was not decided at Camp David, but Begin promised to ask the Knesset to consider relocation of those settlements when he returned to Israel. The Israeli parliament, with some of Begin's former political allies voting against his government, approved the relocation after a bitter debate that did not bode well for future negotiations involving the much larger and more significant settlements on the West Bank and in Gaza.

Those future negotiations would be based on a framework agreed to at Camp David for the next stage of the peace process. The Arab citizens of the West Bank and Gaza were to hold elections and be given "full autonomy" in the near future, with the creation of a "self-governing authority" to replace Israeli military and civilian administrators.[4] During a five-year transition period, representatives of the resident Palestinians would negotiate with Israelis, Egyptians and, hopefully, Jordanians about the borders, se-

3. William B. Quandt, *Peace Process: American Diplomacy and the Arab-Israeli Conflict Since 1967* (Washington, D.C., 1993), 277–83.

4. There were, as one might expect, considerable differences among the parties regarding the meaning of "autonomy," "self-governing," and other key terms in the agreement.

curity arrangements, and political future of the occupied territories. According to Carter, there was an additional concession from Israel—a verbal commitment not to build any new settlements in the occupied territories during the second-stage negotiations on the framework for peace in Gaza and the West Bank.

Any initial hopes for movement toward a general peace in the Middle East after Camp David were short-lived. Even though there was widespread international praise for the Camp David accords (including the awarding of the Nobel Peace Prize to Sadat and Begin), most Arab nations were suspicious of the agreements and critical of the failure to secure firm commitments from Israel to withdraw from all the territories captured in 1967 and suspend settlement expansion. The Golan Heights were not mentioned in the Camp David documents beyond a brief reference to the expectation that Israel would eventually negotiate peace agreements, like the one with Egypt, with its other Arab neighbors—Syria, Lebanon, and Jordan. Of these three, Jordan was the most important, and when an effort was made to bring the Jordanians into the negotiations, which included providing King Hussein with American interpretations of the Camp David terms, Begin became angered and offered very different, and much narrower, interpretations of what had been agreed to at the presidential retreat. Jordan did not join the negotiations.

Moreover, immediately after leaving the summit, Begin began making public statements about the settlement suspension that were at odds with what President Carter believed to have been the Israeli commitment. The moratorium on new settlements was, in Begin's view, to last for only three months while the peace treaty between Egypt and Israel was being finalized, not for the much longer period that it would take to complete negotiations on Gaza and the West Bank. Begin's interpretation of the Camp David settlement commitment took what Americans had thought to be a major Israeli concession and converted it into a minor gesture; and even that gesture was weakened when Israel announced that it would "thicken" existing settlements before the Israeli-Egyptian peace treaty was signed. Begin's statements and actions on settlements were a bad sign for the prospects of further negotiations.

There were bad signs in the Arab world as well. Initial criticisms from Syrian and Iraqi leaders were formalized at a Baghdad summit in November 1978, where radical and moderate Arab states stood together against

Sadat. The Egyptian leader was left alone in the region with growing domestic opposition to some of the concessions he had made to Israel. In the fall of 1978, Sadat was arguably in a weaker domestic and regional political position than he had been before his dramatic trip to Jerusalem.[5] After Camp David it was increasingly difficult for Egypt to make new concessions, or even sign on to the ones that had already been made.

As hopes for a reinvigorated regionwide peace process faded, the completion of the separate Israeli-Egyptian treaty became both more important and more difficult. Those negotiations were supposed to take three months and involve relatively minor matters not fully resolved at Camp David. Instead, they took nearly twice as long and required a second round of high-profile presidential involvement.

Deciding to Go

There were a number of issues related to the Egyptian-Israeli peace treaty that had not been settled at Camp David. One set of questions had to do with the precise dates for Israeli military withdrawal from the Sinai and for an exchange of ambassadors between the two states. The timing of these events was significant because it touched on whether or not the fulfillment of the treaty commitments between Egypt and Israel would be tied to the timetable for negotiations in the next stage of the peace process. The exact relationship between the two agreements made at Camp David was a matter of dispute between Sadat and Begin. Egypt wanted the two agreements to be linked; Israel did not. There were also questions about the oil fields that Israel had developed in the Sinai, and the role that Egypt might play in Gaza during the subsequent stages of the peace process. An issue of particular importance to Israel involved a technical term in international law called the "priority of agreements." Israel wanted assurances that the new commitments Egypt was making with its former enemy would have "priority" over the older defensive treaties that Egypt had with a number of the Arab states bordering Israel. Egypt naturally wanted to avoid any requirement to renounce or withdraw formally from those earlier agreements. Unfortunately, the passage of time tended to make the resolution of all of these problems more difficult.

---

5. For a summary of Sadat's domestic problems and the cabinet changes he made after Camp David, see Melvin Friedlander, *Sadat and Begin: The Domestic Politics of Peacemaking* (Boulder, Colo., 1983), 238–40.

At the broadest level, the technical issues under negotiation for the two-nation peace treaty were less important than lingering suspicions, on each side, that the separate peace they were making would not be long-lasting or genuine. For the Egyptians, there was fear that once Israel had achieved a reconciliation with its most populous and militarily powerful neighbor, it would drag its feet in the next stage of negotiations trying to hold on to the West Bank and Gaza for as long as possible. If this were to occur, Sadat's isolation from the rest of the Arab world would be permanent, not temporary, and the cause of the Palestinians, which Sadat thought he was promoting, would be seriously set back. For the Israelis, any reluctance on Egypt's part to exchange ambassadors promptly, or sell oil to Israel, or give priority to the peace treaty that would soon be signed suggested that the agreement with Egypt might not be strong enough to survive some future Middle East crisis. There was, perhaps understandably, very little trust between two nations that had been at war with each other four times in the previous thirty years. The psychological and political consequences of decades of conflict could not be completely eliminated by Sadat's trip to Jerusalem or by a presidentially brokered agreement at Camp David. The process of establishing normal relations between countries like Israel and Egypt was bound to be slow and difficult.

The overthrow of the shah in Iran at the end of 1978 and during the early weeks of 1979 only made matters worse. Sadat lost one of his closest friends in the region and saw the emergence of a radical Islamic fundamentalism that was potentially threatening to his own regime. The Israelis lost their only reliable supplier of oil in the Middle East and watched the replacement of a government supportive of the United States with one that was hostile to it. The new instability in Iran raised the stakes in the discussions about the oil wells in the Sinai that Israel would soon surrender and highlighted Sadat's weakened relations with his Arab neighbors.

The Israeli and Egyptian negotiating teams working on the final draft of the peace treaty outlined at Camp David met in Washington from mid-October until mid-November, then suspended their talks with most of the outstanding issues still unresolved. At the end of November, just a few weeks before the announced deadline for completion of the treaty, President Carter received two long memos on the Middle East. One was from Brzezinski, the other from Hamilton Jordan.

In Brzezinski's analysis things were coming apart because the president was losing control over the negotiating process. In the seclusion of Camp David, with no press coverage, and the president in the center of discussions between Begin and Sadat, he could dominate both and use the considerable leverage that came from each side not wishing to be blamed for a diplomatic failure. Now that Begin and Sadat were away from Carter and increasingly concerned about their domestic and regional critics, they were less worried about failure and, in many ways, more worried about success. Would Sadat be further ostracized in the Arab world if he went ahead with the signing of a separate peace treaty? Would Begin have to pay too high a price in terms of his domestic political support if he followed through on his Camp David commitments, particularly those involving Gaza and the West Bank? Both sides were becoming more timid and more intransigent, and Brzezinski recommended that the president "adopt a strong public posture, be blunt, and push all sides."[6]

The other memo Carter read in late November made the case for even greater presidential involvement in the negotiations. Hamilton Jordan, in a nine-page message for the president's eyes only, reviewed the post–Camp David scene and argued that it was "logical and reasonable" to assume that both Israel and Egypt had gone so far and had so much at stake in the peace process that they would not let their current differences go unresolved. However, Jordan noted, "there is nothing in our experience to date that would suggest that logic and reason has anything to do with the Middle East or the negotiations."[7] For the president's senior political adviser, there was more at stake in the failure to consummate the peace treaty between Egypt and Israel than the obvious consequences of such a failure for the nations of the Middle East. The continuing negotiations had "created a psychological logjam" for the administration's foreign policy initiatives. Carter needed to complete the peace treaty in order to move on to the recognition of China and to SALT II. Jordan hoped that success on these three issues would allow the president to enter the second half of his administration with a recognized record of international accomplishment. What was needed was some bold action to get things going, and Jordan recommended

6. Zbigniew Brzezinski, *Power and Principle: Memoirs of the National Security Advisor 1977–1981* (New York, 1983), 277.

7. Hamilton Jordan to President Carter, memorandum, November 30, 1978. Hamilton Jordan, Box 49, File Middle East [CF,O/A 414], Carter Library.

that Carter go to Cairo and see Sadat. If the Egyptian leader gave ground on the remaining differences that were blocking the treaty, then the president could decide whether or not to carry Sadat's concessions to Israel personally. This would be risky, Jordan conceded, "but it seems no riskier than the notion several months ago of a Camp David summit."[8]

Carter read Jordan's memo, and may have been inclined to follow its advice, but he waited to do so for several more months. Some of the other members of his administration, particularly the vice president, were not as anxious as Jordan was to see the president take more chances on the Middle East peace process.[9] A failure to complete the bilateral peace treaty called for at Camp David would certainly have diminished the president's earlier diplomatic accomplishment and set back the prospects for greater peace and stability in the region, but a cautious politician might, nevertheless, have decided to leave well enough alone. If Sadat and Begin could not finalize the treaty they had promised to sign at Camp David, one or both of them would bear the blame for missing an opportunity that President Carter had helped to create. If, however, the president of the United States flew to the Middle East, made a second major investment of his time and prestige, and did not bring about the signing of a final treaty, then the United States and its chief executive might lose just as much as the parties directly involved in the negotiations.

Moreover, for Carter to go to the Middle East without knowing in advance that his mission would succeed looked to some of his advisers like a much greater risk than Camp David. When Begin and Sadat came to the United States at presidential invitation, Carter was clearly seen as the mediator trying to build on the good will that Sadat had created with his trip to Jerusalem. If those negotiations had failed, as many commentators expected they would, the president might still have earned some credit for having made the effort and for providing an atmosphere in which progress was possible. But if the president traveled to the capitals of Egypt and Israel before the negotiations were concluded, he might be seen as the supplicant rather than the host, and failure could easily diminish American prestige and the president's personal reputation. There were good reasons to hesitate before following the suggestion that Jordan was making in the fall of 1978.

8. Ibid.
9. Quandt, *Peace Process*, 310–11.

Events elsewhere in the world were also making substantial demands on President Carter's time and attention. In Tehran, Ambassador Sullivan sent a cable early in November 1978 suggesting that it was time to "think the unthinkable"—the shah might lose his throne and the United States might have to deal with his successors. By the time that thought was clearly in the minds of the senior members of the administration, it may well have been too late to do very much about it, but responding to Sullivan's call for new thinking about Iran became a major issue for the administration.[10] Rapid progress was also being made at the end of 1978 in the negotiations to formally recognize the People's Republic of China.[11]

While the Iranian revolution and the formal recognition of China developed, Carter sent Vance to Egypt and Israel in mid-December. The ambassador-at-large for Middle East negotiations, Alfred Atherton, made another round of visits to Cairo and Jerusalem in January. The Egyptians gave ground on a few issues, but the Israelis continued to propose language unacceptable to the Egyptians.[12] The negotiations were, according to Vance, "appallingly tedious," and President Carter recorded in his diary late in January 1979 that both sides were "intransigent and quibbling over details."[13] When in February the Egyptian and Israeli foreign ministers came to the United States for further talks with Vance, the session was billed as Camp David II. But like a bad movie sequel, the second round of negotiations at the presidential retreat, without the original cast, lacked the luster of the earlier version. The Egyptian foreign minister did make some concessions, including a promise to consider an early exchange of ambassadors that was not tied to the second stage of regional negotiations, but his Israeli counterpart, Moshe Dayan, did not have permission from Begin or the Israeli cabinet to conduct independent negotiations. Every detail had to be reported to Jerusalem and evaluated by Begin and his colleagues. That arrangement made progress painfully slow or nearly non-existent. The president then invited Begin to join the negotiations, but the Israeli leader refused unless Sadat also came. Carter responded by asking Begin to come to Washington

10. Gary Sick, *All Fall Down: America's Tragic Encounter with Iran* (New York, 1985), 94–118.

11. Brzezinski, *Power and Principle*, 196–233.

12. Friedlander, *Sadat and Begin*, 269–71.

13. Cyrus Vance, *Hard Choices: Four Critical Years in Managing America's Foreign Policy* (New York, 1983), 236; Carter, *Keeping Faith*, 412.

for talks directly with him, an invitation the Israeli leader could not easily decline.

In 1982, Carter recalled that he almost never had a pleasant surprise in his dealings with Begin.[14] This was certainly true in March of 1979. The Israeli prime minister came to Washington without his defense minister or his foreign minister, despite the fact (or perhaps because of the fact) that both Dayan and Ezer Weizman had been moderating influences in the Israeli delegation to Camp David. In his meetings with the president, Begin gave long speeches about the importance of American support for Israel in the Middle East, the growing Soviet threat in the region, and the need for Israel to replace its lost sources of oil. He continued to object to any language that appeared to tie the peace treaty with Egypt to the future of Gaza and the West Bank and insisted that the Egyptians give unambiguous priority to the new commitments Cairo was preparing to make with her former enemy. Several of the president's advisers were worried, even before Begin came to Washington, that the Israeli leader might have decided to let the Camp David peace process die and hope that Carter would be replaced in the next presidential election by an American chief executive more sympathetic to a Likud agenda.[15] Begin's early statements in Washington gave credence to such suspicions.

Later in the visit, according to Vance, "Begin became less confrontational," and in his meetings with the secretary of state agreed to a new formulation on the priority of agreements issue. The United States would drop its plans to draft a letter containing a legal interpretation of Article VI of the proposed treaty, the article containing language on the priority of agreements. Instead of an American-drafted letter, there would be an interpretative minute added to the end of the treaty. That minute would be intentionally confusing and would say "that there is no assertion that this Treaty prevails over other Treaties or agreements or that other Treaties or agreements prevail over this Treaty." This left Egypt free to claim that the peace treaty with Israel would not have priority over other agreements, while Israel would continue to assert that it did. As Vance observed in his memoirs, it had taken six months to get Menachem Begin to accept an interpretation

14. Jimmy Carter, interview in *Time*, October 11, 1982.
15. According to Quandt, Jordan and Brzezinski shared the view in late February that Begin "wanted Carter not to be reelected." Quandt, *Peace Process*, 298.

on the priority of agreements issue that essentially contained two contradictory statements.[16]

Progress was also made during the Washington talks on new wording that would, in Israel's view, weaken the connection between the peace treaty and the second stage negotiations on autonomy for Gaza and the West Bank. Where there had previously been proposed language setting a "target date" for elections in the occupied territories, there was now to be a "goal" for the completion of the negotiations dealing with the autonomy issue and a promise that elections would follow those completed negotiations as expeditiously as possible.[17] This provided enough loosening of the links between the two Camp David agreements and flexibility about how the second stage of negotiations might proceed to satisfy Begin and his cabinet and to give Carter new confidence that he could now close the small remaining gaps between the two sides.[18] Disagreements remained about future Egyptian oil sales to Israel and the precise timing for the formal exchange of ambassadors, but otherwise the Israelis were willing to accept the latest American proposals for treaty language.

Though most of the president's senior advisers, including Vance, were still hesitant about the advisability of a presidential trip to the Middle East, Carter was now prepared to take what his secretary of state called "a breathtaking gamble and an act of political courage."[19] The president would go to Cairo and then to Jerusalem to complete the negotiations and hopefully sign the peace treaty at the conclusion of his shuttle between the two capitals. Carter's own description of his decision is less complimentary than Vance's; he saw it as "an act of desperation."[20] But whether it was courage or desperation, or some combination of the two, the decision to go put the president in an upbeat mood. Carter, now committed to a venture that many of his closest associates considered politically dangerous, was cheerful and full of good humor.[21] That was the president's characteristic response to a challenge.

16. Vance, *Hard Choices*, 244.
17. Friedlander, *Sadat and Begin*, 277–79.
18. Vance, *Hard Choices*, 244–45.
19. Ibid., 245.
20. Carter, *Keeping Faith*, 416.
21. Brzezinski, *Power and Principle*, 281.

Mission to the Middle East

Following Begin's visit to Washington, Carter sent Brzezinski to Cairo to meet with Sadat, report on the Israeli acceptance of the new American proposals, and to inform the Egyptian leader confidentially that Carter's "domestic political situation was becoming more difficult and that Begin might even wish to see the President defeated."[22] Sadat welcomed the pending presidential visit and made a number of generous proposals designed to ensure the president's success. He agreed to an early exchange of ambassadors between Egypt and Israel and expressed a willingness to invite Begin to Cairo for a dramatic treaty-signing ceremony at the end of the president's personal negotiations.

Carter was pleased with Sadat's customary generosity and arrived in Cairo with high hopes for a successful trip. Though some of Sadat's senior foreign policy advisers had reservations about the wording of the new treaty provisions that Begin had accepted in Washington, the Egyptian leader showed little interest in what he deemed to be minor matters and continued to reassure President Carter that he would do everything he could to bring the negotiations to a triumphant conclusion. Sadat told the president that he was convinced that the Israeli commitment to negotiate on "autonomy" for the Gaza and West Bank, even if Begin persisted in giving autonomy a narrow definition and weakening the ties between the two Camp David agreements, would ultimately become a trap for the Israelis because the world community would take the Palestinian side in any future negotiations about independence and self-determination.[23] That simple version of what had been accomplished at Camp David was much more important to Sadat than any of the details that remained to be worked out. With Sadat's cooperation on the resolution of those details assured, there was very little to discuss in Egypt, and much of the president's time was spent enjoying the ceremonial side of presidential travel. On a train trip from Cairo to Alexandria the crowds were so large and enthusiastic that, as Carter joked to

22. Brzezinski, *Power and Principle,* 282. Quandt reports that Carter in a 1985 interview did not remember asking Brzezinski to convey this sensitive political message, but Brzezinski had a detailed recollection of what the president wanted him to say. Quandt, *Peace Process*, 314 n. 6.

23. President Carter's Diary, March 8, 1979, quoted in Carter, *Keeping Faith*, 418.

Sadat, not even a politician would have to exaggerate the welcome he was receiving.[24]

The president and his entourage left Cairo with Sadat's good wishes and some specific requests from the Egyptian foreign ministry. The Egyptians asked the president to secure new Israeli gestures that would support the claim that Camp David was good for the Palestinians, a changed word in the controversial interpretations regarding the priority of agreements, and some special role for Egypt in Gaza during the subsequent negotiations. They also suggested that if negotiations over the West Bank became bogged down, perhaps the Israelis would agree to allow autonomy for Gaza to take place first. Arriving in Israel just after sunset on Saturday, March 10, Carter had a private meeting with Begin that did not go well. On Saturday night and again the next morning, when the full delegations from both nations met, Begin raised objections to the American plans for a signing ceremony in Jerusalem or Cairo, or in both capitals, at the conclusion of the presidential trip. In typically legalistic fashion, Begin insisted that anything discussed during the president's visit would have to be debated by the cabinet and approved by the Knesset before a formal signing ceremony could take place. This could take days or weeks and would certainly preclude any dramatic conclusion to Carter's Middle East mission. Begin, as it was clearly understood, was willfully denying the president the kind of international media event that he both wanted and deserved for his active role in the Israeli-Egyptian negotiations.

With that Israeli affront announced, the talks turned to the substantive issues that remained to be decided between Israel and Egypt. Here too the Israeli positions were disappointing. Years later, Carter remembered the Jerusalem negotiations with Begin as the "most vituperative confrontation in my political career."[25] The Israeli prime minister insisted that there could be no change in the wording on priority of agreements that had been agreed to in Washington, even though the change the Egyptians requested did little to clarify the contradictory interpretations that constituted the diplomatic compromise on this question. The Israelis also refused to accept the Egyptian proposals regarding a separate schedule for autonomy in Gaza and the

24. Carter, *Keeping Faith*, 419.
25. Jimmy Carter, interview by author, Atlanta, Ga., April 11, 1995.

presence of Egyptian officials there during the next stage of negotiations. Any treaty language that appeared to connect the peace between Egypt and Israel with the future negotiations on Gaza and the West Bank was objectionable to the Israelis. Begin read from Egyptian newspaper stories critical of Israel to prove his contention that the Egyptians really did not want peace and called on Ariel Sharon to deliver a discourse on his standard position that Jordan was the real Palestinian state and that Israeli possession of the West Bank should be permanent. Members of the American delegation, including the president, found themselves interrupted and forced to sit through what were familiar and often irrelevant Israeli speeches that failed to address directly the minor remaining issues in the treaty negotiations.[26]

After a full day of nearly fruitless discussions, including a long session in which the senior American foreign policy makers tried to come up with negotiable synonyms for the new words that the Egyptians wanted in Article VI, expectations for a successful presidential trip were fading.[27] On Monday morning, a tired Israeli delegation, whose members had met throughout the previous night, announced acceptance of the new wording on the priority of agreements, but continued to refuse the Egyptian requests regarding Gaza. Further negotiations took place until Carter and Begin left to speak to the members of the Knesset. The president gave one of his better foreign policy speeches, but the raucous reception that Begin received from some of his right-wing critics, one of whom had to be forcibly removed from the chamber, did little to encourage the American delegation.[28] In the remaining sessions that Monday with Vance and with the president, no progress was made. The Israelis continued to deny the need for giving Egypt anything in Gaza and insisted on unrealistic Egyptian guarantees on the sale of oil from the Sinai. They also found new issues to raise in the controversial language of Article VI, which mentioned the words "comprehensive peace" in a reference to the second-stage negotiations.[29] This was another of those dangerous linkages that the Israelis wanted to avoid, fearing that any failure in the future to produce a "comprehensive peace" or specified steps in Gaza and the West Bank would become an excuse for Egyptian renunciation of the bilateral peace.

26. Quandt, *Peace Process*, 316–20.
27. Quandt, *Camp David*, 306–307.
28. Quandt, *Peace Process*, 319.
29. Quandt, *Camp David*, 308.

When Monday's negotiations proved to be no more fruitful than those on Sunday, the president gave orders to his staff to make plans for travel back to Washington. Carter was prepared to leave that night, but the logistical arrangements for his departure could not be made on such short notice, and the presidential party was scheduled to leave Israel on Tuesday morning. Jody Powell, briefing the press corps Monday evening, gave them an accurate picture of the state of the negotiations and hints that the president might return to Washington without having secured a final agreement between Israel and Egypt. Some newspaper reporters, particularly the Associated Press representative Frank Cormier, took Powell's briefing to heart and wrote stories about the prospective failure of the president's personal Middle East diplomacy. The television journalists, reporting live from Jerusalem, also used Powell's cautious assessment of the state of the negotiations at the conclusion of talks on Monday, with CBS going well beyond Powell's hints to report that "all indications are that Carter's Mideast gamble has failed."[30] However, unbeknownst to Walter Cronkite, or to Jody Powell, the obituaries for the presidential mission were premature.

On Monday evening Vance met with Dayan and learned that some members of the Israeli cabinet had held discussions without their prime minister present and were very concerned about the state of the negotiations and the likelihood that Israel would be blamed for the failure to reach agreement. Together Vance and Dayan worked out a formula for an American guarantee of oil sales to Israel in the event that Egyptian sales of Sinai oil failed to meet Israeli needs.[31] The Israelis asked for a twenty-year American guarantee; Vance proposed fifteen. On Gaza, Dayan suggested that if mention of early autonomy could be omitted from the agreement, it would be possible to discuss that issue in the subsequent negotiations. As to some role for Egyptian liaison officers, Dayan mentioned that after normal diplomatic relations were established, there would be no restrictions on the travel of Egyptians to and from Gaza, and something like what the Egyptians wanted might, in fact, be possible. Vance thought these Israeli promises for future consideration of the Gaza matters might be enough to satisfy Sadat. He and his staff worked through the night on treaty language regarding

30. CBS news and report, quoted in Jody Powell, *The Other Side of the Story* (New York, 1984), 97.
31. Vance, *Hard Choices*, 249–50.

the American oil guarantee, language which Carter approved the next morning.

Dayan and Vance got together early on Tuesday to review the American draft language and to make sure that everything was ready for a hastily scheduled breakfast meeting between Carter and Begin. Though Begin continued to insist that these final arrangements would have to be approved by the cabinet and the Knesset, he accepted the oil guarantee language and agreed to consider some unilateral Israeli steps to improve the political atmosphere on the West Bank. With Begin's approval of the terms that Vance and Dayan had worked out, the president's travel plans were officially redrawn. He would now fly to Cairo to meet with Sadat and report to him on the results of his negotiations with Begin.

The final leg of the president's trip to the Middle East was a brief stop at the Cairo airport. There the president met immediately with Sadat and his senior foreign policy advisers and gave them a very positive report on what had been accomplished. The American delegation had, in reality, achieved very little of what the Egyptians wanted in the final round of negotiations. Instead of firm guarantees for an Egyptian role in Gaza and a possible separate schedule for Gaza's autonomy, the Israelis were offering verbal assurances that these matters could be addressed in subsequent negotiations. The Israelis did accept the modest word change in Article VI that the Egyptian foreign ministry had asked for, but they had proposed some new wording of their own, and the fundamental problem with the priority of agreements language—the fear on both sides that the Middle East peace process would not be comprehensive or long lasting—remained. When the Egyptian foreign minister, Mustafa Khalil, asked Carter if further revisions could be negotiated, the president lost his considerable patience and replied: "For the last 18 months, I, the president of the most powerful nation on earth, have acted the postman. I am not a proud man—I have done the best I could—but I cannot go back to try to change the language."[32] As Carter no doubt expected, Sadat set aside the cautious counsel of his advisers and agreed to the terms that his trusted American friend had secured. A brief call to Begin was followed by the official announcement on the airport tarmac that the final terms for the peace treaty had been concluded.

In Washington, and in much of the world, television viewers were

32. Quandt, *Camp David*, 310 n. 14.

caught off guard by the Cairo announcement and the obvious reversal of fortunes that had taken place between Monday and Tuesday. Perhaps for that reason, and because the completion of a peace treaty between Israel and Egypt had been assumed after the Camp David agreements, the reaction to the president's success was muted. Powell believes that at least part of the modest response that followed the announcement in Cairo was the result of television networks and newspapers not wanting to admit that they had been wrong about the pessimistic stories they had run the day before.[33] It was also true that Powell and the rest of the White House staff had been unable to plan the kind of ceremony that would have drawn more attention to the president's achievement. Begin had precluded such a ceremony, but even if he had not, no one in the presidential delegation had had sufficient confidence that the mission would in fact succeed to give much attention to the staging of its conclusion. An elaborate signing of the Egyptian-Israeli peace treaty did take place on the lawn of the White House about two weeks after the Cairo airport announcement. Neither the president's trip, nor the White House ceremony, had any measurable impact on the president's low standing in public opinion polls.[34]

Conclusions

The successful negotiation of a peace treaty between Egypt and Israel which President Carter brokered at Camp David and later finalized during his travels to Cairo and Jerusalem was arguably the most important foreign policy accomplishment of his administration. Hendrik Hertzberg, the senior speechwriter on the trip to the Middle East, remembers it as the "zenith" of his White House service, the occasion when Carter demonstrated his willingness "to risk everything for peace."[35] But both at home and abroad, the president's accomplishment failed to garner the public praise or political rewards that one might expect from a major foreign policy triumph. During the 1980 campaign, Carter was widely criticized for a minor mishap over how the United States should have voted on a Security Council

---

33. Powell, *The Other Side of the Story*, 99–102.

34. Carter reports that his polls went down in March of 1979. Carter, *Keeping Faith*, 426. Others note an insignificant 1 percent rise. Burton I. Kaufman, *The Presidency of James Earl Carter, Jr.* (Lawrence, Kans., 1993), 132.

35. Hendrik Hertzberg, "Jimmy Carter," in *Character Above All,* ed. Robert A. Wilson (New York, 1995), 197.

resolution involving Israel, and ended up receiving fewer Jewish votes in the general election than his Republican and independent rivals.[36]

Overseas the story was much the same. In his memoirs, Ezer Weizman observed that "as far as I know, no American president has ever helped Israel as much as Jimmy Carter." But, as he went on to admit, "I cannot claim that Israel responded with appropriate gratitude."[37] Anwar Sadat made almost the same observation about reactions to Carter in the Arab world. In his memoirs Sadat confessed that he could not explain "the antagonism of the Arabs toward the only American president who had called for a national homeland for the Palestinian people."[38]

Perhaps it was inevitable that the peacemaker not be rewarded for accomplishments at the time they were achieved. The process of bringing former enemies to some reconciliation usually requires both sides to make immediate concessions in exchange for the long-term benefits of peace. At the time of the initial agreement, the concessions that must be made are perfectly clear and loom large in the minds of the policy makers and citizens on both sides of the negotiations. Compared to the concrete sacrifices that must be made today, the benefits that will accompany a permanent peace are far less tangible and much more problematic. For this reason each side is likely to find that the peace process is opposed by powerful domestic forces suspicious of the established enemy and locked into existing policies and prejudices. The outside mediator who may help to make peace does so by pushing both sides to take chances they might otherwise avoid. As a result, the peacemaker makes enemies among the doubters in both nations. Carter surely did. In Israel, he was the American leader who had pushed the Israelis toward the implementation of the land-for-peace formula that many in the right wing and religious parties rejected or feared. In Egypt, Carter encouraged Sadat's inclinations to break ranks with his Arab neighbors and accept a separate peace that contained what were arguably weak and watered-down promises from Israel to address the important Palestinian territorial and security issues at a later date. To the political extremists and radical religious groups in Egypt, this was an abandonment of the Palestinian cause and the Arab nationalism that was presumably required to advance that cause.

36. Tom Wicker, "Whatever Became of Jimmy Carter?" *Esquire,* July 1984, 82.
37. Ezer Weizman, *The Battle for Peace* (New York, 1981), 382.
38. Anwar Sadat, *Those I Have Known* (New York, 1984), 99.

In the United States, where there was a long-standing tradition of active interest on the part of Jewish voters and lobbyists in Middle East foreign policy issues, Carter's standing was equally uncertain.[39] Though the Camp David accords were clearly good for the security of Israel, and though Begin consistently gave less ground than Sadat at Camp David and during the president's trip to the Middle East, Carter's reputation in the American Jewish community remained mixed. He had come to office without an established record on Middle East issues and from a part of the country with relatively few Jewish voters or politically influential organizations. In his early months in office, he had gone further than other presidents or prominent American politicians in calling for comprehensive Middle East negotiations and an eventual Palestinian homeland.[40] In his early public meetings with Sadat, the shah, and other Middle Eastern leaders, the president appeared to be more comfortable than he was with Rabin and Begin. All of these things raised early doubts about Carter in the American Jewish community that were never fully alleviated by the accomplishments at Camp David and the subsequent negotiations on the Egyptian-Israeli peace treaty. An anti-Israeli vote in the United Nations in 1980 and confusion over how the administration had intended that vote to be cast further alienated Jewish-American voters in the New York Democractic primary and in the November general election.

According to Harold Saunders, the State Department's assistant secretary for Near East and South Asian affairs in the Carter administration and a Middle East expert on Kissinger's National Security Council staff, Carter's newness to the issues related to the Arab-Israeli disputes, which may have contributed to his uneasy relations with the Jewish-American community, also gave him advantages in dealing with these issues. Coming to

39. In June of 1977 Hamilton Jordan prepared a twenty-nine-page memo for the president on the influence of Jewish voters and the American Jewish community, along with a strategy for administration relations with that community. In the introduction he admitted that the role of the American Jewish lobby was "something that was not a part of our Georgia and Southern political experience and consequently not well understood." Hamilton Jordan to the President, memorandum, June 1977, Hamilton Jordan Confidential File, Box 34, "Foreign Policy/Domestic Politics Memo, HJ Memo, 6/77," Carter Library.

40. Early during his first year in office, and shortly after a difficult meeting with Yitzhak Rabin, Carter publicly referred to the need for a "Palestinian homeland" at a town meeting in Clinton, Massachusetts. Quandt, *Camp David*, 48.

Washington as he did without prior foreign policy experience meant that Carter often saw matters in a new light and could more easily than other politicians take a fresh approach. The president, Saunders points out, learned about the Middle East from his own reading of the Bible, from a brief visit he made to Israel in 1973, and later from the studies prepared by his staff. He was an avid reader with a quick mind open to many foreign policy issues that other politicians had learned to avoid. The key for Saunders is that Carter tended to see the Palestinian problem primarily as a human rights concern and never simply as an Israeli security issue.[41] That perspective allowed him to establish good rapport with the Arab leaders he met, particularly with Anwar Sadat, and helped to ensure that he would be accepted as an honest broker in the Middle East negotiations.

The personal relationship between Jimmy Carter and Anwar Sadat was crucial to the developments that led to the Camp David accords and to the signing of an Egyptian-Israeli peace treaty at the end of March 1979. No other foreign leader, and hardly any other person, that Carter worked with during his presidency receives the kind of praise that the president consistently gives to Anwar Sadat. He describes their first encounter in April 1977 as "a shining light that burst on the Middle East scene for me" and later told his wife that meeting Sadat had been his best day as president.[42] In the months and years that followed that meeting, Carter's personal friendship with the Egyptian leader developed and deepened, becoming a fulcrum for much of the heavy diplomatic lifting that was essential to any movement toward peace in the Middle East. The two leaders shared some important personal qualities. Both were deeply religious men who had an essentially optimistic world view. Both were strong-willed, capable of long-range planning, and willing to take genuine political risks in their quest for major accomplishments.

Carter's easy rapport with Sadat at almost every stage of the Middle East negotiations sharply contrasted with his often difficult encounters with Menachem Begin. Yet as Carter's ambassador to Israel, Samuel Lewis, has noted, the relationship between the American president and the Israeli prime minister may have been just as important to the eventual outcome of

41. Saunders comments are in Herbert D. Rosenbaum and Alexej Ugrinsky, eds., *Jimmy Carter: Foreign Policy and Post-presidential Years* (Westport, Conn., 1994), 165–68.

42. Carter, *Keeping Faith*, 282.

the Camp David initiatives as the more celebrated friendship between Carter and Sadat.[43]

Begin was a proud and dour figure who tended to examine almost every aspect of the negotiations in a painstakingly legalistic fashion. When during the Camp David sessions Rosalynn Carter proposed that a joint prayer for the success of the negotiations be used by all three delegations, Moshe Dayan made a joke saying that "you will have to take off your hat for the Christians and your shoes for the Muslims—and then you'll end up putting on a yarmulke for the Jews." The prime minister of Israel did not think the prayer was a joke. His response to the First Lady's idea was to take out a pen, review her draft word by word, and suggest modifications.[44] That was Begin's response to nearly everything, and at times it was difficult to tell whether the Israeli leader was being painfully thorough or masking his rejection of a particular item behind a mountain of minutiae. In his dealings with President Carter, Begin found an interlocutor who could discuss the details of the ongoing negotiations with a mastery that was equal to his own. Perhaps more importantly, according to Ambassador Lewis, President Carter was "a man with an extraordinary degree of self-control and self-discipline." As a result, the president was able to sit through exasperating negotiating sessions with Begin "without ever—except on rare occasions—letting his anger show."[45] Carter found other ways to deal with Begin that went beyond merely enduring his tedious style of negotiation. The president learned that talking with Begin about biblical history, a subject both men knew well, or about their families, to which each was devoted, often made it possible to appeal to Begin's emotional and softer side. Such appeals sometimes broke through the legalistic logjams that Begin had created.

At Camp David, the early meetings between Sadat and Begin went badly and were replaced by separate sessions each leader had with President Carter and by the creation of a committee of lower-level representatives from all three delegations that Carter often chaired. According to the diplomatic historian Gaddis Smith, Carter's immersion in Middle East diplomacy is comparable only to Woodrow Wilson's role at Versailles.[46] Most modern

43. Rosenbaum and Ugrinsky, *Jimmy Carter,* 155–59.

44. Weizman, *The Battle for Peace,* 345.

45. Rosenbaum and Ugrinsky, *Jimmy Carter,* 156–57.

46. Gaddis Smith, *Morality, Reason, and Power: American Diplomacy in the Carter Years* (New York, 1986), 165.

presidents, whether it be Roosevelt at the wartime conferences or Nixon on his trips to Beijing and Moscow, left detailed diplomacy to their subordinates. Carter did not. In the Middle East negotiations at Camp David and in the efforts to finalize the Egyptian-Israeli peace treaty, the president was both master of the minutiae which preoccupied Begin and a holder of the long-term vision that energized Sadat. He was the ideal mediator for these very different national leaders.

At both Camp David and on the trip to the Middle East, Carter was fully in command of a well-coordinated foreign policy team. In the course of his preparations for Camp David and his conduct of the negotiations, he learned a great deal about the villages in the Sinai desert, about the oil that was produced there, and about the different names used by Israelis and Egyptians for the same geographic landmarks. He read Begin's autobiography and even made a brief study of the Koran to better prepare himself for his discussions with Sadat, though he admits that the Egyptian leader knew much more about Judaism and Christianity than he was able to learn about Islam.[47] Some of the crucial language in the final Camp David accords was drafted by President Carter, not because he refused to use staff or delegate authority, but because he was in a unique position given his status and personal relationships with the two heads of state and because his knowledge of the issues, in many cases, made him the best available drafter. He might have delegated more of the work at Camp David, but if he had done so, he might also have lost some of Sadat's trust or encountered even more of Begin's intransigence.

The president's personal diplomacy was staffed and supported by senior officials and area experts who worked exceedingly well together. On issues involving the Middle East peace process, there was no split between the National Security Council and the State Department. At the working level, William Quandt, Harold Saunders, and Alfred Atherton, as well as other Middle East experts in the administration, coordinated the planning for a Geneva conference and supported the president in the Camp David process. The national security adviser and the secretary of state worked without rivalry or jealousy on these issues, and Brzezinski freely admits that, next to Carter, Vance deserves most of the credit for the administration's accomplishments in the Middle East.[48]

47. Rosenbaum and Ugrinsky, *Jimmy Carter,* 156; Jimmy Carter, *The Blood of Abraham: Insights into the Middle East* (Boston, 1985), 9.
48. Brzezinski, *Power and Principle,* 288.

The administration cooperation did not, of course, mean that there was complete agreement among the president's advisers regarding his decisions and actions. There were, in fact, serious debates about how much the president should involve himself in the peace process and whether he should invest his personal prestige in the uncertain diplomatic prospects of both Camp David and the trip to the Middle East. The president's decision to go to Cairo and Jerusalem was actively opposed by Vice President Mondale and press secretary Jody Powell, among others, who feared that failure was too likely and would cost too high a price.

The conventional wisdom among experienced foreign policy experts is that important meetings between heads of state are most useful when no agreements are expected and the national leaders merely have the opportunity to get to know each other or when major agreements have already been negotiated and the national leaders can merely go through the motions of ironing out a few remaining details and then share credit for the success. Substantive sessions between heads of state about important foreign policy issues that have not been carefully choreographed in advance can produce embarrassing results, such as Eisenhower's aborted summit in Paris or Reagan's bizarre bargaining sessions with Gorbachev at Reykjavík.

In his Middle East diplomacy, Carter defied the conventional wisdom. He invited Sadat and Begin to Camp David when the chances for significant progress were widely thought to be slim, and he decided to meet with both of them again five months later when the prospects for finalizing the Egyptian-Israeli peace treaty were still in doubt. The president, who was often described by his critics as weak and indecisive, was, in the conduct of negotiations with Sadat and Begin, bold and fully in command of his own agenda and his own administration. Carter's performance at Camp David and on the mission to the Middle East may be the exception to the rule, or it may be evidence that the rule should be rewritten. In any case, the critiques of Carter's strength and consistency cannot be made on the basis of his involvement in the Middle East peace process. Those claims have much more to do with how he, and his administration, responded to events in Iran and how a minor issue involving an alleged Soviet brigade in Cuba briefly became a major superpower crisis.

8

SHADOWBOXING
The Soviet Brigade in Cuba

It might be said to have started with a pair of pants. According to a communication intercepted in Cuba by the American intelligence community, a Russian soldier was to pick up some trousers from the cleaners and deliver them to brigade headquarters.[1] Of course, the pants themselves did not represent a threat to American national security, but the fact that the word "brigade" was being used in Cuba, in this and other intercepted messages, set in motion a remarkable train of events. In the end, the pair of pants led to a costly delay in Senate action on the SALT II treaty, a series of high-level negotiations between the world's superpowers, and the delivery of two televised speeches to the nation by the president of the United States. American mistakes in the interpretation of Soviet activities in Cuba, and in responding to them, may even have contributed to the Politburo decision to authorize an invasion of Afghanistan.[2]

The Soviet brigade discovered by the United States in the spring and summer of 1979 had been in Cuba since the end of the missile crisis seventeen years earlier. Fidel Castro told the participants at a 1992 international conference on the October 1962 crisis that the troops had been left behind

1. White Burkett Miller Center of Public Affairs, University of Virginia, Project on the Carter Presidency, Robert Beckel Session, November 13, 1981, p. 34.

2. David Newsom, *The Soviet Brigade in Cuba: A Study in Political Diplomacy* (Bloomington, Ind., 1987), 22; Gloria Duffy, "Crisis Prevention in Cuba," in *Managing U.S.-Soviet Rivalry: Problems of Crisis Prevention*, ed. Alexander George (Boulder, Colo., 1983), 308–309.

at Cuban urging, as a way to reinforce the Soviet commitment to defend the island from any future American invasion. "Someone's word is good," Castro said, "but someone's word with four brigades is even better."[3] The four brigades that Castro wanted were negotiated down to one, which remained in place as the rest of the Soviet equipment and military personnel were withdrawn. It was a small force of between two thousand and three thousand men, and though it had some tanks and other modern military equipment and conducted independent military exercises, it lacked any sealift or airlift capacity for rapid deployment off the island. The brigade posed no threat to the United States or to any of Cuba's neighbors; nor did it violate any of the agreements made in 1962 or 1970 concerning the stationing of Soviet offensive nuclear weapons or missile-carrying submarines in Cuba. Its existence was known to American officials in 1963, but the Soviet forces that remained on the island were not considered important, and detailed knowledge about their presence slipped from the institutional memory of the foreign policy bureaucracies. With renewed interest in Cuban overseas military activities in the late 1970s and hypersensitivity to all evidence of Soviet international adventurism in the midst of the SALT II debate, evidence like the laundry errands of Russian soldiers in Cuba was able to create a major domestic political problem and a minor superpower crisis.

The Soviet brigade in Cuba was never particularly important to either the United States or the Soviet Union, and the fact that it briefly received national and international attention completely out of proportion to what, if anything, it might have deserved is hard to understand. When the chief American SALT negotiator, Ralph Earle, tried to explain the series of misjudgments and mistakes that had led the United States to make a major issue out of an old and insignificant Soviet unit in Cuba, the Soviet official he was talking to rejected his explanation. "No government," he said, "could be that stupid."[4]

When Intelligence Is Not Very Intelligent

The stupidity began in the spring of 1979, before the signing of the final SALT II treaty documents at the Vienna summit in June. Zbigniew Brzez-

---

3. James G. Blight, Bruce J. Allyn, and David A. Welch, *Cuba on the Brink: Castro, the Missile Crisis, and the Soviet Collapse* (New York, 1993), 287.

4. Leroy Ashby and Rod Gramer, *Fighting the Odds: The Life of Senator Frank Church* (Pullman, Wash., 1994), 596.

inski called on the intelligence community to give special attention to the question of Soviet military activities in Cuba.[5] There was good reason for the national security adviser to make this request. The nearly completed SALT II agreements would face a ratification debate in the Senate at least as controversial as the debate over the Panama Canal treaties. A wide range of issues could arise in the course of the Senate deliberations, including questions about Soviet overt and covert foreign policy initiatives throughout the world. The role of Soviet-sponsored Cuban troops in various African countries was already a source of tension in U.S.-Soviet relations, and the growing success of the Sandinista movement in Nicaragua and instability in a number of nations in the region made the possibility of Soviet supported subversion in the Western Hemisphere a plausible danger. Earlier in the administration, the delivery of modern Soviet MiG aircraft to Cuba had been an issue for senior foreign policy makers and a topic of discussion between Soviet and American officials.[6] It was resolved when U.S. intelligence experts concluded that the MiGs were not equipped to carry nuclear bombs and, therefore, were not a violation of the 1962 agreements between Kennedy and Khrushchev which brought the missile crisis to an end.

Though the Carter administration had officially abandoned Kissinger-era linkage and argued that SALT II should be evaluated on its merits, there was a realistic recognition that the treaty could not win a two-thirds vote in the Senate if there was substantial evidence of growing Soviet-sponsored aggression in the world, but particularly in the Western Hemisphere. Brzezinski's call for a review of Soviet forces in Cuba was part of a larger concern he had about Soviet assertiveness worldwide that many critics of the SALT II treaty shared. Brzezinski, of course, wanted the SALT treaty ratified and may have been asking for more intelligence on Cuba to make sure that there were no surprises in the course of the upcoming ratification debates. In fact, the Brzezinski request for new information about Soviet-Cuba military activities inadvertently produced the most embarrassing foreign policy surprise of the year.

The National Security Agency (NSA), which has responsibility for signal

5. According to Vance, this request was made in April, but others report that it was made in March. Cyrus Vance, *Hard Choices: Four Critical Years in Managing America's Foreign Policy* (New York, 1983), 358. Duffy, "Crisis Prevention in Cuba," 299.

6. Zbigniew Brzezinski, *Power and Principle: Memoirs of the National Security Advisor 1977–1981* (New York, 1983), 346.

intelligence, responded to the NSC request by monitoring current communications in Cuba and searching its files. The agency discovered—or to be more precise, rediscovered—the word "brigade" in a number of intercepted messages, including the trip to the cleaners.[7] The word had apparently been used in Cuba since at least 1975. In addition, newly collected photographs of Soviet forces stationed in Cuba confirmed that one unit was housed in tents arranged in a fashion similar to a standard Soviet troop deployment.[8] The combination of new and old raw photographic and signal intelligence led analysts in the NSA to conclude that the Soviet military advisers long known to be present in Cuba might now include a combat brigade. They reached this conclusion apparently without checking State Department, Defense Department, or CIA files on the history of Soviet activities in Cuba and could not say how long the brigade had been on the island or precisely what its mission might be. The absence of this historical dimension in the NSA report left the impression that the brigade was new. The use of the word "combat" as an adjective created the impression that it was threatening.[9] Neither impression was correct.

In the normal course of events, this NSA information would have received further analysis in the intelligence community, and indeed, in an interim report prepared by the CIA, there were cautionary notes about continued uncertainty regarding the size, organization, and mission of the unit identified as a brigade by NSA analysts.[10] More investigation of this issue

7. Stansfield Turner, "The Stupidity of Intelligence," *Washington Monthly*, February 1986, p. 30. Most of the material in this article is drawn from Turner's book *Secrecy and Democracy: the CIA in Transition* (Boston, 1985).

8. Gloria Duffy, "Crisis Mangling, " *International Security* 8, no 1 (summer 1983), 72.

9. Turner, "The Stupidity of Intelligence," 30–31. According to a postmortem by journalist Don Oberdorfer, the word *combat* was not used in the initial NSA report as Turner implies. Don Oberdorfer, "Cuban Crisis Mishandled," *Washington Post*, October 16, 1979, p. A14. Newsom also believes that the word *combat* was not used in the July intelligence reports. David Newsom, interview by author, Charlottesville, Va., February 1, 1995. The word was used in some of the media reporting that followed Senator Stone's revelations about the brigade discussed below. On July 18 the *Washington Star* reported that "Sen. Richard Stone, D-Fla., yesterday said Soviet combat troops may be in Cuba," and ABC news described the brigade as containing "combat-ready men." Dan Caldwell, "Senator Church and the Soviet Brigade in Cuba," Pew Case Studies in International Affairs, Case 351, Part A (Washington, D.C., 1992), 2.

10. Duffy, "Crisis Mangling," 73.

was clearly needed and was called for by Brzezinski and others.[11] But before further study could be completed, the NSA preliminary conclusion became a matter of congressional concern and public knowledge.

On July 17, Senator Richard Stone, a conservative Democrat from Florida (the state with the nation's largest Cuban-American community), asked questions in both open and closed hearings of the Foreign Relations Committee about the possibility of new Soviet combat troops in Cuba. CIA Director Stansfield Turner believes that there must have been an intentional leak to the senator by someone in the executive branch, but others report that a member of Stone's staff overheard a conversation between two administration officials discussing the NSA report.[12] Whether the information came to the senator from an accidental or purposeful leak, the result was the same. The senator went public with the information he had.

Stone had made an issue of Soviet military activities in the Caribbean during the Panama Canal debates and took some pride in winning assurances from the Carter administration that it would not permit the introduction of any new Soviet bases in the Western Hemisphere. That concession had given the senator some political cover for his unpopular votes in favor of the Panama treaties. In 1978, when twenty senators who had voted for the treaties were up for reelection, six chose to retire and seven were defeated. Only seven of the twenty treaty supporters were able to win a new six-year term. Stone was up for reelection in 1980.

In a secret session with the Foreign Relations Committee that was scheduled to deal with SALT, Secretary of Defense Brown assured the Florida senator that "there is no evidence of any increase in the size of the Soviet military presence in Cuba over the last several years," and that current "intelligence does not warrant the conclusion that there are any other significant Soviet military forces in Cuba" beyond those on known training missions.[13] Both the Stone allegations and Brown's response were published in the *Washington Star* and used in ABC network news broadcasts. The issue,

11. Brzezinski, *Power and Principle*, 347.

12. Turner, "The Stupidity of Intelligence," 30; Oberdorfer, "Cuban Crisis Mishandled"; Duffy, "Crisis Mangling," 73. A third source may have been an aide to Senator Jesse Helms. Caldwell, "Senator Church and the Soviet Brigade in Cuba," 1–2.

13. Harold Brown, quoted in Turner, "The Stupidity of Intelligence," 30. Turner believes that Brown's denial was a bit too emphatic, given the NSA brigade report and what was known at the time, though, in fact, what Brown said was completely correct.

however, did not receive serious national attention in July, probably because of the immediate administration denial. It also helped that the chairman and the ranking Republican on the Foreign Relations Committee, Senators Frank Church and Jacob Javits, issued a public statement affirming that there was no new Soviet military buildup in Cuba. Senator Stone was not satisfied, and the administration agreed to give him a detailed classified briefing on Soviet activities in Cuba. In addition, at the end of July, Secretary of State Vance wrote a letter to the senator repeating the position already taken by Brown. There was "no evidence of any substantial increase of the Soviet military presence in Cuba over the past several years or of the presence of a Soviet military base."[14] The secretary's letter used the word "base," which was important to Stone, but avoided making any specific reference to a "brigade." Stone dismissed the various administration responses he received to his inquiries about the brigade and called the letter from the secretary of state a "whitewash."[15]

While senior members of the administration were busy denying the rumors about new Soviet troops in Cuba, the CIA was collecting information that would undermine their efforts to downplay the issue. It was learned that in the middle of August the suspect Soviet unit would be conducting field exercises in Cuba, and priority was given to the collection of information about those exercises. In the past, the CIA had not paid close attention to the small number of Russian soldiers in Cuba and knew relatively little about their routines and activities. The military exercises conducted in August were photographed by satellite cameras and did not appear to involve any Cuban observers or trainees. The absence of Cuban participants lent credence to the conclusion that the unit was not engaged in training others and might be properly designated a combat brigade. Of course, it was also possible that a group of soldiers in a foreign country on a training mission would occasionally conduct independent exercises to keep themselves in the general state of readiness that all military units customarily attempt to maintain. Or perhaps the Russians had a special mission in Cuba, like defending the large Soviet communications and intelligence-gathering installation near Havana, or protecting Castro in the event of an internal uprising

14. Vance, *Hard Choices*, 359–60. The full text of the Vance letter to Stone is printed in Newsom, *The Soviet Brigade in Cuba*, 96–97.
15. Caldwell, "Senator Church and the Soviet Brigade in Cuba," 2.

against his regime. As we have already noted, in 1992, Castro claimed that the brigade mission was to guarantee Soviet promises to defend the island. Castro says that he first heard about the brigade's training mission in a message from the Soviets in 1979, after the brigade issue had surfaced, asking if the Soviet troops and facilities in Cuba should be described as a training center.[16] Perhaps there was more than one government in 1979 that had lost track of what the small Soviet troop deployment in the Caribbean was all about.

Certainly the United States government was having difficulty putting its newest Cuban raw intelligence into context. The initial CIA evaluation of the August exercises did not include the important historical information about when Soviet forces arrived on the island or what they had been doing since. Instead, the CIA report summarized the field exercise data and concluded that the analysts at NSA were right. There was a Soviet combat brigade in Cuba.[17] Like the earlier NSA conclusion, the newest classified intelligence report quickly became public.

The CIA review of the Soviet exercises was published in the *National Intelligence Daily*, a fairly widely circulated newsletter that contains current intelligence information for defense and foreign policy makers throughout the executive branch.[18] Within a week, the latest intelligence information about Cuba was in the hands of a reporter for *Aviation Week and Space Technology*—a small-circulation, but influential, technical journal whose stories were often picked up by major newspapers. The reporter who had the brigade information called the State Department for confirmation.

The confirmation request came to the attention of David Newsom, the under secretary of state, on August 29, when many of the senior members of the administration were away from Washington on brief end-of-summer holidays. The president had received a briefing on the new CIA information while on a riverboat trip down the Mississippi River and was planning

16. Blight, Allyn, and Welch, *Cuba on the Brink*, 288.

17. Turner, "The Stupidity of Intelligence," 31. Newsom believes that this was the first internal administration document to use the word *combat* as a modifier for the word *brigade*. Newsom, interview. Stansfield Turner believes that the NSA reporting earlier in the summer also used the phrase "combat brigade." Stansfield Turner, letter to author, March 29, 1995. Neither individual has ready access to the documents that would settle this issue.

18. In 1979, it went to 400 addressees in the federal government. Newsom, *The Soviet Brigade in Cuba*, 22. Duffy reports that the number was 200. Duffy, "Crisis Mangling," 75.

to continue his vacation at Camp David. The vice president was overseas. Brzezinski and Brown were out of town. The Soviet ambassador to the United States, Anatoly Dobrynin, was in Moscow, where his parents were gravely ill. The White House chief of staff, Hamilton Jordan, was in Washington, but he was preoccupied with recently publicized accusations that he had used cocaine while serving as a member of the administration.

The *Aviation Week and Space Technology* reporter was told that the State Department had no comment about the story, and Newsom immediately informed Vance that the brigade intelligence was about to go public. Senator Stone had already been told that there was new information about Cuba and had been promised an updated briefing when he returned to Washington. The Soviet embassy had been asked to respond to the brigade information and urge an early return to Washington for Ambassador Dobrynin. Newsom and Vance now agreed that other senior members of Congress, including the chairman of Stone's committee, should be given the CIA brigade intelligence before it appeared in print. The legislature was in August recess, and like the senior foreign policy officials of the administration, many members were away from Washington. Most of the House and Senate leaders reached by phone thanked Newsom for the update on Cuba and agreed that the story, when it became public, should not be blown out of proportion. There was one significant exception.

Frank Church, the chairman of the Senate Foreign Relations Committee, was up for reelection in Idaho in 1980. Like Senator Stone, Church had voted for the Panama Canal treaties and was fighting a serious conservative backlash against treaty supporters. Unlike Stone, Church had seniority, an important committee chairmanship, and a national reputation based on his leadership of a legislative investigation of intelligence community abuses and his brief run for the presidency in 1976. Nevertheless, those political assets were not enough to keep the senator out of trouble in his home state. Idaho had no significant Cuban-American community, but its citizens held opinions on foreign and defense policy issues that were considerably less liberal than those of their senior senator. Church was one of a number of Democratic senators targeted for defeat by national conservative political organizations. One of the ads being effectively used against him in the early stages of the campaign showed the senator on a visit to Cuba smoking cigars with Castro.[19] Another ad showed an empty missile silo and questioned the

19. Duffy, "Crisis Mangling," 78.

wisdom of Church's role as a promoter of arms control and SALT II.[20] In a conservative western state, these were not the images that would win reelection in 1980, and Frank Church was increasingly worried that his political career might be coming to an end.

Something else influenced the senator's response to Newsom's news that there was a Soviet combat brigade in Cuba. Seventeen years earlier, while campaigning in the fall of 1962, Church had confidently denied speculative press reports that Cuba would become a base for Soviet military operations in the Western Hemisphere. A newsletter downplaying the Castro threat was in the mail to his Idaho constituents when President Kennedy announced the presence of Soviet offensive missiles in Cuba.[21] The missile crisis and Church's 1962 reelection campaign both ended well, but the memory of feeling foolish and politically vulnerable when Soviet actions in Cuba caught him by surprise may have influenced the senator's reaction, or overreaction, to the brigade intelligence.

After talking with Newsom and Vance, and attempting unsuccessfully to reach President Carter, Senator Church decided to call a press conference in Idaho. He thought it would be better if the brigade information came from a Washington official rather than an anonymous leak and told Vance that he would go public with the story if no one in the administration planned to do so. The secretary of state told the senator that a press conference would not be a good idea, but left the final decision with Church.[22] Of course, secretaries of state cannot give orders to members of Congress, and particularly not to the chairman of the committee that reviews most of the department's business. By leaving the matter to the senator's discretion, Church may have thought that Vance was giving him tacit approval to proceed with a press conference. The secretary of state thought he was advising the senator to reconsider before taking that step. "My expectation," Vance recorded in his memoirs, "was that Church would say nothing."[23] The secretary of state was sorely disappointed. Senator Church told all the reporters he could find in Boise that there was a Soviet combat brigade in Cuba and called on President Carter to demand its immediate withdrawal.

20. Ashby and Gramer, *Fighting the Odds,* 592.
21. Ibid., 154–55.
22. Vance, *Hard Choices,* 361.
23. Ibid.

216

Coming from a prominent liberal senator and the chairman of the committee that was still holding hearings on SALT II, the Idaho press conference attracted national attention and speculation that the fate of the strategic arms control agreement might be decided depending on how this issue was resolved. Church had told Newsom that the brigade would "sink SALT" when he first heard about it, but at his press conference he made no explicit linkage between the two issues.[24] Within a few days, however, he was publicly making that connection, as were other senators who were far less sympathetic to SALT than Church. When the Senate reconvened, the Foreign Relations Committee held hearings on Soviet military activities in Cuba, and Church sponsored a resolution calling for a formal delay in Senate action on the treaty pending some settlement of the brigade issue.

The complicated and controversial arms control agreement that had been under negotiation since 1972 by three presidents was now in serious trouble on Capitol Hill, and the administration was caught between the Senate and the Soviets.[25] Ignoring the brigade issue, or treating it as the minor matter that it actually was, would have offended Church, Stone, and other senators whose votes were essential for treaty ratification. But taking the brigade seriously meant demanding its withdrawal or some other concessions from the Soviets that might be difficult to obtain. Given a choice between certain Senate wrath and uncertain Soviet cooperation, the administration chose to take its chances with superpower diplomacy.

Vance at his own press conference on September 5, the day Congress reconvened, said in his planned remarks that "I will not be satisfied with the maintenance of the status quo" in Cuba.[26] He had hoped that this statement would give the administration some credibility with the senators who were making the brigade an issue and some flexibility with the Soviets. If Moscow would accept some change in the brigade—like removing its command structure or relocating its heavy weapons—those actions could be announced as a change in the status quo. Instead, the secretary's statement was interpreted as a call for removal of the brigade from Cuba, and the expecta-

24. Newsom, *The Soviet Brigade in Cuba*, 34.

25. For evaluation of SALT prospects in the midst of the brigade crisis, see Don Oberdorfer, "A Small Soviet Brigade and Its Large Implications," *Washington Post*, September 23, 1979.

26. For a full text of the Vance press conference discussion of Cuba, see Newsom, *The Soviet Brigade in Cuba*, 67–76.

tions of what would come out of forthcoming talks with the Soviets were raised.[27] Two days later the president repeated the Vance language that the "status quo" in Cuba was "unacceptable" in a brief televised report to the nation.[28]

What Carter said on September 7, was, in fact, quite moderate. He reiterated the facts about the brigade as they were then known to the American government. The Soviet unit posed no threat to the United States; it had been in Cuba for an unknown, and perhaps quite long, period of time; and its mission and purpose were not yet clear.[29] Nevertheless, the presence of even a small Soviet combat force in the Western Hemisphere was a matter of concern to the United States, particularly when it was located in a "country which acts as a Soviet proxy in military adventures in other areas of the world like Africa."[30] Inclusion of this brief reference to Cuban military advisers in Africa was favored by Brzezinski and opposed by Vance and Vice President Mondale.[31] Despite the Africa remark and the endorsement of Vance's call for a change in the status quo, the president's statement was intended to dampen the issue. "This is a time for firm diplomacy, not panic or exaggeration," he said. Carter called for "calm and a sense of proportion" and asked the Congress and the American people to await the results of the Vance discussions with Soviet officials. Of course, calling for calm was generally helpful in responding to a minor matter in U.S.-Soviet relations, but doing so in a televised presidential statement was another inflation of the issue's profile and importance.

During the next few weeks Vance met with Soviet ambassador Dobrynin and foreign minister Gromyko in Washington and New York in eight separate sessions. He was unable to win the hoped-for concessions. The Soviets

27. Vance, *Hard Choices,* 362.

28. Jimmy Carter, *Keeping Faith: Memoirs of a President,* (New York, 1982), 263–64.

29. The NSA had reported on September 3 that the Soviet brigade had been in Cuba at least since 1968. Two days later, the CIA confirmed this assessment after a search of human intelligence files from the period 1968 to 1971. Robert M. Gates, *From the Shadows: The Ultimate Insider's Story of Five Presidents and How They Won the Cold War* (New York, 1996), 158.

30. The full text of the president's remarks are in Newsom, *The Soviet Brigade in Cuba,* 79–80.

31. Zbigniew Brzezinski to the president, memorandum: "Cuba Statement," September 7, 1979. Office of the Staff Secretary, President's Handwriting File, Box 144, File 9/7/79, Carter Library.

insisted that the unit in question had been in Cuba since 1962 and that it was not engaged in any new or threatening activities. Further, they insisted that there was no basis for American complaints about the brigade in any of the commitments made in 1962 or 1970 about the placement of Soviet offensive nuclear weapons in Cuba. The United States had troops stationed close to the Soviet border in Turkey and maintained a large number of military advisers in Iran before the fall of the shah. Moreover, it had a combat force of its own stationed in Guantánamo, Cuba, that was roughly the same size as the Soviet brigade.

All of this was true, and Vance could not persuade the Soviets that, given the attention this issue was receiving on Capitol Hill and the dangers it posed for the ratification of SALT II, it would be worthwhile for them to make some minor adjustments in the status of their forces in Cuba. The hoped-for concession that the administration could use to placate senators concerned about the brigade would not be coming from Moscow. The Soviets, perhaps understandably, did not wish to make a change to their forces in Cuba in response to a belated and exaggerated discovery by U.S. intelligence officers that a Soviet brigade was stationed there. In fact, Soviet officials may well have doubted the reality of that belated and exaggerated discovery, and may have feared that the administration was seeking a way out of its SALT II commitments that could be blamed on the Senate.[32]

The failure of diplomacy pushed the issue back on the president's desk and gave Carter some difficult decisions to make. Not only was the fate of a major arms control agreement at stake, but the president's prestige and reputation were also involved in the resolution of the issue. Eventually, the president would have to explain to the satisfaction of selected senators and administration critics what he was going to do about the Soviet "brigade" in Cuba that he and his secretary of state had called "unacceptable." The focus of attention within the administration began to coalesce around the drafting of a second televised address to the nation.

Putting the Matter to Rest
On September 21, the regular foreign policy breakfast meeting included "a major blowup between Vance and Brzezinski" on what to do next in con-

---

32. For evidence that Soviet officials saw the brigade issue in this way, see Caldwell, "Senator Church and the Soviet Brigade in Cuba," 8–9.

nection with the brigade issue. One observer at that meeting described the dispute as three-sided. There were those who wanted to save SALT II as their first priority; those who wanted to build a consensus for a more competitive stance against the Soviet Union (preferably with SALT but without it if necessary); and "those who are primarily concerned with salvaging the Carter presidency, a preoccupation which for the most part inclines them toward the second rather than the first posture."[33]

On the same day, Charles Kirbo, the president's longtime Georgia friend and political adviser, sent Carter a three-page memorandum with a radical proposal.[34] Referring to earlier conversations they had had about the brigade issue, Kirbo suggested that the president go on television, outline the facts about the small number of Soviet troops in Cuba, and blame Senator Church for releasing classified information before matters could be privately resolved in discussions with the Soviets. The president should then argue that the brigade issue can and should be handled without having any effect on the much more important SALT II treaty. Kirbo suggested that the president criticize proposals to delay consideration of SALT, like the resolution sponsored by Church, and urge a prompt vote up or down on the treaty. The president's friend guessed that the Senate would not wish to take responsibility for rejecting a historic arms control agreement, but that even if rejection took place, Carter would be politically better off than he would be if the ratification debate dragged on and the treaty became an issue in the upcoming presidential election.

Carter did not take Kirbo's advice. Instead he began to consider a variety of steps that could be taken by the United States and that could be announced in an address to the nation as the official administration response to the brigade issue. These steps would amount to, as Under Secretary Newsom later wrote, the promised change in the "status quo" in Cuba through "unilateral" American action.[35] This was a weaker response than the one proposed by Kirbo, but it probably had better prospects for saving the SALT II treaty.

Throughout this period, Brzezinski was publicly comparing the brigade

33. Gates, *From the Shadows*, 158–59.

34. Charles Kirbo to President Jimmy Carter, memorandum, September 21, 1979, Office of the Staff Secretary, President's Handwriting File, Box 149, Folder "President's Address to the Nation [2]," Carter Library.

35. Newsom, *The Soviet Brigade in Cuba*, 47.

issue to the Berlin wall, another "unacceptable" Soviet action that the United States accepted, which was answered with a buildup of U.S. forces in Europe.[36] The national security adviser and others in the administration began to develop a list of possible U.S. actions in response to the brigade from which the president might make a selection of those deemed most appropriate.[37] Brzezinski's list contained roughly ten items. Four of them were rather obvious U.S. actions in the circumstances: greater surveillance of Soviet activities in Cuba, assurances to American allies in the region that the United States would defend them against any possible Soviet interventions, increased economic and military aid for some of the Central American and Caribbean nations, and creation of a new Caribbean joint task force to plan and carry out more U.S. military maneuvers in the region than were already done. Three more items involved major moves in defense preparedness: accelerated creation of a rapid-deployment force, a commitment to higher defense spending beyond the 3 percent annual real growth to which the administration was already committed, and a presidential commission to study the reintroduction of the draft. The last two defense-related ideas were favorites of Senator Nunn, another important legislator in the SALT II debate, who was not yet committed to the treaty's ratification. Finally, there were a number of proposed actions that would directly punish the Soviets or threaten their interests elsewhere in the world. These included reconsideration of pending sales of high-technology and computer equipment to the Soviet Union, postponement of any consideration of most-favored-nation (MFN) status for the Soviets (already a nearly dead issue due to the Jackson-Vanik amendment), and a proposal that Congress repeal the Clark amendment restricting American covert action in Angola, one of the locations where Cuban troops were active.

In a long memo written on September 25, another frequent outside adviser, Patrick Caddell, evaluated the possible courses of action suggested by Brzezinski. The president's pollster and campaign adviser told Carter that the American people did not believe that the administration was being

---

36. Brzezinski, *Power and Principle*, 349.

37. One list of the Brzezinski items is contained in Patrick Caddell to the President, memorandum, September 25, 1979, Office of the Staff Secretary, President's Handwriting File, Box 149, Folder "President's Address to the Nation [3]," Carter Library. Other responses proposed by Brzezinski are mentioned in his memoirs and in Oberdorfer, "Cuban Crisis Mishandled."

tough enough with the Soviet Union, but continued to want the progress toward a more peaceful world that SALT had come to represent. Carter's problem in responding to the brigade issue was to sound both tough and hopeful. He needed to clench his fist without crushing SALT, and he needed to get the whole brigade issue behind him before the arrival of the pope in the United States buried anything the president might say or do in a flurry of papal news. Caddell urged Carter to endorse the easy items on Brzezinski's list, such as stepped-up surveillance of Cuba and U.S. exercises in the Caribbean, but shy away from the unpopular or disproportionate responses, such as a study of the draft or asking Congress to repeal the Clark amendment.[38]

While the final unsuccessful negotiating sessions between Vance and Soviet officials were taking place, Brzezinski was supervising the preparation of a possible presidential speech. The national security adviser wanted a measured, but tough, U.S. response that would treat the Cuban issue as the straw that broke the camel's back and have the president talking mostly about the heavy load of Soviet adventurism being carried by the camel and rather less about the straw that was the brigade.[39] In addition to the items listed above, he proposed that the president consider some responses to this broader Soviet threat by approving technology and arms transfers to China and increased Voice of America broadcasts to Soviet minorities.[40]

But while Brzezinski wanted to treat the brigade as a minor matter in a major Soviet global challenge to the United States, Carter continued to focus on how the brigade would affect the prospects for SALT in the Senate. At a meeting with Senate majority leader Robert Byrd on September 23, the president and his two senior foreign policy advisers heard a gloomy picture of the prospects for SALT ratification. Byrd had had his own discussions with Soviet ambassador Dobrynin and warned the ambassador that SALT was in trouble unless the Soviets helped to set the brigade issue aside.

38. Caddell to the President, memorandum, September 25, 1979.

39. The image of the brigade as the straw on the camel's back was suggested to Brzezinski in a handwritten note that the national security adviser passed on to the president. The note is neither dated nor signed, but the initials HO at the conclusion suggest that it was written by Henry Owen. Office of the Staff Secretary, President's Handwriting File, Box 149, Folder "President's Address to Nation [2], Carter Library."

40. Brzezinski, *Power and Principle*, 350.

Dobrynin gave Byrd the same response he had given to Vance, namely, that the whole issue was phony and that it was unrealistic to expect Soviet concessions when the Soviets had, in fact, done nothing new or provocative. Vance, Carter, and Byrd were all talking about finding a face-saving and SALT-saving way out of the mess they were in. This meant hiding Brzezinski's camel instead of parading it before the American people. The national security adviser was not pleased.[41]

At two meetings of the Policy Review Committee (PRC), chaired by the secretary of state and held on September 27 and 28, Vance reported on the results of his unproductive discussions with Dobrynin and Gromyko and on "hotline" communications between Carter and Brezhnev. The most that could be secured from the Soviets were statements that the brigade was engaged in training, that its function and status would not be changed, and that it would not be a threat to the United States or to any other nation. Those Soviet assurances were not really concessions, since they merely restated the Russian version of the brigade facts. The president's senior foreign policy advisers now had to decide where to go from here.

Three issues were addressed at the PRC meetings. Should the president speak to the nation? Carter decided that he would. Should his speech deal with the brigade alone or SALT as well? The linkage between these two issues had been resisted by the administration, but was, by this time, unavoidable. The president would need to talk about both subjects. Finally, what specific unilateral U.S. steps should be taken in response to the brigade? Most of the toughest actions Brzezinski wanted were rejected, and the decision was made to try and put the issue to rest with a full-scale explanation of the available intelligence information, a report on the Soviet assurances that the brigade would not be allowed to create any new threats to security in the Caribbean, and the moderate American responses of increased monitoring and military preparedness in the region.[42]

At the suggestion of Lloyd Cutler, who was counsel to the president, it was also decided that the president should meet with a bipartisan group of prominent former national security officials. The group of sixteen, led by Clark Clifford, included former secretaries of state and defense and foreign

41. Ibid.
42. Martin Schram, "Carter at Meeting's End," *Washington Post*, October 2, 1979, p. A6.

policy experts. Collectively they had served every president from Franklin Roosevelt to Gerald Ford.[43] After receiving a detailed intelligence briefing and discussing the brigade issue with Brzezinski, they met with the president for lunch two days before Carter's scheduled speech to the nation. Here was another inflation of the issue. This kind of session with "wise men" had been used in the Johnson administration when the president wanted endorsement for his controversial actions in Vietnam and later when Secretary of Defense Clifford wanted help in convincing Johnson that it was time to end the war. Both the getting into and out of Vietnam were vastly more important than the Cuban brigade, and Brzezinski objected to the presidential meeting with senior statesmen, predicting that it would result in an appearance of weakness rather than strength.[44] In fact, when news about the meeting between the president and the so-called alumni group became public, it was generally well received.[45]

In the final days of September, the president's speech to the nation went through multiple drafts, with significant contributions from Vance, Brzezinski, Cutler, and head speechwriter Rick Hertzberg. Carter met with his senior political and foreign policy advisers throughout the drafting process and made his own substantive revisions to a near-final version of the speech. Vance provided the language describing the Soviet assurances regarding their military activities in Cuba.[46] Cutler, who had joined the administration about the time the brigade issue broke and was coordinating the SALT ratification fight in the Senate, made his principal contribution to the president's speech by toning down the Brzezinski draft. Where the Brzezinski version said there was "irrefutable" evidence of a Soviet combat unit sta-

43. Besides Clifford the group included George Ball, McGeorge Bundy, Roswell Gilpatrick, Averell Harriman, Henry Kissinger, Nicholas Katzenbach, Sol Linowitz, John McCloy, John McCone, David Packard, William P. Rogers, Dean Rusk, James Schlesinger, William Scranton, and Brent Scowcroft.

44. Brzezinski, *Power and Principle*, 350–51.

45. "Mr. Carter and Cuba," editorial, *Washington Post*, September 30, 1979; "Carter's Cuban Dilemma," *Newsweek*, October 8, 1979.

46. Cyrus Vance to the President, memorandum, September 29, 1979, Office of the Staff Secretary, President's Handwriting File, Box 149, Folder "President's Address to the Nation [1]," Carter Library. Another copy of this memo can be found in Folder [4] as part of the September 30 draft. This copy has handwritten revisions and the notation "The entire group favored this version," which apparently refers to the advisers who met Sunday evening to review the speech.

tioned in Cuba, Cutler substituted "persuasive evidence." Where the draft said that this unit "is" a ground combat brigade, Cutler suggested a more ambiguous "appears to be."[47] Where a reference was made to the Cuban missile crisis "seventeen years ago," Cutler added a qualifying description of that earlier period as "in the era of the Cold War."[48] He also deleted a number of passages having to do with Soviet activities in Africa and North Yemen and a specific proposal to facilitate arms sales to countries around the world menaced by Soviet or Cuban military activities.[49] All of these changes survived the remaining revisions done by the speechwriters and the president and helped set the moderate tone for the president's remarks. Additional deletions proposed by Cutler, which would have eliminated all references to Cuban troops in Africa and the extent of Cuban subservience to Moscow, were not accepted.

As the speech was nearing completion on Sunday, September 30, Rick Hertzberg sent Brzezinski a memo and a last-minute revised draft. Late that night he sent both the memo and draft to the president. Hertzberg was worried that the speech was "whiny" and "topheavy with stuff about the brigade and with overly detailed descriptions of marginal military steps which, thanks to the detail, end up sounding weak." The more important subjects, "Soviet-Cuban mischief in the Third World" and SALT were lost in the detail about the brigade. Hertzberg proposed that a revised version of the speech treat the issue of the brigade "(a) . . . with something bordering on contempt; (b) address the broader issue of Russian mischief in a calm, measured, serious way; and (c) get to SALT before the audience has lapsed into a coma."[50] These were Brzezinski's views as well, though he thought tougher action rather than snappier prose was needed to save the speech. Most of what Hertzberg wrote, including his description of the brigade as "insignificant" and a "pebble" in the path to peace, was dropped. But Carter decided to use the first two pages of Hertzberg's "unauthorized draft" as a

47. Draft THREE (A-l), Lloyd Cutler suggestions, 9/28/79, Office of the Staff Secretary, President's Handwriting File, Box 149, Folder "President's Address to the Nation [4]," p. 5, Carter Library.

48. Ibid., 4.

49. Ibid., 13–15.

50. Rick Hertzberg to Dr. Brzezinski, memorandum, September 30, 1979, Office of the Staff Secretary, President's Handwriting File, Box 149, Folder "President's Address to the Nation [4]," Carter Library.

new and shorter introduction for the speech that included a clear and early connection between the brigade and SALT. He then proceeded to make his own final revisions to the toned-down Brzezinski draft.

Carter's changes were largely stylistic, but style and substance were not far apart in the brigade issue. The detailed litany of Cuban actions in Africa and the Middle East had come out of earlier drafts, but Carter put back into the beginning of the speech a reference to our concern about "Cuban military activities around the world," and he added to the list of responses a reminder that "we have reinforced our naval presence in the Indian Ocean."[51] He deleted several references to the "brigade" in Cuba and replaced them with the phrase "Soviet forces." Where the word "brigade" was left in the text, he crossed out the "combat" modifier.[52] Months after its original discovery, there was still confusion at the highest levels of the Carter administration about what to call the Soviet troops in Cuba.

At a meeting late in the morning on the Monday when the speech was to be delivered, the president approved a final draft. It contained the basic elements that had been discussed for the past week—a detailed description of the brigade intelligence, the Soviet assurances that it would continue to be a non-threatening training center, the list of moderate military measures to be taken in the Caribbean, and the renewed call for Senate ratification of SALT II. In one of the most widely quoted passages, the president said that there was "no reason for a return to the Cold War. A confrontation might be emotionally satisfying for a few days or weeks, but it would be destructive to the national interest and to the security of the United States." In urging the Senate to get on with the business of SALT ratification, and in what may have been read as a veiled criticism of Senator Church, the president said that "politics and nuclear arsenals do not mix."[53] But, of course, they do mix, and that was the central problem the speech attempted to address.

Before the speech was given, Senator Church was invited to the White House for a preview of what the president would say. The Idaho senator, according to one Carter adviser, had "created a minefield through which

51. Untitled draft D-2 with inserts, Office of the Staff Secretary, President's Handwriting File, Box 149, Folder "President's Address to the Nation [1]," pp. 2, 11, Carter Library.
52. Ibid., 4.
53. The full text of the president's speech appears in Newsom, *The Soviet Brigade in Cuba*, 81–86.

we've had to walk every day since this began."[54] Church was not fully satisfied with the president's remarks, but none of his mines exploded. After the speech was delivered, the senator announced that he would schedule a committee markup for the SALT II treaty and began to talk about a reservation to the resolution of ratification that would deal with his Cuban concerns.[55] The issue of the Soviet brigade in Cuba did not disappear completely with the president's televised speech to the nation on October 1, but it did diminish in importance. Nevertheless it remained one of several problems that stood in the way of SALT II ratification.

Conclusions

According to former CIA Director Stansfield Turner, there were two major intelligence failures in the middle years of the Carter administration. One was the inability of the intelligence agencies to predict the fall of the shah; the other was the discovery of a combat brigade in Cuba that had actually been on the island for nearly two decades. In some ways, the brigade fiasco was the bigger mistake. A more accurate picture of events in Iran would have helped the president and his senior advisers in 1978 and 1979, but it might not have led to a fundamentally different American foreign policy. It is possible that the shah would have fallen from power even if the United States had fully understood the dangers he faced in 1978. Earlier and better information about the brigade would have been a different matter. Had the "new" information about Soviet troops in Cuba been properly identified as old and not very important, it could have been shared with the Congress and the public without producing a crisis. With better intelligence the administration could have saved itself from what Warren Christopher correctly called a "self-inflicted wound."[56]

Turner puts much of the blame for the self-inflicted damage on bureaucratic competition within the intelligence community. NSA analysts gave exaggerated interpretation and wide dissemination to fragmentary information about the use of the word "brigade" in Cuba because they wanted to

54. Schram, "Carter at Meeting's End."

55. "Carter Speech May Have Cost SALT Some Uncommitted Senators' Support," *Washington Post*, October 3, 1979, p. A14.

56. Warren Christopher, quoted in Dan Caldwell, *The Dynamics of Domestic Politics and Arms Control: The SALT II Treaty Ratification Debate* (Columbia, S.C., 1991), 169.

be the first ones to deliver the goods that the White House had requested. An agency primarily responsible for the collection of raw intelligence overstepped its role and institutional competence by giving that information a premature and misleading interpretation.[57] The job of interpreting the "new" information should have been performed by CIA analysts and experts in the departments of state and defense who had responsibility for knowing the history of Soviet-Cuban activities and judging the overall significance of the brigade. Those individuals either did not have enough time or did not have easy access to relevant historical information about the Soviet military presence in Cuba to provide the senior foreign policy makers in the administration with an accurate picture of what the NSA intercepts really meant.

Former CIA deputy director Ray Cline argues that the Carter administration contributed to the weak performance of the intelligence community in 1979 by "cancelling aircraft reconnaissance overflights of Cuba" early in 1977, thus sending "the signal that the White House attached no priority to fine points about Soviet forces in Cuba."[58] Other observers argue that the cancellation of SR-71 flights over Cuba made very little difference in the collection of information about the brigade, and that for many years the priority for the intelligence officials monitoring Soviet military forces in Cuba was the introduction of offensive weapon systems that would violate the agreements made at the end of the missile crisis.[59] The fact may be that the U.S. intelligence community was never asked to pay attention to the residual Soviet troops left in Cuba after 1962 and did not do so until the White House and a few members of Congress got interested in the subject in the summer of 1979. Then the intelligence agency performance may have been too good rather than too poor. Once asked, the agency quickly found the word "brigade" and then focused substantial and sophisticated intelligence-collection assets on the observation of what the brigade was doing.

The speed with which that information became available and the leaks to members of Congress and the press complicated efforts to put the new information into perspective. Early piecemeal publicity of nearly raw intelligence data made further study within the executive branch difficult and

57. Turner, "The Stupidity of Intelligence," 32–33.
58. Ray S. Cline, "History Repeated as Farce," *Washington Post,* October 15, 1979.
59. Newsom, *The Soviet Brigade in Cuba*, 54.

largely irrelevant. The administration denials in July had worked well in temporarily dampening congressional and media interest in the issue, but once new information apparently contradicting those denials became available, the president's foreign policy team was in a very embarrassing situation.[60] They needed time to sort things out, and someone who leaked the August CIA conclusions to *Aviation Week and Space Technology*, and one member of Congress, took that time away from them.

President Carter regards Senator Church and his Idaho press conference as the person and event most responsible for the brigade fiasco.[61] Indeed, if Church had remained silent, there might have been a breathing spell for the Soviets to respond to official administration inquiries or for the intelligence experts to give the exercise information a more complete review. The editors of *Aviation Week and Space Technology*, after failing to receive State Department confirmation, did not publish the brigade story in their next issue, and it might have been possible for the administration to keep a lid on the story for a bit longer than was expected. The fact that so many of the principal players were away from Washington did not help the process of evaluating and responding to the CIA conclusions about the brigade exercises and the expectation that they were about to become public.

Both Senators Church and Stone had their own political calculations and motives for publicizing the brigade intelligence that they received. They were correct in believing that they were in political trouble (both failed to win reelection in 1980) and that their votes on the Panama Canal treaties would be used against them. Both senators were seeing in their home states a public unease with the direction of American foreign policy, the military strength of the United States, and the general reputation of the president as an international leader. Despite his success at Camp David and the popular appeal of his human rights campaign, Carter was responsible for "giving away" our canal, pardoning Vietnam-era draft dodgers, canceling the B-1 bomber, and letting the shah and then Somoza fall from power. There was

60. It may be important to note that there was never any serious attempt to suppress the obviously damaging information in the August CIA report. Turner reports that he took the unusual step of clearing the CIA conclusion about the presence of a Soviet brigade in Cuba with the NSC staff before issuing the agency report. He was told to go ahead. Throughout their consideration of the facts and events in Cuba, the members of the Carter administration played the hand they were dealt; they never considered stacking the deck.

61. Carter, *Keeping Faith*, 263.

a growing public impression that the United States was losing military power and political prestige in the world. That impression would be reinforced by subsequent events in Iran and Afghanistan, but even before the hostage crisis and the revival of the cold war, the president's foreign policy record was a political liability for Democratic senators up for reelection.

Members of the Senate inevitably have a different political perspective on international issues than presidents do and are constitutionally involved in the foreign policy process, in part, for that reason. Sometimes their distinct political perspective saves the nation from foreign policy mistakes; sometimes it contributes to them.

David Newsom, a principal participant in the brigade crisis and the author of the book that provides the most detailed and thoughtful analysis of the issue, argues that the crisis was not "a strange aberration in American foreign policy" but instead the product of normal American political processes.[62] To err is human; to really mess things up you need democracy. The sharing of power and the sharing of information between the executive and legislative branches of government are bound to produce occasions when policy is incoherent and information is made available in piecemeal fashion. In the case of the brigade, the natural levels of confusion in democratic foreign policy making processes were worse than usual because the issue arose at a time when a reassertive Congress was seeing more raw intelligence than at any time in its history. The availability of incomplete reports about the brigade, whether leaked to the press or appropriately shared with members of Congress, was at the heart of the crisis. The fact that the brigade was made up of Soviet troops stationed in Cuba, an island ninety miles offshore that had been the scene of previous crisis confrontations, only increased the likelihood that isolated pieces of sensitive intelligence would be misread or misused on Capitol Hill. Of course, it did not help that members of the president's own inner circle had fundamentally different responses to the brigade issue.

The split between Secretary of State Vance and National Security Adviser Brzezinski is a much noted feature of the Carter administration. In this case it was clearly at work, though perhaps in a more complicated fashion than might at first seem to be the case. On the brigade issue Vance, not Brzezinski, took the "hard line" in the early public statements, calling the

62. Newsom, *The Soviet Brigade in Cuba*, 59.

brigade "unacceptable," while the national security adviser told the president that such statements were ill advised.[63] In general, Brzezinski did not regard 3,000 Russians in Cuba as particularly important; he was much more concerned about 40,000 Cubans in Africa. His efforts to use the brigade as an excuse for a public discussion of, and administration response to, the broader problem of Soviet-sponsored activities in the third world largely failed. He himself said some things about these subjects, on and off the record, throughout the crisis, but he usually lost in the internal administration battles over the content and tone of the president's public statements. Brzezinski attributes this failure to the decision to handle the brigade issue through the Policy Review Committee, where Vance was the chair. In his memoirs, the national security adviser argues that the brigade response should have been formulated by the Special Coordinating Committee—the organization designated to deal with crisis situations—where he would have chaired meetings involving a smaller group of presidential advisers. The proposition that a different committee would have produced a different policy is difficult to accept.

Throughout the handling of this issue, Carter and Vance had the same priorities and the same basic reaction to the brigade: they wanted to make sure that it did not destroy the prospects for Senate ratification of the SALT II treaty. If some senators, particularly an influential liberal like Church, were going to tie their SALT support to the Soviet brigade in Cuba, Carter and Vance were going to take the brigade seriously. Their response to the whole issue was rooted in their commitment to strategic arms limitation and to their realization that the political support for SALT was increasingly fragile by the end of 1979. The general public support for arms control that Patrick Caddell reported to the president may have been wide, but it was not deep. The modest and complicated restrictions that SALT II would have placed on the superpower nuclear arsenals were difficult to explain to general audiences and easily criticized. Like the Warnke nomination, the SALT II treaty had problems on both sides of the political spectrum. On the right it was attacked by those who feared that the Soviet Union was winning the arms race and opening a window of vulnerability. On the left it enjoyed less than enthusiastic support because some saw it as too little arms reduction coming too late in an out-of-control arms competition.

63. Brzezinski, *Power and Principle*, 348–49.

The desire to save SALT pushed Carter and Vance into saying that the status quo in Cuba was unacceptable. When the Soviets would not budge in negotiations, both the president and the secretary of state were willing to accept the unacceptable and announce modest U.S. military responses to counteract the unimportant brigade. The whole exercise was an attempt to put the question of Soviet forces in Cuba aside and get on with the important business of arms control. The president's speech on October 1 may have accomplished that purpose. There is no way to know for sure. The Soviet invasion of Afghanistan nine weeks later ended Senate deliberations on SALT II and brought the return to the cold war that was considered inappropriate in the response to the brigade.

Lloyd Cutler believes that SALT could have been ratified without the invasion of Afghanistan.[64] Others disagree, arguing that there were too many senators who had already given the president a politically damaging vote for Panama and were not about to take their chances with another controversial treaty ratification.[65] Whatever the long-term result might have been, it can at least be said that the immediate prospects for approval of SALT II were improved by the president's speech on October 1. Lloyd Cutler and Cyrus Vance were among those who joined Carter after his address to the nation for a celebration of its success and of the president's fifty-fifth birthday. Brzezinski did not attend the festivities.

The national security adviser was despondent about how the brigade issue had been handled, or mishandled, and actually considered submitting a letter of resignation.[66] The only thing that would have been more disproportionate than the brigade issue itself would have been a decision to resign over what it meant for Soviet-American relations. In the end, Brzezinski did not leave the administration, but six months later Vance did. His dramatic departure came about as the result of intense internal debates over how the administration would respond to a real crisis.

64. Lloyd Cutler, White House Staff exit interview, March 2, 1981, Carter White House Staff Exit Interviews, p. 8, Carter Library.
65. For a detailed assessment of SALT II ratification prospects before and after the brigade issue, see Caldwell, *The Dynamics of Domestic Politics and Arms Control*, 181–99.
66. Brzezinski, *Power and Principle*, 351.

9

COMMANDER IN CHIEF
The Hostage Rescue Mission

On the morning of April 25, 1980, President Carter made a brief public statement to the nation announcing that a secret military mission to rescue the American hostages being held in Tehran had failed.[1] Not enough of the helicopters needed to complete the operation had been able to reach a staging area in a remote desert location in Iran, and the mission had been aborted. Worse still, a collision during the refueling of one of the helicopters resulted in casualties. The eight men who died in the Iranian desert were the only military personnel to lose their lives during a mission initiated by President Carter in his service as commander in chief of American armed forces.[2] A president normally reluctant to use force decided to do so in the case of the most frustrating international problem he encountered during his four years in office.

A Presidency Held Hostage
When the shah of Iran left his revolution-torn country in January 1979, he had permission to come to the United States. However, he preferred to stay in the Middle East, first in Egypt, then Morocco, in the hope that the forces opposed to his regime would fail to form a new government and make it

---

1. *Public Papers of the Presidents of the United States, Jimmy Carter 1980* (Washington, D.C., 1981), 771–72.

2. One civilian, an Iranian interpreter, may also have died in the accident. Paul B. Ryan, *The Iranian Rescue Mission: Why It Failed* (Annapolis, Md., 1985), 90.

possible for him to return to power. That hope was futile and as the Ayatollah Khomeini gradually tightened his grip on Iran, the shah became a liability for any nation that offered him asylum. The original invitation to come to the United States was withdrawn as the Carter administration attempted to establish a working relationship with the new Iranian regime for the same strategic reasons that had led Carter, and all his cold war predecessors, to embrace the shah. During his extended exile, arrangements were made, sometimes with active American assistance, for the shah to stay in the Bahamas, Mexico, and later in Panama, but for many months he was not welcome to visit the United States.

To refuse asylum to a former friend and ally ran counter to American sentiments and traditions, but a decision to admit the shah to the United States carried with it obvious dangers for those U.S. citizens who remained in Iran after the revolution. When Brzezinski and Vice President Mondale made forceful recommendations that the shah be free to come to the United States whenever he wished, Carter sided with Vance, who opposed his entry.[3] Orchestrated pressure from outside the administration, which included public and private lobbying by Henry Kissinger, David Rockefeller, and John McCloy, did not persuade Carter to change his mind. At one meeting with Brzezinski, the president made a prophetic, if somewhat mean-spirited, comment that he did not want to see the shah playing tennis in the United States while Americans were being kidnapped or killed in Tehran.[4] In fact, the shah's tennis-playing days were nearly over in 1979; and when Vance and Carter were informed that the shah suffered from cancer and required sophisticated medical attention best provided in the United States, they withdrew their objections to his entry into the country. Within days after the arrival of the shah at a New York hospital, a group of armed Iranian students overran the U.S. embassy in Tehran and took the American personnel stationed there as hostages.

For the next 444 days—all the days that remained in the Carter presi-

3. Cyrus Vance, *Hard Choices: Four Critical Years in Managing America's Foreign Policy* (New York, 1983), 343–44.

4. Zbigniew Brzezinski, *Power and Principle: Memoirs of the National Security Advisor 1977–1981* (New York, 1983), 474; William Shawcross, *The Shah's Last Ride: The True Story of the Emperor's Dreams and Illusions, Exile, and Death at the Hands of His Foes and Friends* (New York, 1988), 126. Carter repeated this observation in a slightly different form at another meeting. Jimmy Carter, *Keeping Faith: Memoirs of a President* (New York, 1982), 455.

dency—resolving the hostage crisis would be the president's highest priority and, at times, his consuming preoccupation. The president would cancel campaign commitments in the 1980 primary season despite a serious challenge for the nomination from Senator Edward Kennedy. That decision could be, and was, cynically described as an attempt to avoid open debate with his Democratic rival. But President Carter did, in fact, give considerable time and attention to the hostage crisis and stayed off the campaign trail much longer than many of his political advisers would have wished.

For Jimmy Carter the hostage crisis was never merely a political or international issue; it was personal as well. He felt the plight of the hostages, met with their families, promised to work for their safe return, and held himself responsible for their welfare. The rest of the country may have needed the reminder that Walter Cronkite provided when he ended his evening news broadcast with a count of the number of days that Americans had been held in Iran. Jimmy Carter did not. In 1982, when he reflected back on the hostage crisis, Carter compared it to an earlier period in his life when he had left his naval career, returned to Plains, and was working to save the family business from bankruptcy. The hostage crisis was like living with the constant fear of financial ruin. "It was a gnawing away at your guts. . . . No matter what else happened, it was always there."[5]

The issue was always there in the media as well. Besides the not-so-subtle reminder at the end of the CBS evening news, ABC broadcast a late-night review of crisis events that eventually became the program *Nightline*, and all the networks gave extensive coverage to the hostage families and the anti-American demonstrations that were a regular ritual in Khomeini's Tehran.[6] Even if the president had wanted to make a low-key response to events in Iran, it is not clear that the American media or his challengers in both political parties would have allowed him to do so.

And, of course, the president's response was anything but low key. During the first days of the crisis he sent a delegation, including former attorney

5. White Burkett Miller Center of Public Affairs, University of Virginia, Project on the Carter Presidency, President Carter Session, November 29, 1982, p. 53.

6. The Cronkite sign-off with the number of days the hostages had been held began on day 74 and became a controversial element in the media coverage of the crisis. For a review of the ways that the Iranians may have intentionally manipulated the American media in the Iranian revolution, see Barry Rubin, *Paved with Good Intentions: The American Experience in Iran* (New York, 1981), 337–64.

general Ramsey Clark, to meet with the ayatollah. He halted all shipments of military spare parts to Iran, called on the UN Security Council to condemn the Iranian action, ordered Iranian students in the United States to report to immigration offices so that those found in violation of their visas could be deported, stopped importation of oil from Iran, ordered pro- and anti-Khomeini demonstrators off the property near the White House, and using emergency powers froze some twelve billion dollars of Iranian assets held in the United States.

At the outset of the crisis there was an expectation that the government of Iran, even the weak government that existed in the aftermath of the shah's departure, would quickly intervene, take control of the hostages, and release them. This is what had occurred in February 1979 when an earlier mob overran the embassy and had to be removed by a second Iranian mob acting on the orders of the ayatollah's Revolutionary Council. Nine months later, with intense debate in Iran over what kind of constitution should be adopted by the new regime, the hostage takers received Khomeini's blessings. For the ayatollah the hostage crisis became a convenient distraction from domestic political disputes and a useful device for sustaining revolutionary enthusiasm at a time when the broad-based anti-shah coalition was coming apart.[7] When the hostage takers received verbal support from Khomeini and when the interim government of Prime Minister Mehdi Bazargan resigned, Carter administration hopes for an early and easy resolution of the crisis disappeared, and the flurry of activity in the early days of the crisis gave way to sustained pursuit of two diplomatic strategies to win the release of the hostages.

First, there was a systematic effort in the United Nations, in the World Court, and among America's allies to isolate and punish the Khomeini regime. Condemnation of Iran's actions was nearly universal, but meaningful international sanctions against a major oil producer in the Persian Gulf were harder to secure. The diplomatic efforts to punish Iran were further complicated by the Soviet invasion of Afghanistan in December 1979, which ended any prospects for a strong UN Security Council role, created new tensions in the Western alliance, and raised fears that too much American pressure against Iran would push Khomeini closer to a Soviet Union that was already dangerously expanding its influence in the region.

7. Robin Wright, *In the Name of God: the Khomeini Decade* (New York, 1989), 60–81.

A second and simultaneous diplomatic effort involved finding reliable private channels of communication with the revolutionary Iranian government and attempting to negotiate acceptable terms for a hostage release. The Iranian demands to turn over the shah or the financial assets he may have held in the United States were clearly unacceptable, but talks about other possible arrangements for the release of the hostages were actively sought. Various intermediaries were used in this effort, and eventually secret meetings took place between senior administration officials, including the White House chief of staff Hamilton Jordan, and the foreign minister of Iran and longtime Khomeini associate, Sadegh Ghotbzadeh. Progress in these private channels was slow and full of frustrations. As it turned out, even highly placed members of Iran's Revolutionary Council could not speak reliably for Khomeini, and everything laboriously negotiated in private channels was subject to his veto. Late in March and early in April 1980, the private negotiations broke down when an elaborately orchestrated plan was rejected by Khomeini at the last minute. The plan had called for the government in Iran to first take control of the hostages and then release them in exchange for a U.S. promise to allow an international commission to investigate past relations between the United States and the shah's regime.

The failure of both public and private diplomacy left very few options for the administration to consider. There were a variety of ways for the United States to unilaterally and militarily punish Iran—by bombing refineries, railroad junctions, power stations, and other economic targets; by blockading or mining Iranian harbors; or by capturing some piece of Iranian territory. Several of these options involved new threats to the flow of oil from the Persian Gulf and were, therefore, objectionable to America's oil-dependent allies. All military action against Iran involved substantial risks that the hostages would be killed or harmed and that Iran would seek closer ties to the Soviet Union. Bombing, mining, or invading were all ideas that were never rejected completely; and from the beginning of the crisis, plans were drawn up for military reprisals that would have been carried out if the hostages had been put on trial or killed. Public and private threats were made to the Iranian regime about what would happen if any harm came to the hostages, and these threats were eventually backed up by the deployment of two aircraft carrier task force groups to the Arabian Sea and the Indian Ocean—the largest naval force that the United States had ever maintained in those waters.[8]

The other military option that had been under consideration since the outset of the crisis was a rescue mission. Planning for a rescue began on November 6, 1979—two days after the hostages were taken—when a full-scale review of all military responses to the crisis was called for by the NSC.[9] In the early stages of the crisis the prospects for a successful rescue operation were remote. The long distances that would have to be traveled in order to reach Tehran, the dangers of operating within a city that had a large and hostile population, and the lack of reliable intelligence about the exact location of the hostages made a rescue appear nearly impossible. But by the time that the diplomatic efforts to secure a release of the hostages were reaching a dead end, a combination of circumstances was also making the rescue mission more feasible and more attractive to the president and his advisers.

The Rescue Plan

Rescuing the hostages held in Tehran was an enormously complicated undertaking, but the United States already had a military unit called Delta Force with specially selected and trained personnel who were expected to carry out anti-terrorist missions. Other nations, including Israel and West Germany, had used military commandos to rescue hostages held by terrorists, and during the Vietnam War the United States had attempted to rescue prisoners held by the North Vietnamese. Getting the U.S. hostages safely out of Iran would be both easier and much more difficult than any of these earlier missions.

The easier part involved the embassy itself, where the student captors, after a few months of holding the American hostages, settled into a routine that left very few armed guards in the embassy compound or in the Iranian Foreign Ministry where Bruce Laingen, the U.S. chargé d'affaires, and two of his associates were being held. In November 1979, CIA operations in Iran were obviously disrupted by the revolution and the hostage crisis. The reintroduction and reorganization of intelligence personnel took some time, but in the confusion of revolutionary Iran, it was easier than expected.[10] When

---

8. Gary Sick, "Military Options and Constraints," in *American Hostages in Iran: The Conduct of a Crisis*, ed. Warren Christopher (New Haven, 1985), 147.

9. Sick, "Military Options and Constraints, " 144–45.

10. David Martin, "Inside the Rescue Mission," *Newsweek*, July 12, 1982; Stansfield Turner, *Terrorism and Democracy* (Boston, 1991), 66–73.

reliable information about the number of people and the procedures inside the embassy became available, the chances that a small number of American soldiers could overpower the Iranians on duty appeared promising.

Using available blueprints, a mock-up of the embassy compound was built in a remote location in the United States, and practice assaults were carried out there by the Delta Force team. Trained to recognize the hostage faces and the kind of clothes they wore, the soldiers assigned to Delta Force did live-ammunition exercises in which they quickly entered rooms where dummies were dressed as hostages and guards. They were expected to shoot the guards and rescue the hostages. Colonel Charles Beckwith, the Delta Force commander nicknamed "Chargin' Charlie" for some of his exploits in Vietnam, occasionally took the place of a hostage dummy in these exercises to demonstrate his own courage and the ability of his men to make rapid and accurate distinctions.[11]

All of this training assumed that the Delta Force team would be able to enter buildings in downtown Tehran in the middle of the night without any prior warning that American troops were in the city or in the country. Like the Apollo missions to the moon, in the hostage rescue operation, getting there would be the hard part. Tehran was hundreds of miles from the open waters of the Arabian Sea where U.S. carriers were operating and farther from any allied airbase that the United States could easily use.

The long distances involved and the need for a secret entry into Tehran meant that the mission would take at least two consecutive nights. On the first night helicopters flying from the Persian Gulf at low altitudes to avoid radar detection would go to a remote location, called by the planners Desert One.[12] There they would rendezvous with C-130 aircraft carrying the Delta Force soldiers and fuel for the helicopters. After the refueling operation, the cargo planes would leave Iran, and Delta Force would proceed to a mountain hideout about fifty miles outside Tehran where team members would rest and the helicopters would be camouflaged for the daylight hours. On the second night, an American agent already placed in the Iranian capital

---

11. For details of the Delta Force training and preparations, see Charlie A. Beckwith and Donald Knox, *Delta Force* (New York, 1983), and Ryan, *The Iranian Rescue Mission*.

12. Other plans for refueling the helicopters were considered, including temporarily capturing an airport in Iran or dropping fuel bladders by parachute in the Iranian desert. In the end these alternatives were judged to be more risky or operationally complex than the Desert One rendezvous.

under cover as an Irish businessman would bring trucks to the mountain hideout for the final trip into the city. Once the raid was ready to begin, the helicopters would be brought in for air cover and to stand by at a stadium across the street from the embassy for a short flight to a little-used airport some miles away. There a second U.S. commando team would land and secure a runway so the rescuers and freed hostages could be airlifted out of Iran.

The arrangements for getting into and out of the Iranian capital city were both complicated and risky, but the failure of diplomacy in the first four months of the crisis and the slim prospects that anything would change on the diplomatic front in the near future made the rescue mission an increasingly attractive option. Not much else was available, except, of course, the easily executed military reprisals that offered certain punishment of Iran and very little prospect of saving hostage lives.

In mid-March of 1980, Secretary of Defense Brown, National Security Adviser Brzezinski, and JCS Chairman General David Jones, who had been meeting regularly to review the development of rescue mission planning, received a full-scale briefing on the current plans and prospects for the mission. Brzezinski, convinced that this was the best option available, decided to share some of this highly secret and sensitive information with Carter's political advisers Jody Powell, Hamilton Jordan, and Vice President Mondale. He was probably enlisting allies for an effort to persuade the president that the rescue operation was needed to end the crisis with reasonable prospects that both hostage lives and America's international reputation would be saved.[13]

The mission planners needed presidential permission to conduct a secret flight into Iran to test the feasibility of landing C-130 aircraft at Desert One and to plant navigational devices for a possible return to the site. Carter rejected this request in late February and again in early March, even after it was jointly recommended by Brzezinski and Vance, who generally disagreed about the use of force in the crisis. Carter was still hoping that private-channel negotiations would lead to a hostage release and probably did not wish to take the risks involved in violating Iranian airspace. During a

13. Brzezinski is sure that he would not have briefed Powell, Jordan, and Mondale without receiving Carter's permission to do so. Zbigniew Brzezinski, interview by author, February 17, 1995.

weekend meeting at Camp David on March 22, Carter reviewed the status of Iranian negotiations with his senior foreign policy advisers and heard a detailed briefing on the elaborate plans for a rescue operation.[14] He recalled years later that despite the "Rube Goldberg" aspects of the rescue plan, the briefing at Camp David convinced him that it could succeed.[15] This time the president authorized the secret flight to inspect Desert One, and, according to Brzezinski, began to shift away from an exclusive concentration on diplomatic means for securing the release of the hostages and to give more serious consideration to military options.[16]

The next day the shah of Iran, who had settled in Panama after his American medical treatments, left that country for Egypt. In the days that followed, a new round of secret negotiations moved toward another major disappointment. On the first of April, Iranian president Abolhassan Bani-Sadr publicly announced that the Revolutionary Council would take control of the hostages from the students in the embassy if the United States promised not to take any hostile action until the Iranian parliament, prescribed in the new constitution, was elected and able to decide what to do with the hostages. This was the Iranian signal, prearranged in private-channel negotiations, that indicated a willingness to resolve the hostage crisis. Carter, on what happened to be the morning of the Wisconsin presidential primary, went on national television to praise this positive step. But one step forward was immediately followed by two in the opposite direction. First the Revolutionary Council failed to take physical control of the hostages, then Khomeini's son announced that it was the ayatollah's wish that the hostages remain in student hands until the not-yet-elected parliament decided their fate. The second announcement sparked another round of U.S. sanctions against Iran. At an April 7 meeting of the NSC, decisions were made to officially sever diplomatic relations with Iran, impose a formal U.S. trade embargo halting the few remaining commercial transactions with Iran, and begin to settle private claims against the Iranian government with the funds frozen earlier in the crisis. Additional pressure was also brought to bear on our European allies to impose or tighten economic sanctions against the Khomeini regime.

14. The Camp David meeting also included a review of the entire Middle East situation as well as Soviet activities in Afghanistan. Turner, *Terrorism and Democracy*, 100–103.

15. Jimmy Carter, interview by author, April 11, 1995.

16. Brzezinski, *Power and Principle*, 490.

But at the April 7 meeting something more than a further turning of the diplomatic screws may have been taking place. According to Brzezinski, Carter listened to plans for blockading Iranian harbors and told his advisers that he should have been more assertive in the past and that it was time to make a fundamental shift in how the crisis was viewed. The earlier notion that the United States was dealing with a weak Iranian government unable to control the hostage holders should now be replaced by the realization that the administration was, in fact, dealing with a hostile government whose actions might justify a forceful response.[17] There were, of course, only two kinds of forceful responses available to the United States—direct attacks on targets in Iran and the rescue mission—and once decision makers began to focus on those two options, the rescue mission looked like the best course of action.[18] There were three National Security Council meetings held in rapid succession in mid-April where the decision to proceed with a rescue attempt was finalized.

The Decision

The first of these meetings was convened on April 11, 1980. In attendance were the president, the vice president, Secretary of Defense Brown, General Jones, CIA Director Stansfield Turner, Brzezinski, Jordan, and Powell.[19] The meeting took place one day after Secretary of State Vance left Washington for a brief and rare vacation, and his place was taken by Deputy Secretary of State Warren Christopher. In Brzezinski's account, the president began the meeting with his assessment that there was no prospect of hostage release any time in the near future and that the time had come for a full review of options and the setting of a timetable. Christopher responded first with a list of additional diplomatic steps that might be taken to further isolate Iran. These included going back to the United Nations for stronger sanctions, blacklisting Iranian ships, and seeking to embargo Iranian access to international telecommunications. Brown replied that such steps were

17. Ibid., 491.

18. Turner reports that at this meeting Mondale, Brown, Brzezinski, and Jones joined him in speaking out in favor of a rescue operation. Christopher preferred the new diplomatic pressures that were agreed to, and the president appeared to favor the mining of Iranian harbors. No decisions about military operations were made at the April 7 meeting. Turner, *Terrorism and Democracy*, 106.

19. Presidential Diary and Appointments, April 11, 1980, Carter Library.

weak and unlikely to prove effective and that the real choice was between punitive military measures and a rescue mission. Because bombing Iran or closing its harbors might push the Iranians closer to the Soviet Union, the only real option was the rescue mission. Vice President Mondale spoke forcefully in favor of a rescue attempt, pointing out that it was the best way to end the continuing humiliation of the United States.[20]

Brzezinski, who had given the president a long memo the day before with his own arguments in support of a rescue mission, reminded the group that there was a certain urgency in their deliberations, since the existing plans required long moonless nights for secret helicopter flights into Iran and that the coming summer months would not be as favorable as the spring. Brzezinski made two additional recommendations. Iranian hostages should be taken during any rescue mission, since they might be useful as bargaining chips if additional Americans were captured in Iran. Furthermore, punitive military measures should be scheduled for roughly the same time as the rescue mission to punish Iran and to provide some face-saving if the rescue attempt failed.[21] Brzezinski appears to have been the only one at the meeting to raise the subject of planning for a possible failure. He did not anticipate the problems that actually occurred at Desert One, but had reservations about the prospects for an easy raid on the embassy in Tehran and a successful flight out of the country. The president, Brzezinski recalls, was somewhat taken aback by the brief discussion of a failed rescue, and no decisions were made on the proposals regarding hostage taking or punitive raids.[22]

On the core issue facing the group that met on April 11, Brzezinski, Brown, Powell, Jordan, Jones, and Turner all supported making the rescue attempt.[23] Several of the meeting participants not only wanted the military operation to take place, but wanted it to happen soon. Brzezinski was concerned about the limited availability of moonless nights, and Turner cautioned that any change in the location of the hostages would greatly complicate a mission that was specifically planned for the embassy compound.[24]

20. Brzezinski, *Power and Principle*, 492–93.

21. Ibid., 493.

22. Brzezinski, interview.

23. According to Turner, Powell and Jordan sat in on the April 11 meeting, but did not express their views about a rescue mission, though both supported this option. Turner, *Terrorism and Democracy*, 107.

24. Brzezinski, *Power and Principle*, 492–93.

During the April 11 meeting, Warren Christopher asked Hamilton Jordan in an aside if Vance knew how far the rescue planning had gone and how close the president was to endorsing such a mission.[25] Jordan assumed that the president had spoken to Vance, but did not know in what detail the subject had been reviewed. Christopher then told the president that he did not feel comfortable representing the absent secretary of state, who had given him no guidance on this important issue. That neutral and procedural statement was the closest anyone came to expressing a reservation about proceeding with a rescue attempt. Carter was aware that Vance was opposed to any military action against Iran as long as there was no immediate threat to the hostages and was ready, despite those reservations, to go ahead with the rescue mission.[26]

Political scientist and Carter biographer Betty Glad describes the April 11 meeting as a classic case of "groupthink,"[27] a concept developed by Irving Janis to describe the psychological pressures among presidential advisers that can lead to unwarranted conformity about a flawed course of action.[28] The classic case of this phenomenon is found in the deliberations early in the Kennedy administration leading up to the Bay of Pigs invasion. In those meetings a number of Kennedy's aides who had questions or reservations about the Cuban operation failed to raise them and instead went along with a plan developed by Eisenhower's CIA and apparently endorsed by the new president. The Carter administration deliberations about the rescue mission would appear to be rather different from those involving the Bay of Pigs. There is no evidence that anyone at the NSC meeting on April 11 suppressed reservations they had about the admittedly risky rescue mission.

---

25. Hamilton Jordan, *Crisis: The Last Year of the Carter Presidency* (New York, 1982), 251.

26. Zbigniew Brzezinski, "The Failed Mission," *New York Times Magazine*, April 18, 1982, p. 62. Hamilton Jordan reports in his memoirs that no final decision was made at the April 11 meeting and instead the president asked his advisers to give the subject further consideration and prayer and reassemble after the weekend. Jordan, *Crisis*, 251. In the Carter, Brzezinski, and Turner versions of this meeting, the decision to proceed with a rescue attempt was made. Carter, *Keeping Faith*, 507; Brzezinski, *Power and Principle*, 493; Turner, *Terrorism and Democracy*, 107.

27. Betty Glad, "Personality, Political and Group Process Variable in Foreign Policy Decisionmaking: Jimmy Carter's Handling of the Iranian Hostage Crisis," *International Political Science Review* 10 (1989).

28. Irving Janis, *Victims of Groupthink: A Psychological Study of Foreign-Policy Decisions and Fiascoes* (Boston, 1972).

Christopher did not know how Secretary Vance would respond to this proposal, and he made that fact known. Carter himself reportedly mentioned that Vance was not in favor of military action, but if forced to choose, preferred a rescue attempt to some sort of blockade.[29] Though the secretary of state was not present, there is no evidence that the meeting was scheduled for a date when he would be unable to express his concerns. The agenda and scheduling of the April 11 meeting followed logically from the president's call on April 7 for a rethinking of the crisis and for new attention to be given to options involving the use of force.

There was a general feeling of the majority at the April 11 meeting that centered on the point made at the outset by Secretary of Defense Brown—the basic choice for the administration in the spring of 1980 was between punitive military measures and a rescue effort. Only Christopher expressed a contrary opinion and argued that further diplomatic steps to isolate Iran might be worthwhile. No one else took that position. If Brown was correct in identifying the two basic alternatives, the rescue mission was the obvious choice. It had fewer strategic risks and better prospects for saving at least some of the hostage lives. Brzezinski's suggestion that punitive measures be combined with a rescue attempt did not garner much support and would later be rejected by the president. Carter apparently used the April 11 meeting to make it clear that he was planning to proceed with the rescue operation and to invite criticism of that decision.[30] He would not hear any until Secretary of State Vance returned to Washington.

When Vance came back from his weekend in Florida, he asked for, and received, an opportunity to express his opposition to the rescue mission. The second meeting of the National Security Council to discuss the rescue plans took place over lunch on Tuesday, April 15. Vance first met in private with Carter and then with the larger group.[31] His reservations were easily stated.

29. Brzezinski, *Power and Principle*, 493.

30. Again, Hamilton Jordan gives a slightly different account of this meeting, with the president less sure of his decision to go ahead with a rescue mission. Jordan, *Crisis,* 251. Powell, writing about the April 11 meeting, reports that "the President said he was tentatively inclined to proceed with the mission, but would defer a final decision until he had discussed it with Vance." Jody Powell, *The Other Side of the Story* (New York, 1984), 227–28.

31. Vance met with the president alone from 12:10 to 12:47. There was then a two-hour meeting attended by Vance, Brown, Turner, Jones, Christopher, Graham Claytor, Jordan, Powell, and Brzezinski. President's Diary and Appointments, April 15, 1980.

First, he thought that a rescue attempt at this time would interfere with efforts to secure allied support for new sanctions. Second, since recent reports from the Red Cross indicated that the hostages were in good health, the United States should wait until the Iranian parliament was put in place and then resume negotiations. Attempting a rescue now would probably involve substantial casualties among the hostages as well as the Iranians encountered in Tehran. Even if there were no hostage deaths, a successful rescue operation would push Khomeini closer to the Soviet Union, inflame the Arab world, and probably result in new hostages being taken from among the large number of American journalists and other U.S. citizens still living and working in Iran.[32]

Brzezinski reports that Harold Brown was the first to respond to Vance's argument and that he did so with a pointed question. "When do you expect the hostages to be released?"[33] Naturally, the secretary of state could offer no assurances that the hostages would be freed anytime in the near future. No one knew how long it would take to elect and organize the new Iranian parliament or what its political makeup would be. Vance's only response was to reiterate his fear that at least some hostages would be killed in a rescue attempt. Hamilton Jordan remembers the meeting differently, with President Carter offering the first and only response to Vance. The president, in Jordan's account, pointed out that the Joint Chiefs had little confidence in the early rescue mission planning, but had spent the last four months improving the plan until it now had a reasonable chance for success. It was true that other Americans might be taken hostage, but the U.S. government had been warning all U.S. citizens to leave Iran for some time, and the diplomats had been in Tehran in the service of their country, not for personal or business reasons. As to foreign reaction to a successful rescue, U.S. allies would probably be relieved that the crisis was over, and though some leaders in the Arab world would publicly complain about unilateral American military actions, privately they would be snickering behind Khomeini's back.[34] After a clear presentation of Vance's opposition to the rescue mission and the responses that were made to his arguments, neither the

32. Vance, *Hard Choices*, 410; Jordan, *Crisis,* 252–53; Brzezinski, *Power and Principle*, 494.
33. Harold Brown, quoted in Brzezinski, *Power and Principle*, 494.
34. Jordan, *Crisis,* 253–54.

president nor any of his advisers changed their minds about proceeding with a rescue attempt.[35]

Vance's personal decision to resign over this issue, which he conveyed to the president on April 17, may have added weight to his criticisms, but did not diminish Carter's commitment to the rescue option.[36] The Vance resignation probably had more consequences in terms of personal relations than policy deliberations. The president found his secretary of state's decision to leave the administration if a rescue mission went forward deeply wounding. Vance was the cabinet member who was philosophically closest to Carter, and the president felt that his friend and adviser was putting a "knife in my back" by threatening to leave the administration on the eve of one of its most risky ventures.[37] Carter understood Vance's general reservations about military responses to the hostage crisis and shared those reservations throughout the early months of the crisis. But he had assumed that Vance's thinking on how to handle the situation in Iran was moving in the same direction as his own. The secretary of state had recommended the secret test flight to Desert One and heard the same briefings Carter heard about the rescue plans. Moreover, he had no real alternative to the rescue attempt which offered any prospects for success.

According to Brzezinski, the April 15 meeting also included some inconclusive discussions of his earlier suggestions that the rescue team take hostages and that punitive measures against Iran be ordered after either a successful or a failed rescue mission.[38] A decision was made to take Iranian hostages if it were necessary in order to complete the mission and to release them just before leaving Iran. Contingency plans for broader use of military power against Iran were to be prepared, but a final decision on this matter

35. Again there are some discrepancies among the various accounts of this meeting. Brzezinski, Turner, and Vance have the president announcing that he would stick with his earlier decision to attempt a rescue at the earliest possible date. Powell implies that the decision was made at the April 15 meeting. Jordan has the president deferring a final decision, but expressing an inclination to go ahead. Brzezinski, *Power and Principle*, 494; Turner, *Secrecy and Democracy*, 109; Vance, *Hard Choices*, 410; Powell, *The Other Side of the Story*, 228; Jordan, *Crisis*, 254.

36. This was Vance's fourth threatened resignation and the one that Carter would accept.

37. Carter, interview by author, April 11, 1995.

38. Brzezinski, *Power and Principle*, 494–95.

was postponed. On the day before the mission Carter decided not to complicate an already complex operation with the additional attacks that Brzezinski had recommended.

The third meeting of the National Security Council on the rescue issue
took place on the evening of April 16. This was the only occasion prior to
the rescue attempt when the president would meet personally with the mission commanders: General James B. Vaught, overall commander of the operation, who would monitor events from Egypt; General Philip C. Gast, in
charge of air logistics; and Colonel Beckwith. The three officers drove to
the White House in a private car wearing civilian clothes to avoid attracting
attention. They proceeded to give the president and his senior advisers one
more detailed briefing on the rendezvous and refueling that was to take
place at Desert One, the pre-positioning of Delta Force in the mountains
just outside Tehran, the final trip to the embassy walls, the assault on the
compound and the Foreign Ministry, and the airlift out of Iran. Jordan reports that President Carter carefully took notes throughout the meeting and
frequently questioned the briefers.[39] Most questions were easily answered,
and all accounts of the April 16 meeting agree that the single most important substantive subject in the discussions was the matter of casualties.

When Carter asked how many there might be, General Vaught admitted
that there was no way to tell, but that deaths and injuries among both the
rescue team and the hostages were probable.[40] Because the Delta Force personnel were planning to shoot anyone in the embassy compound carrying a
weapon, there was special concern about what might happen if, in the confusion of the raid, some of the hostages overpowered their guards and
picked up their weapons. Beckwith was direct and honest in reporting the
possibility that American hostages might be killed by their rescuers. Ac-

39. Beckwith and Knox, *Delta Force*, 5; Jordan, *Crisis*, 254–64. Brzezinski suggests that
a decision may have been made at this meeting to increase the number of helicopters assigned to the mission from seven to eight. Brzezinski, "Failed Mission," 64.

40. Turner, who did not attend the April 16 meeting but was represented by his deputy,
Frank Carlucci, reports that General Vaught had estimated that 4 hostages and 8 members
of Delta Force might be wounded. Turner, *Terrorism and Democracy*, 113. Ryan reports that
unidentified Pentagon sources estimated 30 casualties in the rescue team and 15 among the
hostages. Ryan, *The Iranian Rescue Mission*, 127. Jody Powell reports that there was a disin-
formation campaign in 1980 that involved false accusations that Pentagon casualty estimates
were very high. Powell, *The Other Side of the Story*, 256–57.

cording to Beckwith, Carter acknowledged this risk and said, "I understand. And I accept it."[41] The president also cautioned the team against any temptations they may have felt to "settle some scores for our nation," and asked them to keep the mission focused on the objective of safely returning the American hostages.[42] Christopher pursued the subject of casualties further, asking what the phrase "taking the guards out" meant and whether they would be shot in the shoulder or otherwise immobilized. "No sir," replied Beckwith, "we're going to shoot each of them twice, right between the eyes."[43]

At the end of the April 16 meeting, there was some discussion of pre-positioning forces for execution of the plan, and President Carter interrupted to make it clear that the decision to go forward was final. Beckwith records his comments: "I do not want to undertake this operation, but we have no other recourse. The only way I will call it off now is if the International Red Cross hands back our Americans. There's not going to be just pre-positioning forward. We're going to do this operation."[44] Colonel Beckwith, despite the fact that he grew up in Georgia not very far from Plains, admits that he had not voted for Jimmy Carter and did not think the president had the guts to order a high-risk rescue mission. On hearing the president's decisive statement that the mission would go forward, Beckwith reports that he almost fell out of his chair.[45]

The Delta Force commander was also impressed by two other decisions Carter announced at this meeting. The planes carrying the freed hostages and their rescuers out of Iran would have tactical air cover, and the mission would be run by the military in the normal chain of command, without any civilian interference. "This is a military operation," Carter said speaking to the chairman of the Joint Chiefs of Staff. "You will run it. By law you will keep the Secretary of Defense Dr. Brown informed; and I'd appreciate it if you'd do the same with me. I don't want anyone else in this room in-

---

41. Beckwith and Knox, *Delta Force*, 7.

42. Turner, *Terrorism and Democracy*, 113.

43. Ibid.

44. Beckwith and Knox, *Delta Force*, 9.

45. Ibid. Once again, Hamilton Jordan gives a different report. He says that the president thanked the mission commanders for their answers and promised to make a final decision about the rescue attempt in a few days. Jordan, *Crisis,* 263.

volved."[46] Then the president took Beckwith aside and gave him two additional instructions. One was to tell the members of his team that if the mission failed it would not be their fault, it would be the president's. The second was that if there were casualties, and if it was possible to do so without risking further loss of life, the bodies of hostages or rescuers should be brought home.[47]

President Carter wanted the mission commanders to avoid wanton killing, but clearly recognized that this operation involved the certainty of Iranian deaths and the probability of American casualties.[48] For the first, and only, time in the hostage crisis Carter did not place preservation of hostage lives at the very top of his agenda. This is a significant departure from his otherwise consistent position that everything should be done to minimize danger to the hostages. Of course, the hostages were in constant danger and under considerable stress throughout their ordeal, and Carter in ordering a rescue mission may well have been balancing the risks of hostage death and injury in the rescue attempt against the risks that they would suffer other kinds of harm in their continued captivity. Carter never fully embraced the Brzezinski position that the lives and health of the hostages were less important than the power and prestige of the United States. For Brzezinski, ending the crisis with a display of force would have enhanced our international reputation and national morale, with good effects on a variety of other foreign policy problems. For Carter, there was apparently less inclination to think of the hostage crisis in connection with other international or domestic events.[49]

After months of futile negotiations and with no diplomatic solution in sight, the president wanted the crisis brought to an end, even if that end

46. Beckwith and Knox, *Delta Force*, 9. Turner also praises Carter for these statements, Turner, *Terrorism and Democracy*, 113–14.

47. Beckwith and Knox, *Delta Force*, 10.

48. The president's admonition to avoid wanton killing is remembered by Brzezinski, "Failed Mission," 69. Some reports indicate that the helicopters assigned to provide ground cover for the operation in Tehran would have used a special ammunition less lethal than regular bullets but more likely to produce sparks and flames when it hit objects or the ground. This would presumably have had a dramatic effect on bystanders who might have tried to interfere with the mission. Ryan, *The Iranian Rescue Mission*, 61.

49. Brzezinski reports that there were never any discussions of domestic politics during any of the rescue mission meetings or at other times in the crisis. Brzezinski, *Power and Principle*, 490.

entailed substantial risks for the hostages. His military advisers were eager to see their highly trained personnel and elaborately planned operation put into action. His political advisers, no doubt, also wanted the crisis ended so that their candidate could resume normal activities in a hotly contested election year. All would be deeply disappointed.

Disaster in the Desert

Between April 16 and the first available moonless night later in the month, one final round of high-level meetings between Hamilton Jordan and Sadegh Ghotbzadeh took place in Europe. The purpose of the meeting was to discuss the failed scenario of early April and the possibility of renewed negotiations on the hostage issue. For Jordan, it was a last chance for the Iranians to avert the pending military action against the hostage holders. Without giving any warning about what might be coming, Jordan asked his Iranian counterparts when they thought the hostages might be released. The answer was the same one Cyrus Vance gave at the April 15 meeting; the Iranian foreign minister had no idea when the hostages might be able to go home. That information answered any doubts that Jordan or Carter may have had about proceeding with the rescue mission and in Jordan's account led to Carter's final decision to authorize the mission.[50]

Jordan's trip to Europe and all of the preparations for the pending rescue mission naturally took place in strictest secrecy. Nevertheless, there was growing speculation that some sort of military action might be in the offing. The United States was escalating public pressure against Iran in the formal suspension of diplomatic relations and the open efforts to win allied support for stronger sanctions against the Khomeini regime. At the April 17 press conference where the president announced the newest sanctions, he hinted that if they were not successful, future steps might involve military action.[51]

A number of White House staff members not involved in the rescue decision were concerned that some sort of military action was in the works, and at a senior staff meeting on April 22 Jordan assured his colleagues that

---

50. Jordan, *Crisis,* 265–67.

51. *Public Papers of the Presidents of the United States, Jimmy Carter 1980,* 704–14. According to Jody Powell, the announcement of possible future military action was part of the cover story that had been prepared to explain any of the military movements connected with the rescue mission that might have been discovered by the press. Powell, *The Other Side of the Story,* 228–30.

there were no immediate plans to mine Iranian harbors or blockade Iranian shipping. When asked directly if there would be a rescue attempt, Jordan, for the second time in a week, lied. His first lie had been to Ghotbzadeh in Europe when the subject of U.S. military action against Iran had come up.[52] The second lie to the White House staff quickly leaked to the press and was reinforced by Jody Powell when he was approached by the *Los Angeles Times'* Washington reporter Jack Nelson.[53] The story Nelson wrote may well have helped to ensure that Iranian officials would be surprised by the rescue attempt. Unfortunately, the rescuers encountered some surprises of their own.

On April 24 eight helicopters took off from the aircraft carrier *Nimitz* for the long flight to Desert One. They were flying at low altitude and in complete radio silence. Limited communications with the mission commander in Egypt were available, but there were no direct communications among the pilots. One helicopter landed and was left in the desert after a warning light indicated danger of a cracked rotor blade. The crew of the abandoned helicopter was picked up by another helicopter, whose pilot saw the emergency landing, but not all the pilots were aware that their numbers had been reduced by one. The seven remaining helicopters encountered a severe dust storm that eliminated almost all visibility and lasted for nearly two hours. The lead helicopter briefly landed and reported the bad weather to General Vaught before resuming flight. After clearing the first dust storm, the fleet flew in clear skies for some time and then entered a second and even worse cloud of dust. One pilot described the storms as something "like flying in a bowl of milk."[54] Just minutes before exiting the second storm, the pilot of a helicopter that was experiencing equipment problems with its navigation systems turned back and safely returned to the *Nimitz*.

The C-130 aircraft arrived at Desert One on time without encountering any weather problems and quickly discovered that a road near the landing site was much busier than expected. The American troops stopped a bus with forty-four Iranian passengers, disabled a truck carrying fuel and shot at an accompanying pickup truck, probably driven by fuel smugglers. The pickup got away. Since smugglers were unlikely to notify anyone that they

52. Jordan, *Crisis,* 267.
53. Powell, *The Other Side of the Story*, 231–32.
54. Helicopter pilot, quoted in Ryan, *The Iranian Rescue Mission*, 70.

had been attacked and would probably assume that their attackers were Iranian authorities, a decision was made to go ahead with the mission.

When the six remaining helicopters landed, one of them was confirmed to have a major hydraulic system failure that would make it very dangerous for that aircraft to go on. According to the plan, six was the minimum number of helicopters needed for the next stage of the operation, which involved moving more than ninety men and their equipment to the mountain hideout near Tehran. There was considerable confusion at Desert One about which of the officers present was in charge, but no question that Colonel Beckwith would make the critical decisions about the assault team. Beckwith recommended that the mission be aborted. Canceling the mission at this stage did not completely preclude trying again at a later date, though at least two U.S. helicopters would be abandoned on Iranian territory and forty-four Iranian bus passengers would either be witnesses to what had happened at Desert One or would mysteriously disappear if they were taken to Egypt with the Delta Force personnel.

When news of the abort reached Washington, Brzezinski was tempted to violate the president's injunction that there be no civilian second-guessing of military decisions. Brzezinski contemplated pushing for an order to continue the mission with five helicopters.[55] Instead, he asked the president to verify that Beckwith, the on-scene commander, wanted the mission to be terminated. When that confirmation was received, a disappointed Carter accepted cancellation of the attempted rescue. An hour after learning that the mission would be aborted, even more disheartening news arrived in Washington. One of the last of the helicopters to complete refueling crashed into a C-130, producing a large explosion and fire that killed eight servicemen and injured several others. The rescue team left Desert One, leaving all the helicopters and the damaged C-130 behind. In their rush to go they also left some planning documents that the Iranians could use to determine how the rest of the mission would have been conducted.

In the desert and in Washington everyone was crushed. Carter calls the day of the failed rescue mission one of the worst in his life.[56] He called his wife, who was taking his place at a campaign commitment, and asked her to return to Washington without explaining why.[57] He instructed his staff

---

55. Brzezinski, *Power and Principle*, 497–98.
56. Carter, *Keeping Faith*, 514.
57. Rosalynn Carter, *First Lady from Plains* (New York, 1984), 308.

to review the public statements President Kennedy had made after the Bay of Pigs fiasco and, like Kennedy, prepared to take full responsibility for the failure. His appearance on national television was postponed as long as possible to give the CIA agents in Tehran an opportunity to get out of the country or go into hiding, but not so long as to allow Iranian discovery of the desert debris to generate false fears of an American invasion. In the interim, congressional leaders and foreign governments were given belated notification of the mission and its failure.

Conclusions

Carter attributes the failure of the mission to bad luck and completely unpredictable mishaps.[58] A postmortem investigation conducted by Admiral James L. Holloway III for the Pentagon concurred that bad luck plagued the mission, but also found evidence of planning errors. Most of the criticisms in the Holloway report involve secrecy and excessive compartmentalization of information. Meteorologists, who might have provided more information about the likelihood of dust storms in the Iranian desert, rarely met with the helicopter pilots, who were not shown the weather annex to the operation plan. No full-scale rehearsal of the Desert One rendezvous was ever conducted, and the helicopter pilots, may not have been prepared for how difficult the first stage of the mission would be.[59] The crew of the first abandoned helicopter may not have known that in the history of the model they were flying, there were frequent cases of faulty warning lights indicating a pending rotor blade crack, but no instances of actual cracks. With restricted radio communications and compartmentalization of the information given to pilots and repair personnel, they could not check this issue in flight. Radio silence also prevented the helicopter crew that turned back from learning that there was good visibility just ahead and that one of the other helicopters was already down—information that probably would have led to a different decision.[60]

58. Diary entry, April 24–25, 1980, quoted in Carter, *Keeping Faith*, 518.

59. Beckwith is particularly critical of the helicopter pilot selection and training. Ryan, *The Iranian Rescue Mission*, 128–29.

60. Turner believes that an important factor in the failure of the mission was a peacetime military culture that emphasized safety in the training of military personnel instead of risk taking to accomplish a vital mission. He questions all three of the decisions that reduced the number of helicopters from eight to five and Beckwith's decision not to proceed with fewer than six helicopters. Turner, *Secrecy and Democracy*, 132–45.

Secrecy was, of course, important to the success of the mission. Delta Force had to travel to the center of the Iranian capital without prior detection. Though Iranian intelligence-gathering capacities against the United States were probably very limited, there was real fear that the Soviet Union might discover the military movements associated with the operation and share their information with the Khomeini regime.[61] Despite these legitimate fears, the secrecy surrounding the mission was probably carried to extremes. Early on, the senior group of presidential advisers regularly reviewing rescue mission planning was limited to Brzezinski, Brown, and Jones. Stansfield Turner had to insist that he be included in those meetings, even though it was obvious from the outset that the CIA and its agents would play a critical role in the planning and execution of the mission.[62]

Concern for secrecy at the highest levels of the administration sometimes led to bizarre behavior. Brzezinski, at one point, recommended that the president hold a phony National Security Council meeting with a large number of persons in attendance where the president would announce that he had decided against a rescue mission. This meeting would then be followed by a rump session involving a much smaller number of persons where the real decision to proceed would be made.[63] Carter did not carry out this recommended charade, but he took care to write his own diary (presumably seen only by the secretary who typed it) in a way that would not reveal that a rescue operation was about to take place.[64] Neither the president nor any of his senior advisers conducted serious consultations with congressional leaders, though they were arguably required by law to do so.[65] Perhaps more importantly, the JCS, which monitored mission planning, never assembled a group of outside experts to review and critique the planning documents, though that was a common practice in less sensitive operations.[66]

61. Ryan, *The Iranian Rescue Mission*, 37.

62. Turner, *Terrorism and Democracy*, 38.

63. Brzezinski, "Failed Mission," 61. Something like the Brzezinski suggestion did take place in the case of the White House senior staff meeting on April 22 and the leak to the press that indicated that no military action would take place soon.

64. Carter, *Keeping Faith*, 507.

65. Frank J. Smist, Jr., "The Iranian Rescue Mission: A Case Study in Executive Distrust of Congress," *Jimmy Carter: Foreign Policy and Post-Presidential Years*, ed. Herbert D. Rosenbaum and Alexej Ugrinsky (Westport, Conn., 1994), 221–30.

66. Ryan, *The Iranian Rescue Mission*, 123–24.

The limited number of people familiar with all aspects of the plan and the complexity of the logistics it entailed meant that a number of important mission features were not adequately reviewed. The role of weather conditions in the flight to Desert One is an obvious example. So was the volume of traffic on the road near Desert One, which led to the detention of forty-four Iranians. In a number of these instances, senior decision makers who did carefully evaluate the plans did not have sufficient expertise or incentives to identify the possible weaknesses in the operation. Brzezinski reports that the decision to increase the number of helicopters for the initial flight from seven to eight was made in a haphazard fashion after an air force officer passed a note to David Aaron, Brzezinski's deputy, during one high-level meeting.[67] On another occasion Vance warned Jordan that, in his experience, "generals will rarely tell you they can't do something."[68] Of course, that warning by itself did not lead to the identification of weak points in the plan. Whatever planning failures may have existed were not the result of groupthink. They came mostly from the difficult trade-offs between sharing information among experts and making sure that news of the pending mission did not become available to the Iranians.[69]

For the purposes of understanding Jimmy Carter and his foreign policy, second-guessing the rescue mission planners is probably less important than understanding the president's decision to go ahead with the plans he saw in March and April of 1980.[70] Though there is some dispute among the president's senior advisers about precisely when the commander in chief officially ordered a rescue attempt, there is no doubt that in the spring of 1980 Carter made a major change in his handling of the hostage crisis. After long and complicated private-channel negotiations failed to produce real progress, and after there were repeated instances in which Khomeini made it

67. Brzezinski, *Power and Principle*, 495.

68. Jordan, *Crisis*, 264.

69. In addition, one critic of the mission planning argues that an attempt to involve all the military services led to the selection of marine pilots for the helicopters, when air force pilots, who had more experience in long-distance overland flying, were not chosen. Richard A. Gabriel, *Military Incompetence: Why the American Military Doesn't Win* (New York, 1985), 85–116.

70. Almost all of the criticism after the rescue attempt was about its failure to succeed, not about the intent to rescue the hostages. White Burkett Miller Center of Public Affairs, University of Virginia, Project on the Carter Presidency, Cutler Session, October 23, 1982, p. 24.

clear that he had no real interest in resolving the issue, Carter temporarily gave up on a negotiated settlement of the crisis. Why did he do so?

The rescue decision came nearly five months after the hostages were taken and after extensive diplomatic efforts had been made to secure their release. Everyone in the president's inner circle, except perhaps Cyrus Vance and Warren Christopher, had lost patience with diplomacy. Khomeini appeared to be unaffected by international condemnations, indifferent to economic sanctions, inaccessible through normal channels of communication, and unwilling to delegate any decision-making authority to his representatives in private negotiations. Despite the high costs of keeping the hostages in terms of international reputation and economic sanctions, in Iranian domestic affairs the continued confrontation with the United States apparently served a useful, if sometimes hard to fathom, purpose. Diplomacy was a dead end.

At that dead-end point, Carter turned to military force and exercised his responsibilities as commander in chief. Though there was extensive planning for the mining of Iranian harbors, for blocking Iranian use of the Persian Gulf, and for bombing a variety of targets in Iran, there is no evidence that the administration was ever close to executing any of these options (except, of course, as retaliation for harm to the hostages).[71] For most of his presidency Jimmy Carter was reluctant to use force or to encourage the leaders of other nations to do so. He wanted the United States to stay out of the conflict in the Horn of Africa and did not encourage the shah to crack down on his revolutionary opponents. He did supply arms to Afghan rebels after the Soviet invasion and issued a stern public warning that the United States would use force to defend Western economic interests in the Persian Gulf against any further Soviet expansion. But military force for Carter was clearly a last resort and not a first-choice course of action. In his post-presidency he would oppose the invasion of Panama, the threatened invasion of Haiti, and the Gulf War, believing in all of those cases that diplomacy and peaceful means of resolution, like the use of economic sanctions, had not been exhausted. But Carter, despite a persistent desire to serve as an international peacemaker, had his limits. In the spring of 1980, Khomeini had pushed him to the end of his considerable tolerance.

71. There is good reason to suspect that the threats of force made early in the hostage crisis had the desired effect of reducing the likelihood that the hostages would be put on trial or harmed. Sick, "Military Options and Constraints," 148–49.

Once the use of force was in the forefront of the president's agenda, there was little doubt that the rescue mission would be the favored course of action. It offered the best chances that hostage lives could be saved (though the risk of hostage deaths and injuries was real and understood) with minimal killing of civilians in Iran. The rescue mission would not, of course, have ended the conflict in U.S.-Iranian relations, and Vance's prediction that new hostages would have been taken was a distinct possibility. But a successful rescue would have ended the immediate source of confrontation between the two countries and made it clear to the Iranians that military force might be used in the future. Indeed, if more hostages had been taken, something Carter did not expect to happen,[72] further military action against Iran would have been a likely consequence.

Even the failed rescue mission had the advantage of conveying to the Iranians the important message that the United States was willing to use force in some circumstances. It also released pressures that were building within the Carter administration and within the country to do something that would bring the crisis to an end and punish the Iranians. In Brzezinski's view, the rescue attempt "lanced the boil" that could easily have exploded into much larger acts of violence between the United States and Iran.[73] After April 1980, there was less public demand for military action against Iran, and in due course it was possible for the administration to resume the negotiations that would eventually bring the hostages home.

In the execution of his responsibilities as commander in chief, Carter made two decisions that give some indication about how he would have performed on other occasions when military forces were ordered into action. First, he made it perfectly clear that he took full responsibility for the mission. The rescue attempt was in that sense directly under his command. This is what he said publicly to the American people after the disaster at Desert One and what he said privately to Colonel Beckwith before the mission began. Second, though he was fully briefed on the details of the operation and asked numerous questions about the plans, he avoided any micromanagement of the mission once it was under way. He gave the order to go ahead, but did not interfere thereafter. The only minor exception to this

72. Carter, interview by author, April 11, 1995.
73. Brzezinski, "Failed Mission," 64, and *Power and Principle*, 500. Cutler shares this judgment. Project on the Carter Presidency, Cutler Session, 24.

rule was his acceptance of Brzezinski's recommendation to confirm that cancellation of the mission was Beckwith's preference. Carter avoided the kind of White House control over operational details that characterized the Ford administration handling of the *Mayaguez* incident, the last-minute Kennedy decisions about the Bay of Pigs, and the day-to-day direction of various aspects of the Vietnam War during the Johnson and Nixon administrations. Carter wanted to be commander in chief, but not commander on the scene. Like President Bush in the operations against Iraq, Carter gave his professional military advisers the freedom to exercise their best judgment in carrying out the presidential orders he gave. Unfortunately for President Carter, his desert storm was not at all like the one that became associated with President Bush.

Conclusion

The failed rescue mission and continuing hostage crisis sealed the fate of the Carter presidency. With the decisive Republican victory in the November 1980 election, the Democrats lost control of the White House for the next twelve years. During those years. Republicans repeatedly reminded the American public about the mistakes and misfortunes of the Carter era. In their indictment of the Georgia Democrat, his political opponents usually mentioned the high inflation and interest rates during Carter's last year in office, the much maligned "malaise" speech that he gave in the summer of 1979,[1] the president's image as a weak and indecisive leader, and his failures in foreign policy.

Throughout the 1980s and 1990s, Jimmy Carter's standing with the American people rose, but this was largely a product of his exemplary post-presidency, in which he took on some difficult diplomatic assignments and built the Carter Center to promote and carry out worthy projects at home and abroad.[2] The general impression that Carter's was a failed presidency,

1. The speech did not contain the word "malaise," though it has become almost universally known by that word. For a detailed account of the speech, see Robert A. Strong, "Recapturing Leadership: The Carter Administration and the Crisis of Confidence," *Presidential Studies Quarterly* 16, no. 4 (fall 1986).

2. For a review of Carter's post-presidency, see Peter G. Bourne, *Jimmy Carter: A Comprehensive Biography from Plains to Post-presidency* (New York, 1997), Chapters 28–29; Rod Troester, *Jimmy Carter as Peacemaker: A Post-presidential Biography* (New York, 1996); and

or at best a mediocre one, has remained the prevailing public and professional opinion.[3] Looking back on the style and substance of Carter's conduct of foreign policy with twenty years' perspective and looking carefully, as we have done in the preceding case studies, may justify a reconsideration of Carter's presidential performance; it certainly justifies a reexamination of his record in foreign affairs.

Carter Revisionism

Though he came to the White House with less international experience than most presidents in the modern era, Jimmy Carter took an immediate interest in foreign policy, outlined an ambitious international agenda for his administration, and proceeded to accomplish many of the items that were placed on that agenda.[4] He devoted considerable time to foreign affairs, even when there was no crisis at hand forcing him to do so, and with a modest electoral mandate took on some of the most difficult and obviously controversial issues on the international scene.

His administration completed the process of normalizing relations with China, negotiated a SALT II agreement with the Soviet Union, promoted majority rule in southern Africa, worked to reduce the prospects of nuclear proliferation, gradually increased defense spending in response to the continuing military threat posed by the Soviet Union, publicly committed the United States to defend the independence of the nations in the Persian Gulf, punished the Soviets for their invasion of Afghanistan, and dealt with the early emergence of the Solidarity movement in Poland. And, of course, on the last day of the administration and the first day of Ronald Reagan's presidency, Carter and his senior foreign policy team secured the safe return of

---

particularly Douglas Brinkley, *Unfinished Presidency: Jimmy Carter's Journey Beyond the White House* (New York, 1998).

3. Arthur Schlesinger, Jr., "The Ultimate Approval Rating" *New York Times Magazine*, December 15, 1996, pp. 46–51.

4. Brzezinski reminds us that one of his first memos to the newly elected Carter listed ten major foreign policy goals for the new administration, which included a comprehensive Middle East peace settlement, enhanced attention to human rights, formal recognition of China, completion of a SALT II treaty, greater cooperation among the industrialized democracies, improved North-South relations, reduced arms sales to the third world, a strong defense and more attention to the issue of nuclear proliferation. Zbigniew Brzezinski, *Power and Principle: Memoirs of the National Security Advisor 1977–1981* (New York, 1982), 52–54.

the American hostages held in Iran. Any, or all, of these issues could have served as raw material for revealing case studies about Carter's conduct in the making of American foreign policy. Equally good cases could have been developed from some of the Carter administration initiatives that failed— the proposed withdrawal of U.S. troops from South Korea, the attempts to normalize relations with Vietnam and Cuba, or the unsuccessful efforts to negotiate a comprehensive test-ban agreement and significant reductions in superpower conventional arms transfers.

The foreign policy issues that were reviewed in this book, though they were selected to show the variety of situations and settings in which presidential foreign policy making takes place, touch on some of Carter's major international accomplishments. The president fundamentally changed the American relationship with Panama, and by doing so also changed America's reputation in Latin America and among developing nations. In the Middle East he served as an instigator, and then a mediator, in the peace process that transformed the relationship between Israel and Egypt. Finally, and perhaps most importantly to him, President Carter advanced the cause of human rights on the American political agenda and in the world community. These were significant accomplishments in terms of both the agenda he had set for himself and the impact these policies have had on international politics.

So why is it still common to refer to the Carter years as an era of failure in foreign affairs? One reason is that many of the major foreign policy goals Carter set for himself and subsequently achieved were either consistently unpopular, like the Panama Canal treaties, or entangled in long-standing controversies, like those surrounding arms control, détente, the recognition of China, and the Middle East. On those controversial issues, there were often interest groups or expert communities whose members were hostile to Carter's policies or convinced that a novice statesman would be unable to make meaningful progress on the vexing problems that only the properly initiated could be trusted to manage. When he was elected in 1976, Carter was largely unknown to people like Paul Warnke and Paul Nitze, and to the other prominent members of the foreign policy establishment. When he subsequently accomplished significant diplomatic feats, as he did at Camp David, with the ratification of the Panama Canal treaties, or in the tortuous negotiation of a SALT II agreement, Carter rarely earned the kind of praise or trust that might have been given to a president who had enjoyed a longer career on the national scene or a better relationship with the foreign policy elites.

Beyond Carter's newness to international politics and the unpopularity of some of the items on his agenda, two basic critiques dominate the commentary on Carter's performance in foreign affairs. One criticism involves his style of decision making; the other the substance of the decisions he made, particularly about U.S.-Soviet relations. With regard to style, the president's critics have argued that he paid too much attention to detail without thinking about, or articulating, a broad strategic vision. They have charged, moreover, that he failed to resolve the important differences between his secretary of state and his national security adviser that contributed to inconsistency in the development and implementation of his foreign policy agenda.

As the case studies in this book make clear, President Carter did pay attention to details, particularly for the issues to which he attached a high priority. He literally led the negotiating team at Camp David and in the final stages of the Israeli-Egyptian peace treaty talks. He gave equally careful attention to the SALT negotiations and remembers spending more time on Rhodesia and southern Africa than he ever did on the Middle East.[5] Though he largely delegated the negotiation of the Panama Canal treaties, he conducted many of the public and private lobbying activities that were needed to win ratification of those controversial agreements and, along with his personal assistant Hamilton Jordan, persuaded Omar Torrijos to give the administration enough time to deal with the most difficult of the senators in the majority coalition. In connection with human rights, Carter was both the principal spokesman for the broad themes that the human rights campaign involved and a kind of senior administration caseworker for selected individuals around the world whose torture, harassment, imprisonment, censorship, expulsion, or threatened execution became the subject of high-level diplomacy.[6] Even in lesser matters—like preparing for the visit of a head of state, or drafting an important foreign policy speech—the presi-

---

5. Jimmy Carter, interview by author, Atlanta, Ga., April 11, 1995.

6. To this day, he remembers the human rights campaign in terms of both its broad thematic messages and the effects it had on the lives of individuals whose personal circumstances received presidential attention. Carter, *Keeping Faith: Memoirs of a President* (New York, 1982), 141–51.

dent often reviewed a great deal of written material and listened attentively to expert briefings.[7]

Paying attention to detail had been part of Carter's administrative style long before he came to the White House, and he, no doubt, felt that it was part of his responsibility as president to learn the essential facts related to the major issues on his foreign policy agenda. Those who worked closely with him uniformly report that he was an intelligent and diligent individual who did this kind of work easily and well. On his last day in office, in the final stages of the hostage-release negotiations, it was the president who noticed that one of the many international banks taking part in the complicated arrangements to return a portion of Iran's frozen assets had not sent a message agreeing to the transaction procedures.[8]

The president's attention to detail and capacity to master complicated subjects did not mean that he was unable or unwilling to delegate authority, or that he constantly micro-managed his subordinates. On the contrary, many of the members of his foreign policy team report that while the president was knowledgeable about the issues they were working on, he often left them free to make their own decisions about how best to fulfill the general instructions he gave. Sol Linowitz, for example, reports that in the negotiation of the Panama Canal treaties, he rarely took questions to the president and was given considerable leeway in producing treaty language that would be "generous, fair and appropriate."[9] The planners of the hostage-rescue mission report much the same thing. When they briefed the president, he listened carefully, took notes, asked numerous questions, but after approving the plan made sure that neither he, nor any of his senior staff members, interfered with its implementation.

There is no question about Carter's attention to detail; the question to be answered about this feature of his presidential style is whether or not it

---

7. Madeleine Albright, who served on Brzezinski's NSC staff, found Carter to be "a brilliant person to brief." He was "very good on facts" and paid careful attention to his talking points. White Burkett Miller Center of Public Affairs, University of Virginia, Project on the Carter Presidency, Brzezinski Session, February 18, 1982, p. 50. For a discussion of how candidate and president-elect Carter responded to CIA briefings and how his responses contrasted with those of his successor, see John L. Helgerson, *Getting to Know the President: CIA Briefings of Presidential Candidates 1952–1992* (Washington, D.C., 1995).

8. Carter, *Keeping Faith*, 8.

9. Sol M. Linowitz, *The Making of a Public Man: A Memoir* (Boston, 1985), 152.

served him well. There can be little doubt that Carter's command of factual information was decisive in the Middle East peace process and in various negotiations that he personally conducted in his meetings with other heads of state. But it is probably true that in some cases he learned more than he needed to about issues that never came to fruition and was tempted to push such a large agenda of controversial items that it should have been evident from the outset of his administration that he would never be able to win public or congressional support for all of them. In this connection, his mistake may not have been devoting himself to the study of large amounts of detailed information, but his unwillingness to prioritize the agenda items that would most benefit from his close examination.

Pursuing a large and ambitious foreign policy agenda, as President Carter did, and working hard to master many of the issues on that agenda, as he also did, may have led him to neglect the strategic planning that might have given his foreign policy more coherence. He may also have given less time than he should have to the kind of sustained public education that would have impressed opinion makers and helped to generate solid support from the American people. President Carter only rarely gave his full attention to the preparation and presentation of his foreign policy speeches. He closely supervised the writing of his commencement address at Notre Dame, where he outlined the basic foreign policy goals for the administration; and, as we saw, he played a central role in the drafting of an important speech on U.S.-Soviet relations in the summer of 1978. But the failure of the Annapolis speech to end confusion about the administration's policy toward the Soviet Union, and the ease with which a distorted version of how that speech was drafted became widely accepted, may be evidence that Carter lacked the interest or ability to craft memorable rhetorical appeals.

The persuasive articulation of a strategic vision was obviously not one of Carter's strengths, but most critics of his conduct of foreign affairs do not claim that his foreign policy was utterly without vision and coherence—that it was all trees and no forest. Instead, they usually argue that there were two conflicting strategic plans in his conduct of foreign affairs that came from his secretary of state and his national security adviser, and that the president's greatest failing was his inability to decide whose forest he was in— Vance's or Brzezinski's.

The Vance-Brzezinski split is perhaps the most often noted feature in commentary on Carter administration foreign policy decision making. The split was, of course, a real one. It was partly a matter of conflicting personal styles and customary institutional rivalries that have been present in other modern presidencies, but it was also related to substantive differences involving important issues. Brzezinski once observed, in an effort to discount the emphasis placed on his disputes with Vance, that he and the secretary of state really only disagreed on two things: how to respond to the Iranian revolution and how the administration should deal with the Soviet Union.[10] That is a bit like saying that a couple I know have a wonderful marriage; they only argue about religion and sex. Nevertheless, there is a point in Brzezinski's observation. Commentators during the Carter administration, and after, have exaggerated the differences between the national security adviser and the secretary of state, often finding conflict in instances where it simply did not exist.

The president's leaked letter to Somoza is the best example in the case studies of how some observers presumed that nearly everything could be explained in terms of the dispute between the president's two senior foreign policy advisers and their staffs. When it came to giving advice about the president's correspondence with a minor Central American dictator, Vance and Brzezinski had precisely the same position—the letter was not very important, and if the president wanted to send it, he should do so. Moreover, the staff specialists in Latin American affairs who worked in the White House and at Foggy Bottom also had the same position—given Somoza's track record, the letter should not be sent. Somehow, that situation got reported as yet another dispute between the NSC and the Department of State. Newspaper reporters and commentators, once they had identified the existence of real tensions between the president's principal foreign policy advisers, saw those tensions at play nearly everywhere. So did junior members of the administration, who did not always have access to what went on at the highest levels of deliberation. In this regard, the events surrounding the drafting of the president's speech in Annapolis demonstrate how misunderstood and misreported events that conform to an existing interpretative framework carry the day against facts that inconveniently complicate the prevailing interpretation. Throughout the case studies, there is evidence to confirm the complaints of President Carter and his senior staff members that media reports about their administration often failed to tell the full

10. Project on the Carter Presidency, Brzezinski Session, 68.

story, or even an accurate story, about what went on in the Carter White House.

The Vance-Brzezinski relationship and its consequences for the Carter administration were much more complicated than most observers recognized while the administration was in office. The two senior members of the president's foreign policy team worked together on a number of important issues. They both supported and lobbied for the Panama Canal treaties; they shared the president's concern for human rights; they favored majority rule in southern Africa; and they saw an opportunity and responsibility for the United States to promote peace in the Middle East. They met with Carter every Friday morning along with the secretary of defense, and later the White House chief of staff, to discuss the foreign policy issues of the day and to receive instructions from the president. Both Vance and Brzezinski understood, as many outside observers did not, that Jimmy Carter was in charge of the foreign policy decisions in his administration and that each of them was there to serve the president's needs. When they failed to serve Carter's policy preferences, as occurred in the implementation of decisions about the neutron bomb, their combined advice was insufficient to change the president's mind.

When the differences between Vance and Brzezinski, real and presumed, became the prevailing interpretation of foreign policy making in the Carter administration, the president did display an apparent indifference, or perhaps an arrogant indifference, toward the public perception of disarray among his senior foreign policy advisers. He read the exaggerated accounts of disputes between Vance and Brzezinski, understood that those accounts were damaging to the reputation and effectiveness of his administration, complained about the leaks that were often involved in the distorted reporting about internal foreign policy deliberations, but in the final analysis Carter did relatively little to change the public perception. Early on in the administration, he mostly sided with Vance when his advice was at odds with Brzezinski's, and occasionally tried, as he did in the drafting of the Annapolis speech, to reconcile the differences between the two. But the president never decided that firing one or the other in an effort to repair the public perception problem would be worthwhile. When he finally did accept Vance's resignation, it was near the end of the administration and only after the secretary of state had placed the president in an impossible situation by opposing a major decision to use force in the Iranian hostage crisis.

Brzezinski reports that after Vance announced his resignation, the two of them were together in the national security adviser's office when the newly named secretary of state, Senator Edmund Muskie, gave a press conference with the president and clearly attempted to upstage Carter. Both reportedly laughed at Muskie's presumptuous performance.[11] Each of them knew that Jimmy Carter would continue to be the dominant foreign policy decision maker in his administration. While that reality was perfectly clear to insiders, it was not always clear to those on the outside, and President Carter apparently never gave a high priority to fixing the prevailing misperception.

The heart of the substantive dispute between Vance and Brzezinski, and the most important internal foreign policy debate during the Carter years, involved U.S. relations with the Soviet Union and the status of the cold war. For many commentators and interpreters of the Carter years, this is the crucial problem with the president's conduct of foreign policy.[12] He began his administration by declaring that the era of "inordinate fear of communism" was over and ended it with a traditional cold war response to the Soviet invasion of Afghanistan. The critics who focus attention on U.S.-Soviet relations in the Carter years are loosely divided between those who favor the new international agenda of the early Carter years and wish that it had prevailed and those who prefer the cold war realism at the end of the administration and wish that it had come sooner. Critics on both sides of that division agree that the key to Carter's failure was his mismanagement of the American relationship with the Soviet Union and the fact that he did not have a consistent approach to this fundamental foreign policy problem.

While there is a clear dividing line between early and later Carter administration foreign policy regarding the nature and importance of the Soviet threat, the debate about the two Carter foreign policy agendas and the emphasis given to the split between Vance and Brzezinski glosses over some important continuities in Carter's world view and approach to American

11. Ibid., 76.
12. This is particularly true for Richard C. Thornton, *The Carter Years: Toward a New Global Order* (New York, 1991).

foreign policy.[13] When he arrived in the White House, Jimmy Carter was genuinely committed to human rights, to the peaceful resolution of international disputes, to ambitious arms control agreements, to the use of military force only as a last resort, and to the spread of democratic institutions and values throughout the world. He remained committed to these things before and after the Soviet invasion of Afghanistan. He has remained committed to them throughout his post-presidency. Carter's view of the world, and the role the United States should play in it, were consistent with many of the conventional American opinions on these subjects and resonated with a tradition of idealistic thinking about international politics that has deep roots in the American experience.[14] Perhaps he did not give a high priority to the articulation of a grand strategy for the conduct of foreign policy in his administration because he thought that his strategic thinking was already in line with what most Americans believed.

If there is more consistency to Carter's basic thinking about international politics over time than his critics have been willing to recognize, there may also be fewer consequences to his mid-term shift on U.S.-Soviet relations than has frequently been claimed. Now that the cold war is over, the two Carter administration foreign policy periods—the early one emphasizing human rights and an end to the exaggerated fear of communism and the later one with its military buildup and sanctions against Soviet aggression in Afghanistan—may have more in common than was appreciated twenty years ago. The foreign policies pursued in both Carter periods, and the Reagan administration decisions to build on those policies by accelerating defense spending and continuing public criticism of Soviet and Eastern European human rights practices, made real contributions (however hard they might be to measure) to the eventual collapse of communism.[15]

13. For a discussion of the shift in U.S.-Soviet relations and its significance in the Carter administration, see David Skidmore, *Reversing Course: Carter's Foreign Policy, Domestic Politics, and the Failure of Reform* (Nashville, 1996), and Jerel A. Rosati, *The Carter Administration's Quest for Global Community: Beliefs and Their Impact on Behavior* (Columbia, S.C., 1987).

14. For a thoughtful discussion of the role of morality in Carter's world view, see Gaddis Smith, *Morality, Reason, and Power: American Diplomacy in the Carter Years* (New York, 1986).

15. Robert Gates, in a memoir about the intelligence community in the second half of

The intellectual adjustments that are still being made to the end of the cold war may well lead to a less critical view of Carter's foreign policy toward the Soviet Union, but that new view will not change the fact that while he was in office, President Carter acquired a reputation for indecision and weakness. Part of that reputation came from his statements and decisions concerning U.S.-Soviet relations and from his inability to bring the hostages home for more than a year. But the president's reputed indecision had other sources as well. Though Carter's thinking about world politics may have been consistent and conventional, it was never doctrinaire or ideological. He accepted compromises and tolerated contradictions when they appeared to be necessary; and he often changed his mind when new evidence became available. Carter expected that there would be both cooperation and competition in American relations with the Soviet Union and saw no reason why he could not answer a letter from Andrei Sakharov in the same month that he was preparing a new arms control proposal for Soviet consideration. He was not uncomfortable raising serious human rights concerns with the shah in private while publicly praising him as the important American ally that he was. In these and other instances, Carter was criticized for each side of the compromise he chose to make. What he probably saw as necessary steps to balance the complicated elements of his foreign policy agenda contributed to the emergence of a reputation for inconsistency and indecision. The president allowed that reputation to take hold in the public mind.

He also changed his mind about a number of important subjects. During the 1976 campaign, he was evasive about what he would do regarding the B-1 bomber or the ongoing negotiations with Panama; and then, after the election, he made clear commitments to cancel the bomber and push for new canal treaties. He began his administration calling for cuts in defense spending, but was soon persuaded that gradual increases in military expenditures by the United States and by our NATO allies were necessary. After the shah fell from power, he opposed his entry into the United States until he learned about the medical conditions that made the need for such a visit

the cold war, argues that Carter's reputation with historians is likely to rise as we come to understand the full effects of the Helsinki accords and the Carter human rights campaign on the eventual collapse of the Soviet empire. Robert Gates, *From the Shadows: The Ultimate Insider's Story of Five Presidents and How They Won the Cold War* (New York, 1996).

compelling. He resisted the use of force in the hostage crisis until the diplomatic options had apparently run their course; and as we saw in the case of the neutron bomb controversy, Carter let the negotiations with our NATO allies move beyond the policy parameters he set and then abruptly canceled the announcement of an allied agreement when he finally realized that the agreement did not conform with his original instructions. On the neutron bomb issue, Carter was a decisive, independent, obstinate, and powerful leader at precisely the time that his actions were producing a public impression of indecision and weakness. There is more than a little irony in this observation, and perhaps an important key to understanding Carter and his conduct of American foreign policy.

Carter appears to have been at his best when he was clearly in command of his own substantive issues. At Camp David and on the trip to the Middle East to finalize the Egyptian-Israeli peace treaty, Carter was energized, engaged, well informed, willing to take risks, and fully in charge of an effective and loyal staff. On those occasions he was capable of impressive accomplishments. When he had a clearly defined goal, like winning sixty-seven Senate votes for the Panama Canal treaties, he could be dedicated, determined, and diligent in pursuit of his objective. On other issues that seemed to come out of nowhere, like the original newspaper story about the neutron bomb or the fragmentary intelligence on the Cuban brigade, Carter was much less effective. He treated both of those issues as substantive matters worthy of further study and made preliminary statements shortly after they became public issues that later constrained and complicated his ability to achieve the policies he eventually selected. Only late in the day, if at all, did he see these issues, and treat them, as the public relations fiascoes that they were.

In general, Carter was more interested in the substance of foreign policy problems than in how they would play out in media commentary or short-term shifts in public opinion. When he finally focused on what had transpired in the negotiations with our NATO allies over the neutron bomb in March 1978, he stood up to stiff opposition from allied governments and from virtually all of his senior political and foreign policy advisers. Those advisers told him that he would have to pay a very high price in terms of alliance relations and his own political reputation in order to get the policy outcome he wanted. The president paid the price. He did much the same thing on Panama, where the domestic political costs were even higher.

Throughout the hostage crisis he insisted that the safe return of the American officials held in Tehran was his highest priority and resisted temptations that must have been present to use military force against Iran as either a demonstration of our great power status or as a way to relieve domestic political frustrations.[16] Carter's one decision to use military force in the hostage crisis was the risky, and ultimately unsuccessful, rescue mission.

Carter's closest advisers have often said that he did not want to hear how a particular action would affect his standing in the polls or his prospects for reelection; he wanted his staff to provide him with substantive policy analysis.[17] Other presidents have said the same thing, but perhaps not as often or as sincerely as Carter. Charles O. Jones has called Carter's administration a "trusteeship presidency," recalling a tradition in political representation in which the elected official does what he or she thinks best for the community without regard to immediate public opinion.[18]

Carter may well have been a trustee, but he was also a politician, and a politician who wanted to be elected president in both 1976 and 1980. He was successful on only one of those occasions, and in 1981 he turned the White House over to a very different chief executive, whose habits of work in foreign affairs were radically at odds with those that Carter had exhibited. Ronald Reagan would be a president rarely accused of being mired in the details of complicated foreign policy issues. Unlike Carter, Reagan narrowed his agenda and paid extraordinary attention to his speeches, public appearances, and the ceremonial duties of his office.[19] Meanwhile, he delegated many of the substantive, and controversial, policy decisions that Carter would have insisted on making himself. Reagan and his team would

16. Project on the Carter Presidency, Brzezinski Session, 90.

17. One of his advisers said in an interview that "we used to joke that the worst way to convince the President to go along with your position was to say that this would help you politically." Quoted in Erwin C. Hargrove, *Jimmy Carter as President: Leadership and the Politics of the Public Good* (Baton Rouge, 1988), 17. Hargrove is an excellent source on Carter's leadership style and the efforts he did make to integrate political advice with substantive policy analysis.

18. Charles O. Jones, *The Trusteeship Presidency: Jimmy Carter and the United States Congress* (Baton Rouge, 1988).

19. Reagan's administration has come to exemplify both the virtues and vices of what Jeffrey Tulis has called the "rhetorical presidency," in which effective appeals to the public become the essence of presidential leadership. Jeffrey K. Tulis, *The Rhetorical Presidency* (Princeton, N.J., 1987).

regard the management of the media and the maintenance of the president's popularity as vital to their success and probably welcomed the unusual comparison of the president to the coating on non-stick cookware. But if Reagan's was the "Teflon" presidency, Carter's may be remembered as the "flypaper" presidency—an administration that performed necessary, and sometimes unpleasant, functions rather well, but one that also found that its many successes tended to diminish rather than enhance its overall appearance.

Whatever attempts may be made to reduce the Carter or the Reagan presidencies to a single clever adjective need not be taken seriously, but a vital question in the comparison of these two administrations cannot be avoided. In this book we have examined, in a variety of situations, how one president did his foreign policy work. We found Carter to have been an intelligent and conscientious decision maker who mastered the sum and substance of a number of complicated and controversial policy initiatives. He worked hard and took chances; he sometimes succeeded and sometimes failed. What happened when he was replaced by a chief executive who was almost certainly more ideological and less intellectually curious, more willing to delegate and less in command of the issues he encountered? Could it be that Reagan's electoral successes and good standing with the American people were, at least in part, related to the very different way he went about doing his foreign policy work? Or are the skills and work habits of presidents simply less important than other factors that contribute to success or failure in presidential performance?[20] Or do we know too little about how to recognize success and failure in presidential behavior beyond the obvious tests provided by polls and elections?

Historians and presidential scholars have a great deal to consider in evaluating Jimmy Carter's conduct of American foreign policy. For a little-known presidential candidate who won a narrow electoral victory and

20. For example, in the work of Stephen Skowronek the political structure that a president encounters may be more important than the personal skills he brings to bear on the problems of his day. Therefore, the fact that Carter won a narrow election in 1976 and led a tired and divided Democratic Party severely constrained his ability to introduce important political and policy changes, while Reagan's larger victory in 1980 and the surprising Republican capture of the Senate provided an entirely different set of structural political opportunities. Stephen Skowronek, *The Politics Presidents Make: Leadership from John Adams to George Bush* (Cambridge, Mass., 1993).

served for only one term, Carter left a legacy of significant achievements including the Camp David accords, the Panama Canal treaties, the formal recognition of China, the peaceful transition to majority rule in Rhodesia, the negotiation of a complicated SALT II agreement, and the enhancement of both international and domestic attention to human rights. The world is clearly a different place, and many would argue a better one, for the work that President Carter did in it. Yet there is a temptation to speculate that had he done his work differently—with more rhetorical flair, with fewer controversial initiatives, with a less complicated policy toward the Soviet Union, with greater attention to winning favorable media coverage—he might have been able to enjoy both substantive foreign policy accomplishments and sustained political success.[21] Whether Carter could have done these things and remained true to himself is, of course, another question.

That question is connected to a larger debate among modern presidential scholars. For some students of the presidency, success in the highest office of the land is a matter of skills that can be learned by careful observation of past masters; for others, presidential success is rooted in fundamental elements of character and style that presidents bring with them to the Oval Office.[22] In the long run, it may not matter if we study the presidency by learning the tricks of the trade or by uncovering the traits of the tricksters. Substantive accomplishments that stand the test of time are likely to play a larger role in the making of ultimate presidential reputations than the evaluations of decision making processes or personality traits that often preoccupy the commentators who paint the earliest portraits of presidential performance. This book has attempted to challenge some of the initial accounts of Carter's conduct of American foreign policy that found him to be weak, indecisive, inconsistent, and the victim of conflicts among his advisers. That is a portrait that does not conform with the evidence now available. In its place the case studies in this collection show us an active, intelligent, and

21. Of course, domestic policy—and particularly the state of the economy—has much more to do with presidential performance in reelection campaigns than almost any actions on the international scene. President Bush in 1992, with major foreign policy accomplishments in the Gulf War and in the resolution of delicate issues that arose in connection with the breakup of the Soviet empire, could not translate these successes into a reelection victory.

22. Richard E. Neustadt, *Presidential Power: The Politics of Leadership* (New York, 1960), and James David Barber, *The Presidential Character: Predicting Performance in the White House*, 4th ed. (Englewood Cliffs, N.J., 1992).

sincere individual in command of a complicated foreign policy agenda that often involved the conscious acceptance of substantial political risks. Whether the results of the risks that President Carter willingly took will impress future evaluators of presidential performance remains to be seen. For now it may be enough to recognize that the time has come to begin the process of reassessing Carter's foreign policy accomplishments and international legacy.[23]

Presidential Work and Foreign Policy

Carter revisionism was only one objective for this research project. The other, and broader, task was to ask what might be learned by examining how one recent president went about doing the different kinds of work that nearly all presidents do in exercising their foreign policy responsibilities. Of course, it is problematic to make any statements about the presidency based on evidence that involves only one holder of that office. Nevertheless, there are some themes in the case studies developed from Carter's experiences that would appear to involve generic problems for modern presidents.

The first of these themes draws our attention to the large and complicated part that the news media play in the processes by which foreign policy issues emerge and are addressed. In almost all of the cases in this book, media reporting about foreign policy events had a significant, and sometimes a central, role. The most obvious example of dramatic media impact would be the neutron bomb—an issue that was disclosed, distorted, and, to some extent, driven by media reports.[24] The initial *Washington Post* stories about the previously little known development program gave the new weapon its lasting name and an overly simplified characterization of its nature that profoundly affected both the American and European public responses to the new NATO warheads. Later the leaks about Carter's preference for an outright cancellation of the controversial program made the

23. The revisionism of Carter's foreign policy legacy may already be under way. See Douglas Brinkley, "The Rising Stock of Jimmy Carter: The 'Hands On' Legacy of Our Thirty-Ninth President," *Diplomatic History* 20, no. 4 (fall 1996), 505–29.

24. The most important source in the chapter on the neutron bomb controversy was the study by Whitman, which focused on the media role in the issue. David Whitman, "The Press and the Neutron Bomb," in *How the Press Affects Federal Policy Making: Six Case Studies*, by Martin Linskey et al. (New York, 1986).

desperate last-minute attempts to develop a new policy in Washington, and among the allies, utterly impossible to achieve.

From start to finish, the neutron bomb controversy has to be considered in the context of when, why, and how information that could legitimately be classified for some period of time entered the public domain. In this instance, the accidental release of a seemingly arcane budgetary fact, and the active pursuit of the matter by an influential and well-informed journalist, converted the new weapon from a minor research-and-development project into a major symbolic and emotional issue for the entire Western alliance. Perhaps this transformation was inevitable and would have occurred without Walter Pincus or the *Washington Post* whenever enhanced-radiation technology reached the point of open public discussion about the construction and deployment of new warheads based on an inherently objectionable design. But the timing of this controversy, its intensity, and the difficulty the administration had in formulating an effective public relations strategy were all clearly affected by how the news media perceived and performed its functions. Once the issue came to command significant public attention and intense media scrutiny on both sides of the Atlantic, it became difficult, if not impossible, for the administration and the alliance to maintain secrecy during the final round of policy deliberations.

Leaks involving sensitive foreign policy information are ubiquitous in our nation's capital, and a great deal of routine communication among actors in the foreign policy making process apparently takes place on the pages of national newspapers. In the case of the alleged Soviet brigade in Cuba, the premature release of incomplete intelligence information by members of Congress, and the fear that such information would appear in the press, constituted the substance of a crisis that otherwise had very little substance of any kind. In President Carter's correspondence with Sakharov and Somoza, the press played a major role in both sets of communication. Jimmy Carter never saw the two messages that Andrei Sakharov sent to him while he was a presidential candidate, but he certainly saw the one that arrived after his inauguration when it became a headline on the front page of the *New York Times*. In Sakharov's memoirs, it is clear that he either misread, or was misled, by early press accounts of Carter's response to the Soviet crackdown against dissidents in the Eastern bloc. Sakharov's false first impression about the president's commitment to human rights was corrected by the letter he received at the American embassy in Moscow. In Carter's memoirs, the president remembers the news media photograph of Sakharov holding up his sheet of White House stationery better than he remembers what the letter actually said. In Latin America, Venezuelan president Pérez dismissed Carter's correspondence with Somoza when the Nicaraguan dictator tried to show it to him in their private meeting, but he became furious, as did Carter, when a partial account of the letter's contents was reported in the *Washington Post*. That presidential correspondence, like many other pieces of paper in Washington, had very little significance until it was written about in a major American newspaper.

Modern presidents, and not just Carter, constantly complain about press coverage and leaks. They consistently threaten to fire the leakers, if and when they are found. Almost always they are not. On a more abstract level, there is a long-standing debate in American politics about what the limits of First Amendment freedoms ought be in connection with national security and intelligence information. There are legitimate fears that political leaders will abuse the right to withhold information or control its release to avoid embarrassment or otherwise gain political advantage. On the other side, there is concern that the apparent decline in the ability of the government to keep secrets will make it difficult for presidents to conduct private deliberations, consider unconventional policy options, and exchange confidential diplomatic communications.[25] The debate about the relationship between freedom of the press and the proper boundaries of government secrecy may, however, be beside the point. The working assumption of many high-level American policy makers is very likely to be that nearly any sensitive piece of information could, at any time, become publicly known.

In the chapter on the hostage-rescue mission (one of the most tightly and successfully held secrets of the Carter administration),[26] it was noted that there is some question about when President Carter actually made up his mind to carry out the rescue attempt. Hamilton Jordan describes the presi-

25. For a classic and comparative treatment of this subject, see Thomas M. Franck and Edward Weisband, eds., *Secrecy and Foreign Policy* (New York, 1974). A detailed discussion of how leaks play a role in the modern foreign policy making process can be found in Barry Rubin, *Secrets of State: The State Department and the Struggle over U.S. Foreign Policy* (New York, 1985).

26. And, of course, it should be remembered that the secrecy surrounding the rescue mission was maintained, in part, by the leaking of fraudent disclaimers that any rescue attempt was in the works. Jody Powell, *The Other Side of the Story* (New York, 1984), 231–32.

dent making his decision late in the series of high-level deliberations; Brzezinski suggests that he did so early on. When interviewed about the timing of Carter's decision, the president's former press secretary, Jody Powell, expressed some surprise that such a question would need to be asked. In Powell's view, as soon as Carter elected to put the rescue mission option on the table at NSC meetings in late March and early April of 1980, he was more or less committing himself to go forward. Otherwise, the fact that the president had rejected a rescue option reviewed at the highest levels of the government would, when that fact became known, have serious political consequences that would have been obvious to everyone concerned.[27] Perhaps Powell, because of his responsibilities and experiences, thought more automatically about the eventuality of leaks than did other members of the president's senior staff, but there is a compelling logic to his train of thought and clear evidence that concern for the secrecy surrounding the rescue mission constrained the ability of mission planners, and senior administration officials, to explore all the problematic aspects of the proposed rescue attempt.

There should be nothing new or newsworthy in drawing attention to the importance of leaks, and the fear of leaks, in the political life of Washington. But there may be a tendency among some political scientists to construct models of foreign policy decision making that overemphasize internal administration deliberations without treating members of the news media as ever-present, independent, and important actors in those processes.[28] The movement of information from official secrecy to public discourse, which usually involves both the formal and informal interactions among government officials and news organization reporters, and the efforts to manage and manipulate that movement of information, ought to be matters of continuing interest to students of American foreign policy and presidential behavior.[29]

27. Jody Powell, telephone interview by author, March 14, 1995.

28. See, for example, Alexander George, *Presidential Decisionmaking in Foreign Policy: The Effective Use of Information and Advice* (Boulder, Colo., 1980). The bureaucratic politics literature does treat the media and leaks as important factors in foreign policy decision making. See, particularly, Morton H. Halperin, *Bureaucratic Politics and Foreign Policy* (Washington, D.C., 1974).

29. In Jimmy Carter's post-presidential career as an international mediator, election observer, and maverick diplomat, he has been able to enhance his effectiveness, and generate

A second theme in the case study materials is related to both the role of the media in American politics and the need for revisionism in the evaluation of Carter's performance in foreign affairs. Calling for a new and revised assessment of a particular presidency, as is commonly done in the decades after almost every administration, requires some explanation of why the original assessment was wrong.

Part of the reason that revisionism occurs is relatively easy to understand. When we know how events have turned out, we are bound to look back on how they unfolded in new and different ways. Carter's teargassed reception of the shah and his toast in Tehran were not particularly important events until the revolution in Iran changed almost all of the previous assumptions about the shah and the stability of his regime. Critics of the early Carter administration's search for a comprehensive peace agreement in the Middle East thought that the president's plans were overly ambitious; critics of the subsequent Camp David accords thought that those agreements were excessively vague about the prospects for a resolution of the Palestinian problem. After Madrid and Oslo—at least on days when acts of terrorism are not making headlines—the Carter administration efforts on behalf of peace in the Middle East look more realistic and substantial than they did to some of their contemporary critics. This sort of revisionism is bound to take place and appears, on the whole, to be helping Carter's reputation.

But the case studies in this book suggest that there is another kind of revisionism that is necessary when original accounts of what the president may have said or done are incomplete or inaccurate. Revisionism in these cases occurs when scholars read more documents, do more interviews, and collect more evidence about what actually transpired in connection with a given issue or decision. Sometimes careful research into presidential behavior reveals things that White House occupants have actively sought to hide, like the true state of Kennedy's health, or the accumulation of Johnson's personal wealth. More often, thorough research simply recovers details, nuances, and complexities that get lost in the rush to label and judge a sitting president. It is that rush to judgment, perhaps even more than changing events in the world, that makes revision of Carter's reputation worth considering.

---

considerable controversy, by talking to CNN before he talks with the White House or the State Department. See Brinkley, *Unfinished Presidency*, especially the chapters on North Korea and Haiti.

Jimmy Carter did not slap together contradictory memos in the creation of an important foreign policy speech. He did not, in some important ways, change his mind about the neutron bomb. Nor was he alone in suffering from public misperceptions. He was not a weak and indecisive president any more than Gerald Ford was clumsy, or Ronald Reagan asleep, or George Bush a wimp. Elements of presidential character and behavior that may have some basis in reality appear almost invariably to get simplified for mass consumption, repeated in a steady stream of repetitious commentary, and absorbed by a public audience that wants to believe that it truly knows the person who holds the highest office in the land. Presidents of the United States are by no means innocent parties in this process of simplification, having often won the presidency by the skillful use of techniques in modern campaigning that involve putting a candidate's best face (and only that face) forward. Campaigns help to raise the expectations that are usually dashed by the realities of holding office and making decisions.

But whether the blame for distorted and overly simplified pictures of presidential performance ultimately lies with candidates, or commentators, or a public craving for easy answers to complicated questions about our highest public officials may not matter a great deal. What should matter is the recognition that such distortion is a potential phenomenon and that both scholars and citizens need to look with care at the work our presidents do, and, if we possibly can, to look with care when they are doing it.

Selected Bibliography

Anderson, Patrick. *Electing Jimmy Carter: The Campaign of 1976.* Baton Rouge: Louisiana State University Press, 1994.

Andrianopoulos, Gerry Argyris. *Kissinger and Brzezinski: The NSC and the Struggle for Control of U.S. National Security Policy.* New York: St. Martin's Press, 1991.

Aquino, Michael A. *The Neutron Bomb.* Ann Arbor, Mich.: University Microfilms, 1982.

Ashby, Leroy, and Rod Gramer. *Fighting the Odds: The Life of Senator Frank Church.* Pullman, Wash.: Washington State University Press, 1994.

Auger, Vincent A. *The Dynamics of Foreign Policy Analysis: The Carter Administration and the Neutron Bomb.* Lanham, Md.: Rowman and Littlefield, 1996.

Beckwith, Charlie A., and Donald Knox. *Delta Force.* San Diego: Harcourt, Brace, and Jovanovich, 1983.

Bell, Coral. *President Carter and Foreign Policy: The Costs of Virtue.* Canberra Studies in World Affairs, no. 1. Canberra: Australian National University, 1980.

Bourne, Peter G. *Jimmy Carter: A Comprehensive Biography from Plains to Post-presidency.* New York: Scribner's, 1997.

Brady, C. Paul. *The Camp David Peace Process: A Study of Carter Administration Policies (1977–1980).* Grantham, N.H.: Tompson and Rutter, 1981.

Brinkley, Douglas. *The Unfinished Presidency: Jimmy Carter's Journey Beyond the White House.* New York: Viking Penguin, 1998.

Brown, Harold. *Thinking About National Security: Defense and Foreign Policy in a Dangerous World.* Boulder, Colo.: Westview Press, 1983.

Brzezinski, Zbigniew. *Power and Principle: Memoirs of the National Security Advisor 1977–1981*. New York: Farrar, Straus, Giroux, 1983.

Caldwell, Dan. *The Dynamics of Domestic Politics and Arms Control: The SALT II Treaty Ratification Debate*. Columbia, S.C.: University of South Carolina Press, 1991.

Carter, Jimmy. *Keeping Faith: Memoirs of a President*. New York: Bantam Books, 1982.

———. *Turning Point: A Candidate, a State, a Nation Come of Age*. New York: Times Books, 1992.

———. *Why Not the Best*. Nashville: Broadman Press, 1976.

Carter, Rosalynn. *First Lady from Plains*. Boston: Houghton Mifflin, 1984.

Christopher, Warren, ed. *American Hostages in Iran: The Conduct of a Crisis*. New Haven, Conn.: Yale University Press, 1985.

Clifford, Clark, with Richard C. Holbrooke. *Counsel to the President: A Memoir*. New York: Random House, 1991.

Dayan, Moshe. *Breakthrough: A Personal Account of the Egypt-Israel Peace Negotiations*. New York: Alfred A. Knopf, 1981.

Dobrynin, Anatoly. *In Confidence: Moscow's Ambassador to America's Six Cold War Presidents*. New York: Times Books, 1995.

Dumbrell, John. *American Foreign Policy: Carter to Clinton*. London: Macmillan, 1997.

———. *The Carter Presidency: A Re-evaluation*. Manchester, Eng.: Manchester University Press, 1993.

Fallows, James. "The Passionless Presidency." *Atlantic Monthly,* May and June 1979.

Fosdick, Dorothy, ed. *Staying the Course: Henry M. Jackson and National Security.* Seattle: University of Washington Press, 1987.

Franck, Thomas M., and Edward Weisband. *Foreign Policy by Congress*. New York: Oxford University Press, 1979.

Friedlander, Melvin. *Sadat and Begin: The Domestic Politics of Peacemaking*. Boulder, Colo.: Westview Press, 1983.

Garthoff, Raymond. *Détente and Confrontation: American-Soviet Relations from Nixon to Reagan*. Washington, D.C.: Brookings Institution, 1985.

Gates, Robert M. *From the Shadows: The Ultimate Insider's Story of Five Presidents and How They Won the Cold War*. New York: Simon and Schuster, 1996.

George, Alexander, ed. *Managing U.S.-Soviet Rivalry: Problems of Crisis Prevention*. Boulder, Colo.: Westview Press, 1983.

Glad, Betty. *Jimmy Carter: In Search of the Great White House*. New York: W. W. Norton, 1980.

Grover, William F. *The President as Prisoner: A Structural Critique of the Carter and Reagan Years*. Albany: State University of New York Press, 1989.

Haas, Garland A. *Jimmy Carter and the Politics of Frustration*. Jefferson, N.C.: McFarland, 1992.

Hargrove, Erwin C. *Jimmy Carter as President: Leadership and the Politics of the Public Good*. Baton Rouge: Louisiana State University Press, 1988.

Harvey, Mose L. *Soviet Combat Troops in Cuba: Implications of the Carter Solution for the USSR*. Monographs in International Affairs, Advanced International Studies Institute. Miami: University of Miami, 1979.

Hyland, William G. *Mortal Rivals: Superpower Relations from Nixon to Reagan*. New York: Random House, 1987.

Jones, Charles O. *The Trusteeship Presidency: Jimmy Carter and the United States Congress*. Baton Rouge: Louisiana State University Press, 1988.

Jordan, Hamilton. *Crisis: The Last Year of the Carter Presidency*. New York: G. Putnam's Sons, 1982.

Jorden, William J. *Panama Odyssey*. Austin: University of Texas Press, 1984.

Kaufman, Burton I. *The Presidency of James Earl Carter, Jr.* Lawrence: University of Kansas Press, 1993.

Lake, Anthony. *Somoza Falling: A Case Study in the Making of U.S. Foreign Policy*. Boston: Houghton Mifflin, 1989.

————. *Third World Radical Regimes: U.S. Policy Under Carter and Reagan*. Foreign Policy Association Headline Series, no. 272. New York: Foreign Policy Association, 1985.

Lance, Bert, with Bill Gilbert. *The Truth of the Matter: My Life In and Out of Politics*. New York: Summit Books, 1991.

Linowitz, Sol. M. *The Making of a Public Man: A Memoir*. Boston: Little, Brown, 1985.

McLellan, David S. *Cyrus Vance*. Totowa, N.J.: Rowman and Allanheld, 1985.

Maga, Timothy. *The World of Jimmy Carter: U.S. Foreign Policy, 1977–1981*. West Haven, Conn.: University of New Haven Press, 1994.

Mazlish, Bruce, and Edwin Diamond. *Jimmy Carter: An Interpretive Biography*. New York: Simon and Schuster, 1979.

Miller, William Lee. *Yankee from Georgia: The Emergence of Jimmy Carter*. New York: New York Times Books, 1978.

Moffett, George D. *The Limits of Victory: The Ratification of the Panama Canal Treaties*. Ithaca, N.Y.: Cornell University Press, 1985.

Morris, Kenneth E. *Jimmy Carter: American Moralist*. Athens: University of Georgia Press, 1996.

Mower, A. Glenn, Jr. *Human Rights and American Foreign Policy: The Carter and Reagan Experiences*. Studies in Human Rights, no. 7. New York: Greenwood Press, 1987.

Muravchik, Joshua. *The Uncertain Crusade: Jimmy Carter and the Dilemmas of Human Rights Policy*. Lanham, Md.: Hamilton Press, 1986.

Neustadt, Richard E., and Ernest R. May. *Thinking in Time: The Uses of History for Decision Makers*. New York: Free Press, 1986.

Newsom, David D., ed. *The Diplomacy of Human Rights*. Lanham, Md.: University Press of America, 1986.

——— . *The Soviet Brigade in Cuba: A Study in Political Diplomacy*. Bloomington: Indiana University Press, 1987.

Nitze, Paul. *From Hiroshima to Glasnost: At the Center of Decision: A Memoir*. New York: Weidenfeld and Nicolson, 1989.

Orman, John. *Comparing Presidential Behavior: Carter, Reagan, and the Macho Presidential Style*. New York: Greenwood Press, 1987.

Pastor, Robert A. *Condemned to Repetition: The United States and Nicaragua*. Princeton, N.J.: Princeton University Press, 1987.

Powell, Jody. *The Other Side of the Story*. New York: William Morrow, 1984.

Prados, John. *Keepers of the Keys: A History of the National Security Council from Truman to Bush*. New York: William Morrow, 1991.

Public Papers of the Presidents of the United States, Jimmy Carter 1977–80. Washington, D.C.: Government Printing Office, 1977–1981.

Quandt, William B. *Camp David: Peacemaking and Politics*. Washington, D.C.: Brookings Institution, 1986.

——— . *Peace Process: American Diplomacy and the Arab-Israeli Conflict Since 1967*. Washington, D.C.: Brookings Institution, 1993.

Rosati, Jerel. *The Carter Administration's Quest for Global Community: Beliefs and Their Impact on Behavior*. Columbia, S.C.: University of South Carolina Press, 1987.

Rose, Clive. *Campaigns Against Western Defense: NATO's Adversaries and Critics*. New York: St. Martin's Press, 1985.

Rosenbaum, Herbert D., and Alexej Ugrinsky, eds., *Jimmy Carter: Foreign Policy and Post-presidential Years*. Westport, Conn.: Greenwood Press, 1994.

Rubin, Barry. *Paved with Good Intentions: The American Experience in Iran*. New York: Penguin, 1981.

Ryan, Paul. *The Iranian Rescue Mission: Why It Failed*. Annapolis, Md.: Naval Institute Press, 1985.

Sadat, Anwar el. *Those I Have Known*. New York: Continuum, 1984.

Sakharov, Andrei. *Memoirs*. New York: Alfred A. Knopf, 1990.

Schwartz, David N. *NATO's Nuclear Dilemmas*. Washington, D.C.: Brookings Institution, 1983.

Shawcross, William. *The Shah's Last Ride: The True Story of the Emperor's Dreams and Illusions, Exile, and Death at the Hands of His Foes and Friends*. New York: Simon and Schuster, 1988.

Sick, Gary. *All Fall Down: America's Tragic Encounter with Iran*. New York: Random House, 1985.

Silver, Eric. *Begin: The Haunted Prophet*. New York: Random House, 1984.

Skidmore, David. *Reversing Course: Carter's Foreign Policy, Domestic Politics, and the Failure of Reform*. Nashville: Vanderbilt University Press, 1996.

Smith, Gaddis. *Morality, Reason, and Power: American Diplomacy in the Carter Years*. New York: Hill and Wang, 1986.

Somoza, Anastasio. *Nicaragua Betrayed*. Boston: Western Islands, 1980.

Spencer, Donald S. *The Carter Implosion: Jimmy Carter and the Amateur Style of Diplomacy*. New York: Praeger, 1988.

Sullivan, William. *Mission to Iran*. New York: W. W. Norton, 1981.

Talbott, Strobe. *Endgame: The Inside Story of SALT II*. New York: Harper and Row, 1979.

———. *The Master of the Game: Paul Nitze and the Nuclear Peace*. New York: Alfred A. Knopf, 1989.

Thompson, Kenneth W., ed. *The Carter Presidency*. Portraits of American Presidents, vol. 8. Lanham, Md.: University Press of America, 1990.

Thornton, Richard C. *The Carter Years: Toward a New Global Order*. New York: Paragon House, 1991.

Turner, Stansfield. *Secrecy and Democracy: The CIA in Transition*. Boston: Houghton Mifflin, 1985.

———. *Terrorism and Democracy*. Boston: Houghton Mifflin, 1991.

Vance, Cyrus. *Hard Choices: Four Critical Years in Managing America's Foreign Policy*. New York: Simon and Schuster, 1983.

Wasserman, Sherri L. *The Neutron Bomb Controversy: A Study in Alliance Politics*. New York: Praeger, 1983.

Weizman, Ezer. *The Battle for Peace*. New York: Bantam, 1981.

Whitman, David, "The Press and the Neutron Bomb." In *How the Press Affects Federal Policymaking: Six Case Studies,* by Martin Linsky, et. al. New York: W. W. Norton, 1986.

Wilson, Robert A., ed. *Character Above All*. New York: Simon and Schuster, 1995.

Witcover, Jules. *Marathon: The Pursuit of the Presidency, 1972–1976*. New York: Viking, 1977.

Wright, Robin. *In the Name of God: The Khomeini Decade*. New York: Simon and Schuster, 1989.

Zonis, Marvin. *Majestic Failure: The Fall of the Shah*. Chicago: University of Chicago Press, 1991.

Index